RELIGION AND CULTURE IN THE MIDDLE AGES

Holiness and Masculinity in the Middle Ages

Series Editors
Denis Renevey (Universities of Fribourg and Geneva)
Diane Watt (University of Wales, Aberystwyth)

Editorial Board
Miri Rubin (Queen Mary, University of London)
Jean-Claude Schmitt (École des Hautes
Études en Sciences Sociales, Paris)
Fiona Somerset (Duke University)
Christiania Whitehead (University of Warwick)

RELIGION AND CULTURE IN THE MIDDLE AGES

Holiness and Masculinity in the Middle Ages

Edited by

P. H. CULLUM and KATHERINE J. LEWIS

UNIVERSITY OF WALES PRESS
CARDIFF
2004

© The Contributors, 2004

All rights reserved. No part of this book may be reproduced, stored in a retrieval system, or transmitted, in any form or by any means, electronic, mechanical, photocopying, recording or otherwise, without clearance from the University of Wales Press, 10 Columbus Walk, Brigantine Place, Cardiff, CF10 4UP.
www.wales.ac.uk/press

British Library Cataloguing-in-Publication Data
A catalogue record for this book is available from the British Library.

ISBN 0–7083–1894–0

The right of the Contributors to be identified separately as authors of their work has been asserted by them in accordance with the Copyright, Designs and Patents Act 1988.

Printed in Great Britain by Cromwell Press Ltd, Trowbridge, Wiltshire

Contents

List of Illustrations   vii
Series Editors' Preface   ix
Acknowledgements   xi
Notes on Contributors   xiii
Abbreviations   xvi

1   Introduction: Holiness and Masculinity in Medieval Europe
    P. H. Cullum   1

2   Holiness and Masculinity in Aldhelm's *Opus Geminatum De virginitate*
    Emma Pettit   8

3   Masculinizing Religious Life: Sexual Prowess, the Battle for Chastity and Monastic Identity
    Jacqueline Murray   24

4   Matronly Monks: Theodoret of Cyrrhus' Sexual Imagery in the *Historia Religiosa*
    Christopher C. Craun   43

5   Bride or Bridegroom? Masculine Identity in Mystic Marriages
    Carolyn Diskant Muir   58

6   Henry Suso and the Divine Knighthood
    Meri Heinonen   79

7   Holy Eunuchs! Masculinity and Eunuch Saints in Byzantium
    Shaun Tougher   93

8	The Signification of the Tonsure *Robert Mills*	109
9	Christian Sanctuary and Repository of France's Political Culture: The Construction of Holiness and Masculinity at the Royal Abbey of Saint-Denis, 987–1328 *Dawn Marie Hayes*	127
10	Self-Mastery and Submission: Holiness and Masculinity in the Lives of Anglo-Saxon Martyr-Kings *Edward Christie*	143
11	Edmund of East Anglia, Henry VI and Ideals of Kingly Masculinity *Katherine J. Lewis*	158
12	Monarchy, Martyrdom and Masculinity: England in the Later Middle Ages *W. M. Ormrod*	174
13	Making Youth Holy: Holiness and Masculinity in *The Interlude of Youth* *Fiona S. Dunlop*	192
14	The Catholic Gentlemen of the North: Unreformed in the Age of Reformation? *Sarah L. Bastow*	206
Index		222

List of Illustrations

5.1. *The Exemplar*, MS 2.929, fo. 28^v — 63

5.2. 'Heinrich Seuse with the Vision of Eternal Wisdom', woodcut, *c*.1470–80 — 64

5.3. 'The Spiritual Marriage of Sapientia and the Disciple', *Horloge de sapience*, MS IV, 111, fo. 127^v — 66

5.4. *The Exemplar*, Anton Sorg, Augsburg, 1482, Inc. 447, fo. 89^r — 67

5.5. *The Exemplar*, MS 2.929, fo. 1^v — 68

7.1. Mosaic of St Ignatios, Hagia Sophia, Istanbul — 99

8.1. Heidelberg Sachsenspiegel (1300). MS cod. pal. ger. 164, fo. 12^v — 112

8.2. Wild man, in *The Luttrell Psalter* (*c*.1335–40). MS Add. 42130, fo. 70^r — 117

8.3. A bird monster cracks a monastic nut, in *The Luttrell Psalter* (*c*.1335–40). MS Add. 42130, fo. 179^v — 118

8.4. A fighting cleric with a tonsure and a naked cleric, in *The Luttrell Psalter* (*c*.1335–40). MS Add. 42130, fo. 54^r — 119

8.5. Artist in Rueland Frueauf the Elder's circle, *Carrying of the Cross* (*c*.1440–1507) — 121

9.1. Sumner McKnight Crosby's reconstruction of Saint-Denis's west façade as imagined by Suger — 131

9.2. F. N. Martinet's engraving of the main entrance to the abbey as it may have looked during Suger's abbacy — 132

9.3. Christ on the tympanum of the west façade's central portal — 133

9.4. Louis IX cures scrofula, *Grandes chroniques de France* — 136

SERIES EDITORS' PREFACE

Religion and Culture in the Middle Ages aims to explore the interface between medieval religion and culture, with as broad an understanding of those terms as possible. It puts to the forefront studies which engage with works that significantly contributed to the shaping of medieval culture. However, it also gives attention to studies dealing with works that reflect and highlight aspects of medieval culture that have been neglected in the past by scholars of the medieval disciplines. For example, devotional works and the practice they infer illuminate our understanding of the medieval subject and its culture in remarkable ways, while studies of the material space designed and inhabited by medieval subjects yield new evidence on the period and the people who shaped it and lived in it. In the larger field of religion and culture, we also want to explore further the roles played by women as authors, readers and owners of books, thereby defining them more precisely as actors in the cultural field. The series as a whole investigates the European Middle Ages, from c.500 to c.1500. Our aim is to explore medieval religion and culture with the tools belonging to such disciplines as, among others, art history, philosophy, theology, history, musicology, the history of medicine, and literature. In particular, we would like to promote interdisciplinary studies, as we believe strongly that our modern understanding of the term applies fascinatingly well to a cultural period marked by a less tight confinement and categorization of its disciplines than the modern period. However, our only criterion is academic excellence, with the belief that the use of a large diversity of critical tools and theoretical approaches enables a deeper understanding of medieval culture. We want the series to reflect this diversity, as we believe that, as a collection of outstanding contributions, it offers a more subtle representation of a period that is marked by paradoxes and contradictions and which necessarily reflects diversity and difference, however difficult it may sometimes have proved for medieval culture to accept these notions.

Acknowledgements

We would like to thank all those who attended the original conference 'Holiness and Masculinity in the Middle Ages', held at the University of Huddersfield in July 2001, especially the following for their papers: John Arnold, Bjorn Bandlien, Santha Bhattacharji, Michael Calabrese, Isabel Davis, Kate Giles, Yelena Matsusevitch, Liz Herbert McAvoy, Victoria Thompson and Robert Wright. We would also like to thank the Division of History at the University of Huddersfield for its support with the conference and Heloise Brown and Samantha Riches for help with its organization. Final thanks go to all of those with whom we have discussed issues of medieval masculinity, particularly the students who have taken our 'Gender and Society' module.

Notes on Contributors

SARAH L. BASTOW lectures in medieval and early modern history at the University of Huddersfield and the Trinity and All Saints College, Leeds. She also teaches A-level History at Greenhead College, Huddersfield. Her research interests are in early modern religious history and her Ph.D. was entitled 'Aspects of the History of the Catholic Gentry of Yorkshire from the Pilgrimage of Grace to the First Civil War' (2002). She has also published two articles, ' "Worth Nothing but Very Wilful": Catholic Recusant Women of Yorkshire, 1536–1642', *Recusant History*, 25 (2001) and 'The Catholic Gentry and the Catholic Community of the City of York, 1536–1642: The Focus of a Catholic County?', *The York Historian*, 18 (2001). These examine the role played by women in maintaining the Catholic religion and the position that the city of York held as a focus for Catholicism in the Tudor and Stuart eras.

EDWARD CHRISTIE took his Ph.D. from West Virginia University, where his research focused on the representation of the alphabetical letter as an atomic unit of text and a medium of cultural memory from the grammatical culture of Anglo-Saxon England to later typographical and digital remediations of Anglo-Saxon manuscripts. He continues to research in Anglo-Saxon representations of literacy, history and the materiality of the sign.

CHRISTOPHER C. CRAUN is a doctoral student in Medieval History at the University of St Andrews, Scotland. He is currently finishing his thesis entitled 'A Contextualization of the *Martyrologium Hrabani*' and plans on submitting it later in 2004. While his Ph.D. focuses upon the Carolingian West, Christopher is also deeply interested in early asceticism throughout the Mediterranean world of Late Antiquity. Aside from academic labours he and his wife, Kala, are busy raising their three children and the family currently resides in the USA.

P. H. CULLUM is Head of History at the University of Huddersfield. She has published widely on hospitals and charity in late medieval England, and has interests in female piety and clerical masculinity.

FIONA S. DUNLOP has recently completed a Ph.D. at the Centre for Medieval Studies at the University of York, with a thesis on the representation of young noblemen in the early Tudor interlude. She teaches English at Bootham School, York.

DAWN MARIE HAYES received her Ph.D. in medieval European history from New York University in 1998. Having taught at Iona College and for the City University of New York, she joined the history faculty at Montclair State University in the fall of 2003. She is the author of *Body and Sacred Place in Medieval Europe, 1100–1389* (2003) and will soon publish 'Body as Champion of Church Authority and Sacred Place: The Murder of Thomas Becket', a chapter deconstructing accounts of the archbishop's murder in *'A Great Effusion of Blood'?: Interpreting Medieval Violence* (2004). She is currently working on *Medieval Maternity*, an examination of pregnancy and childbirth in medieval Europe. She has been a Speaker in the Humanities for the New York Council for the Humanities and a participant in a National Endowment for the Humanities Summer Seminar on Gothic architecture in the Ile-de-France.

MERI HEINONEN is a Phil. Lic. (Licentiate of Philosophy) at the University of Turku, Finland. She is currently completing her dissertation which is entitled 'Mystical Experience and Gender in German Mysticism, 1200–1400'.

KATHERINE J. LEWIS is a Lecturer in History at the University of Huddersfield. She is the author of *The Cult of St Katherine of Alexandria in Late Medieval England* (2000) and co-editor of *A Companion to Margery Kempe* (2004). She is currently working on a study of gender and society in late medieval England (forthcoming, 2005).

ROBERT MILLS is a lecturer in English at King's College London. His research interests include medieval visual culture, late medieval literature in the vernacular and modern critical theory. Recent publications include *The Monstrous Middle Ages*, co-edited with Bettina Bildhauer (2003) and *Troubled Vision: Gender, Sexuality, and Sight in Medieval Text and Image*, co-edited with Emma Campbell (2004). His book on medieval punishment iconography is forthcoming, and he is now working on a new project: a study of the links between eroticism and religious devotion in medieval culture.

NOTES ON CONTRIBUTORS

CAROLYN DISKANT MUIR received her BA from Wellesley College and her MA from the University of Pennsylvania. She is an Associate Professor in the Department of Fine Arts of the University of Hong Kong, where she teaches European art of the Renaissance and Baroque periods. Her research focuses on issues of religious iconography in early European art, especially the imagery of saints. Recent publications include articles on St Catherine of Alexandria and St Hermann-Joseph. She is currently working on a large-scale study of mystic marriage imagery of male and female saints in Northern Renaissance art.

JACQUELINE MURRAY is Professor of History and Dean of the College of Arts at the University of Guelph. She has published widely on ideas about sexuality and gender and marriage and family in medieval society. Her publications include *Love, Marriage and the Family in the Middle Ages* (2002) and *Conflicted Identities and Multiple Masculinities: Men in the Medieval West* (1999). Her current work focuses on masculinity and male embodiment.

W. M. ORMROD is professor of Medieval History at the University of York. He is the author of *The Reign of Edward III* (1990), *Political Life in Medieval England, 1300–1450* (1995) and numerous articles on the politics, government and political culture of later medieval England.

EMMA PETTIT has recently completed a Ph.D. at the University of York. Her thesis is entitled 'Aldhelm's *opus geminatum De virginitate* in its Early Anglo-Saxon Context'. She considered how this double treatise on sexual renunciation related to Aldhelm's influential ecclesiastical and political career, the composition of the text's audience and the purpose and nature of its spiritual advice.

SHAUN TOUGHER is Lecturer in Ancient History in the Cardiff School of History and Archaeology at Cardiff University, and has also taught at the Queen's University of Belfast and the University of St Andrews. He specializes in late Roman and Byzantine history, and has written several articles on subjects such as eunuchs, Julian the Apostate and Leo VI. He is the author of *The Reign of Leo VI (886–912)* (1997) and the editor of *Eunuchs in Antiquity and Beyond* (2002).

Abbreviations

CRS   Catholic Record Society

EETS   Early English Text Society
ES   extra series
OS   original series

PG   Patrologia Graeca

PL   Patrologia Latina

SS   Special Series

1

Introduction: Holiness and Masculinity in Medieval Europe

P. H. CULLUM

This collection is the product of a conference called 'Holiness and Masculinity in the Middle Ages' organized by the editors at the University of Huddersfield in 2001. We had recently taught a new final year course for the first time, entitled 'Gender and Society: Men and Women in the Middle Ages'. Both course and conference had grown out of a long conversation conducted on the drive back from the annual 'Gender and Medieval Studies' conference, which was held at Canterbury in January 2000. That drive, from the senior ecclesiastical centre of medieval England to the next most senior (York), gave us time and space to consider relationships of gender and religion. For both of us our research was extending from considerations of women's religiosity to include that of men. We wanted to be able to teach issues that we were researching, but we did not think that our (or indeed anyone's) library resources were at that point sufficiently developed to be able to sustain a course only in aspects of the history of medieval masculinity.[1] Although we had both written on and taught women's history, we believed that gender history, as a properly integrated subject and not just as a euphemism for women's studies, was what we could and should develop, hence the subtitle of our course. There has been a significant expansion in published work on medieval masculinity since the beginning of the current millennium, but at its dawn on that early January 2000 drive there was very little that we could give to students.[2] So we decided to add to it ourselves.

Our own research interests were focused on intersections of gender and religion, and although we knew other people who were interested in aspects of medieval masculinity, we felt that the issue of holiness and masculinity was an area that had not had much attention yet paid to it. We knew that there were both established scholars and graduate students working in the field but no conference had brought them together, and little had been published in the field. Moreover the intersection of women's history and religion has been a very fruitful one in medieval studies, and we thought that could also be the case for studies of masculinity.[3] To adapt a formula used by Samantha J. E. Riches and Sarah Salih, we were particularly interested in exploring the ways in which holiness has a bearing on masculinity, and masculinity has a bearing on holiness.[4] Another focus was consideration of the ways in which the performance of both holiness and masculinity intersected with, and was informed by other categories such as monasticism, kingship, mysticism, sanctity, body and age. We felt that a conference and a collection of essays devoted to holiness and masculinity would answer our needs, those of our students and those of others in the field. We deliberately threw our net as wide as possible in seeking contributions. As we are both products of the Centre for Medieval Studies at the University of York we have taken an interdisciplinary approach to our research and we wanted to bring together scholars not just of history, but of literature and art history as well, so that different disciplines could throw light on each other. We also wanted as broad a geographical and chronological range as we could, to highlight the ways in which masculinity and masculinities varied across time and place, and could be contested or diversified even in relation to a single individual. (For instance, the essays by Carolyn Diskant Muir and Meri Heinonen explore the differing means which Henry Suso used to conceive his own identity and relationship to the divine, and the changing ways in which he could be represented, by looking at visual and literary representations of him, respectively.) Thus the current collection, while focusing primarily on northern Europe and on the high and late Middle Ages, also draws on other periods, for instance fifth-century Syria, divided by a serious theological controversy that had crucial implications for perceptions of the embodiment of holiness and the divine. It also includes essays which examine other traditions that informed ideas both of masculinity and forms of holiness, from the Byzantine tradition of eunuchism which produced a rather different gender system to that of the West, to

Reformation England where Catholic gentlemen were faced with the disappearance of Catholicism as the dominant culture. The chapters address the experiences of lay and clergy, the saintly and the secular, the royal and the obscure. In most cases the body, although sometimes problematic in its submission to the will, remained in other respects unproblematically male, but two papers address the altered male body: Shaun Tougher considers the extent to which the post-male physical body of the eunuch might continue to house a masculine spirit, while Robert Mills addresses how and with what purpose the tonsure could be a physical sign to both the cleric and laity of the particular status of the career holy man, and a site of anxiety at the same time.

For women in the Middle Ages religion offered both opportunities and problems in establishing themselves as authorized and authoritative holy persons. For women, authority was often particularly difficult; to claim to speak authoritatively on matters of religion and to have that claim validated was a difficult act to manage. One of the ways in which women might do this was through use of conventional ideas of female submission such as the prophetic claim merely to voice the word of God in a form of ventriloquism in which the female speaker was merely the puppet through whom God's voice was transmitted to the world. In this case the woman sidestepped all claims to personal authority. In a slightly different way the female mystic who sought union with God could use the fact of her female body to position herself as the Bride of Christ entering into a 'natural' relationship of courtship or marriage.

By contrast men could find these kinds of relationships with God difficult precisely because they might challenge conventional ideas of masculine autonomy. Thus Carolyn Diskant Muir and Christopher C. Craun explore the extent to which male hermits and mystics might, in seeing God as male, choose to place themselves in a female subject position and the effect that this had on representations of their gender identities. Muir also explores instances where men such as Henry Suso and St Hermann-Joseph contracted mystical marriages to a female figure as the male partner. In the case of Suso this involved a masculine subject position which is rather at odds with much current scholarship which tends to emphasize the female-centred nature of his spirituality. Meri Heinonen's essay provides a challenge to this approach as she focuses instead on one text in which Suso used male and female characters to delineate forms of holy life appropriate to men and women, borrowing from contemporary aristocratic secular models of masculinity to emphasize that only men should attempt the endeavours of holy masculinity.

Indeed, this emphasis of Suso's on the divine knighthood leads us to consideration of the other side of the problem; namely that aspects of the religious life required the setting aside of emblems of masculine authority or autonomy which might have implications for the subject's sense of his own masculinity, and others' views of it. Emma Pettit argues that Aldhelm constructed a model of active masculine sanctity for his monastic audience precisely because Anglo-Saxon monks had to leave a warrior lifestyle behind. Jacqueline Murray explores the problem of the monk who, in relinquishing sexual activity and accepting submission to the will of others, might have been thought to have relinquished masculinity itself. But instead the 'struggle for chastity' was re-envisioned as a specifically masculine arena of battle, again borrowing from secular and aristocratic codes. Thus the willed abandonment of conventional male behaviour was used as a sign of the specifically masculine spiritual endeavour. Knights might see themselves as the truly masculine 'hard men', but their lives were soft in comparison to the spiritual battles to be fought by monks and clerics in ensuring the submission of the body to the will, in the practice of chastity and in the triumph of martyrdom.

For kings the meshing of religious values with the practice of authority presented other demands, as it was necessary to balance the requirements of religious observance with the proper practice of regality. This was a blend successfully achieved by Louis IX, whose canonization made a statement not just about his holy kingship, but about the nature of the French royal line more widely. The enhancement and blazoning of the reputations of France's male royals was made possible through their physical location in the monastery of Saint-Denis, surrounded both by the monks and earlier emblems of French royal sanctity, as Dawn Marie Hayes shows. However, other king-saints present more awkward models; an overly religious king, like Edward the Confessor, who was believed to have placed his inclination towards chastity before his duty of providing an heir to the throne, could create extreme difficulties for himself and for his kingdom. Even more problematic were those kings who met death in the defence of their kingdoms or rule, for they could all too easily be seen as failures. The ignominious end of a king such as Edward II not only cast shadows on his own reputation but that of his dynasty. W. M. Ormrod argues that Edward III's concern for Edward II's posthumous reputation was a matter that not only reflected on his father but on his mother, and thus himself as well. The attempts to have both Edward II and Henry VI officially recognized as saints also provided a means of re-masculinizing rulers whose equivocal gender identities had provided important ammunition for those who sought to depose and disgrace them. Rewriting both kings as martyrs had an important recuperative effect on their masculinity. Similarly Edward Christie argues that the deaths of Anglo-Saxon kings embodied contemporary values because they knew that they faced death and actively chose both it and submission to the will of God. They could thus be presented not as failed kings, but as successful martyrs. To die was an act of masculine will and enhanced rather than detracted from the king-saint's authority. The posthumous creation and recreation of a king's reputation allowed the representation of events in the light of an understanding of his holiness of life.

Holiness had to be learned before it could be willed, and Fiona S. Dunlop's paper explores the use of drama as a didactic method for the instruction of young laymen on the brink of manhood, through analysis of a play which offers them status-specific lessons about desirable masculinity. She considers the role of didactic literature such as mirrors for princes, and these are also examined in Katherine J. Lewis's discussion of the model of holy kingship offered to Henry VI in St Edmund of East Anglia. Henry perhaps demonstrates that the lesson learned was not always the one offered, but it is nevertheless clear that his keepers were concerned to offer him appropriate role models who incorporated both the holy and the military. The Catholic gentlemen of the northern English Reformation by contrast preferred a quietist response which involved (on the whole) neither a military reaction nor a martyrdom but the survival of the family and its faith in the face of difficult circumstances. Nevertheless, the behaviour of their wives and daughters, who were apparently less willing to conform than their menfolk, could have been and sometimes was seen as evidence that the men were unable to exercise proper patriarchal authority over their households. In these cases Sarah L. Bastow argues the apparent failure of masculine authority was nothing of the kind, for the female civil disobedience was tolerated, if not encouraged, by the men of the family.

This collection is necessarily limited in scope. The majority of the papers relate to monks and to a lesser extent secular clergy, and to elite laymen. These are a well-documented but small minority of the population. There is much work still to be done, for example, on lower status or peasant men's piety, and the ways in which it intersected with issues of gender. Some of the papers signal interactions between clerical and aristocratic ideals, but we were unfortunately not offered a paper on one of the potentially most fruitful areas for the examination of this topic, the military orders. Indeed, issues of holiness and masculinity underpin the events and ethos of the Crusades, but this is an area that has seen very little research to date.[5] This is an exploration of Christian masculinity and holiness, but neither category is confined to Christians, there is much to be said about Muslim, Jewish and indeed pagan conceptions of the intersection of holiness and masculinity in medieval Europe. We look forward to further work in this field.

Whatever the specific forms of holy masculinity under discussion, throughout there is a strong emphasis on the masculine ability to exercise self-mastery. Even those who apparently preferred to adopt a feminine subject position chose this as an act of will. The abandonment of authority and submission to the will of God or to an earthly superior was also a willed choice, in which the subject exercised a form of power. The practice of holiness embodied the masculine capacities of self-control (whether physical or mental) and intellectual decision. No man could be holy who did not choose to be so, however much he might consider himself to be dependent on the will of God.

Notes

[1] There were of course a number of individual articles in collections and journals, but the main body of work was focused in a small number of collections: Nancy F. Partner (ed.), *Studying Medieval Women: Sex, Gender, Feminism* (Cambridge, MA, 1993), a special edition of *Speculum*; D. M. Hadley (ed.), *Masculinity in Medieval Europe* (London and New York, 1997); Judith C. Brown and Robert C. Davis (eds), *Gender and Society in Renaissance Italy* (London and New York, 1998); Claire A. Lees (ed.), *Medieval Masculinities: Regarding Men in the Middle Ages* (Minneapolis, 1994); Jeffrey Jerome Cohen and Bonnie Wheeler (eds), *Becoming Male in the Middle Ages* (New York and London, 1997); Vern L. Bullough and James A. Brundage (eds), *Handbook of Medieval Sexuality* (New York and London, 1996); Jacqueline Murray (ed.), *Conflicted Identities and Multiple Masculinities: Men in the Medieval World* (New York, 1999).

[2] Since then a small number of useful collections and monographs have appeared: Matthew Kuefler, *The Manly Eunuch: Masculinity, Gender Ambiguity and Christian Ideology in Late Antiquity* (Chicago and London,

2001); Ruth Mazo Karras, *From Boys to Men: Formations of Masculinity in Late Medieval Europe* (Philadelphia, 2002); Kim M. Phillips and Barry Reay (eds), *Sexualities in History: A Reader* (New York, 2002); Glenn Burger and Stephen F. Kruger (eds), *Queering the Middle Ages* (Minneapolis, 2001); Samantha J. E. Riches and Sarah Salih (eds), *Gender and Holiness: Men, Women and Saints in Late Medieval Europe* (London, 2002); Sharon Farmer and Carol Braun Pasternack (eds), *Gender and Difference in the Middle Ages* (Minneapolis and London, 2003). There are also other relevant individual articles and essays elsewhere, but there is not space to list them all here.

[3] See, for example, Eileen Power, *Medieval English Nunneries* (Cambridge, 1922); Penny Schine Gold, *The Lady and the Virgin: Image, Attitude and Experience in Twelfth-Century France* (Chicago, 1985); Caroline Walker Bynum, *Holy Feast and Holy Fast: The Religious Significance of Food to Medieval Women* (Berkeley, CA, and London, 1987); Barbara Newman, *Sister of Wisdom: St Hildegard's Theology of the Feminine* (Berkeley, CA, and Aldershot, 1987); Sharon K. Elkins, *Holy Women of Twelfth-Century England* (Chapel Hill, NC, and London, 1988); W. J. Sheils and Diana Wood (eds), *Women in the Church*, Studies in Church History, 27 (Oxford, 1990); Lynn Staley, *Margery Kempe's Dissenting Fictions* (University Park, Pennsylvania, 1994); Diane Watt, *Secretaries of God: Women Prophets in Late Medieval and Early Modern England* (Woodbridge, 1997); Rosalynn Voaden, *God's Words, Women's Voices: The Discernment of Spirits in the Writing of Late-Medieval Women Visionaries* (York, 1999); Sarah Salih, *Versions of Virginity in Late Medieval England* (Cambridge, 2001).

[4] Riches and Salih, 'Introduction' to *Gender and Holiness*, pp. 1–8 (p. 5).

[5] The recent collection, Susan B. Edgington and Sarah Lambert (eds), *Gendering the Crusades* (Cardiff, 2001), while invaluable in its consideration of women's roles, does not include any essays dealing specifically with masculinity.

2

Holiness and Masculinity in Aldhelm's *Opus Geminatum De virginitate*

EMMA PETTIT

In the early seventh century Sigebert of East Anglia renounced his kingship and entered a monastery. Bede, in his *Historia ecclesiastica* (731), tells us that this able warrior and leader had chosen to serve the kingdom of God as a spiritual soldier. Nonetheless when the East Angles came under attack from the kingdom of Mercia, Sigebert's people dragged him from the monastery to encourage their fearful army. Mindful of his monastic profession, however, Sigebert carried only a staff and in the battle that followed he was killed and his army defeated.[1] Since Bede's account clearly demonstrates the incompatibility between the roles of secular warrior and spiritual monk, this episode serves to illustrate the tensions that arose in seventh-century Anglo-Saxon England as existing Germanic codes of behaviour met with inherited Christian traditions. Although the conversion of the English was begun in earnest in the late sixth century, even so, it was a piecemeal process. By the late seventh century, the period with which this chapter is concerned, adult Christians were perhaps only two generations away from their 'pagan' antecedents. With respect to monastic life, the church had to accommodate differences not only in entrants' religious convictions, but also in their sexual histories and biological sex, all of which threatened the unity of the newly formed and rapidly expanding monasteries.[2] Churchmen therefore had the challenging task of formulating and introducing new statuses, identities and codes of behaviour that would unite mainly adult aristocratic recruits, as well as distinguish them from the nominally Christian laity.[3]

To this end it is significant that men's and women's transitions from the secular to the religious life seem to have been different. Both had to forsake the secular status conferred by marriage and sexual relations, yet for most high-status women, there appears to have been much continuity between the types of activities associated with their religious and secular lives. Both religious and secular women could therefore undertake a number of similar, socially important roles, such as those of influential diplomat and counsellor, domestic host to guests, commemorator of the dead and crafter of textiles.[4] In contrast, men were expected to make a more radical break with their secular lifestyles when they entered the religious life; in particular they had to forsake the military duties of warrior service.[5] Men were prohibited not only from carrying weapons and engaging in active combat (including hunting), but also from the physical potency, aggression and heroism associated with the warrior status. It was therefore important for ecclesiastical writers to redirect male warrior energies towards a new type of service for Christ.[6] As priests, some male religious could assume a new form of authority through their exclusive access to certain sacramental rites, yet the church still had to teach men that the relinquishment of their secular status did not necessarily mean a concomitant loss of masculinity. This period of religious and social transition therefore provides a fruitful context in which to examine the culturally changeable concepts of holiness and masculinity.

An ideal Anglo-Saxon text to explore these concepts is offered by Aldhelm's late seventh-century *opus geminatum*, that is, 'work of two paired parts', the prose *De virginitate* and its verse counterpart, the *Carmen de virginitate*.[7] Aldhelm (c.640–709) was abbot of Malmesbury in Wiltshire and subsequently bishop of Sherborne in Dorset.[8] This double treatise, written in Anglo-Latin, was intended to provide guidance on sexual and social renunciation for people entering a monastic life and, as this chapter will argue, can be seen to respond to the contemporary issues and anxieties outlined above. Contemporary authors' indebtedness to the double treatise's Latin and densely glossed extant manuscripts of the prose text both provide evidence for their rapid dissemination and popularity.[9] Aldhelm's double treatise may have been popular precisely because it edified and entertained male and female religious in equal measure. The texts begin and end with advice on how individuals of both sexes can achieve religious perfection, as well as providing a lengthy catalogue of male and female saints, presented as illustrative models.[10] That Aldhelm certainly envisaged a mixed audience for the texts is suggested by internal evidence, for at times he specifically counsels 'ecclesiastics', 'brothers' and individuals of 'either sex'.[11] Indeed, it has long been assumed that the double treatise was intended specifically for Abbess Hildelith and the nuns of Barking Abbey in Essex, but Scott Gwara has recently made a persuasive case for Aldhelm's intended audience in fact being a whole 'constellation' of double monasteries in Wessex.[12] In early Anglo-Saxon England these communities, over which abbesses normally presided, housed nuns, monks and clerics, who lived together in varying degrees of proximity.[13] This chapter seeks to investigate Aldhelm's attitude to masculinity by examining both his passages of spiritual advice and his representation of male and female saints. Gender here is understood to be a relational concept, in which masculinity and femininity pertains both to 'perceived differences' as well as to parallels 'between the sexes'.[14] The fact that individuals might be subject to 'variant notions of masculinity' also underpins this analysis.[15] Aldhelm's construction of gender identities will be related to the cultural experiences of his male and female religious addressees.

Aldhelm's remarkable guidance, as a number of scholarly studies have shown, drew upon patristic literature on sexual continence and asceticism, yet carefully selected and transmitted its ideas with a view to contemporary circumstances.[16] One of Aldhelm's most striking departures from his patristic sources was his unprecedented use of male saints as *exempla* to illustrate the spiritual rewards of sexual continence.[17] In significant contrast, the patristic literary model which greatly influenced Aldhelm's work and its structure, namely Ambrose's *De virginibus ad Marcellinam* (a long letter concerning virginity addressed to his sister Marcellina and dated 377), concentrated on exemplary female virgins.[18] In fact Aldhelm not merely selects holy males as *exempla*, but his male saints are also given considerably more prominence than the females. Thus, in both texts Aldhelm lists the males first, and in the prose text even follows his female accounts with those of five Old Testament patriarchs. Furthermore, in total, Aldhelm catalogues seventy-three male saints compared to forty-three female saints across both texts, as well as giving these males almost twice as much space as the females. Despite this, to date, scholars have focused largely on a gendered analysis of Aldhelm's female saints in relation to the female component of his audience.[19] The male saints and male audience have yet to receive the same attention, an area of research to which this essay seeks to contribute. But first, it would be useful to rehearse some of the arguments that have been made in relation to Aldhelm's gendered treatment of sanctity.

Gwara has recently observed that Aldhelm's thematic treatment of sanctity differs in his portraits of male and female saints. Whereas saints of both sexes endure persecution and are martyred, the males typically achieve holiness through zealously proselytizing, the females by rejecting their pagan suitors. Gwara relates this to the different roles that Aldhelm expected men and women to assume in the conversion of England.[20] Alternatively, a number of scholars have focused on Aldhelm's varied approach to women in the double treatise. On the one hand, these scholars suggest that his depiction of male and female virgins as equally holy individuals illustrates women's influential involvement in the early church alongside men. On the other hand they use his misogynistic clichés against women to illustrate the Anglo-Saxon clergy's transmission of negative patristic views of the female sex.[21] Thus for Aldhelm, Sinead O'Sullivan argues, virginity enables both men and women to transcend earthly gender divisions and 'to participate in the oneness of Christ'. Nonetheless, to achieve this coequal state women must reject what are deemed typically 'female preoccupations' of worldliness and carnality and instead 'become male' by adopting 'masculine spirituality'.[22] Furthermore, a recent study by Claire Lees and Gillian Overing suggests that, through his figurations of the female body, Aldhelm 'encouraged' his female audience 'to think of themselves as sometimes embodied and gendered – sometimes male, other times female'.[23] Thus scholars generally agree that Aldhelm represents women as both masculine and feminine, but what about his representation of men?

Interior men

Throughout his double treatise Aldhelm instructs his audience that they must focus upon the 'actions of the inner man', that is upon their invisible spiritual selves.[24] A ceaseless battle against personified and animalistic vices is one of the contemplative acts he exhorts them to undertake.[25] Aldhelm encourages his audience to engage in mental warfare in the prose text and devotes 314 lines to providing them with a battle plan at the end of its poetic counterpart.[26] The savage power and virulence with which Aldhelm associates the vices makes it clear that they can only be thwarted with extreme mental violence. 'With savage armies of foes' the vices thus ceaselessly battle against the religious.[27] They also wield an array of weaponry with which to injure spiritually the religious fighters. As a result, Aldhelm commands his audience to trample, whip and strike these vices into submission 'with muscular energy', indeed, as if fighting 'the most ferocious armies of barbarians'.[28] All religious are expected to brandish such specialized spiritual arms as 'the shield of modesty', as well as those essential weapons of 'the sword of the Holy Word and the impenetrable breast-plate of faith'.[29] The use of metaphorical armed force is in fact crucial since these vices, Aldhelm warns, will prey upon those individuals who are 'unarmed'.[30] In this way all the members of his audience are cast as 'warriors of the Lord'.[31] All religious therefore, regardless of biological sex, sexual status (whether a virgin or chaste) and level of monastic experience, are expected to undertake the same duties in the spiritual battle and to fight with comparable vigour. This is important, for Aldhelm not only associates all members of his audience, male and female, with the spiritual strength that patristic authors ordinarily identify as a male quality, but also with physical strength, aggressive warrior action and weapon-bearing, which in Anglo-Saxon culture was chiefly associated with men.

If such aggressive imagery did not suffice to encourage both male and female religious to adopt masculine strength in these inner battles, then Aldhelm taught this more explicitly. His addressees are therefore told to act 'viriliter', 'manfully', in their chaste lives.[32] More revealingly, Aldhelm mocks womanly behaviour in warfare by berating those faint-hearted soldiers who would rather flee from the battlefield than face the enemy because they fear war 'muliebriter', that is, 'in the manner of women', something Aldhelm describes as shameful.[33] Arguably Aldhelm was encouraging his audience to achieve masculine holiness in their invisible inner selves, with the aim of creating unity in the cloister through this shared spiritual endeavour.[34] It is also important to note that Aldhelm not only exhorts his audience to adopt masculine inner strength in their contemplative spiritual battles, but also provides them with concrete examples of both sexes to imitate in this respect, because his catalogue of male and female saints also exemplifies the virtue of iron-willed minds.[35]

Aldhelm's saintly exempla

Whilst Aldhelm depicts both male and female religious as masculine combatants in their internal spiritual battles, his double treatise recognizes gendered distinctions between men's and women's external acts and demeanours. Aldhelm's representation of miracle stories in his saintly *exempla* illustrates this contention. A systematic survey of this lengthy catalogue reveals that, in the outward act of miracle performance, only male saints are masculinized, whereas female saints are aligned with culturally feminine characteristics. Aldhelm's depiction of sanctity partly derives from the nature of his sources of course. Male saints in the double treatise include early Christian prophets, apostles, popes, bishops, monks and abbots, spanning the period from the Old Testament to the sixth century, whereas his female saints are nearly all third- and fourth-century virgin martyrs. Because the celebration of women in the early Christian church is largely confined to the martyrial literature, Aldhelm's selection of saints partly reflects an actual distribution and this lends a natural bias to the themes that he offers in his saints' accounts.[36] For example, the fact that many of his female saints were virgin martyrs explains why they principally achieve sanctity by rejecting pagan marriages and suffering torture and death as a result. However, we must recall that Aldhelm selected these saintly *exempla* and since his portraits were digests of more expansive textual accounts, he chose which material to transmit and how to present it. Studies have indeed shown that Aldhelm's saints accounts do differ – sometimes radically – from their literary sources.[37] Furthermore, comparative evidence from Carolingian Europe suggests that even writers who were well-acquainted with a female saint, either personally or through extant written evidence, often disregarded this material when they wrote the saint's *vita*. Instead, they constructed these texts according to male hagiographical traditions.[38] Arguably, therefore, Aldhelm's decision over which aspects of his male and female saints' accounts to select and emphasize illuminates our understanding of his concept of gender identity, and within this context, his concept of holiness and masculinity in particular.

Miracles, essential qualifiers of sanctity, are overwhelmingly a male activity in the double treatise. If we consider Aldhelm's use of repeated miracle motifs, he provides only thirty-eight female saints' miracle stories across both treatises, while his male saints can be credited with no less than one hundred and fourteen. Proportionately, male saints thus perform almost twice as many miracles per individual as female saints. In addition, while the miracle stories associated with both male and female saints range across the miracle spectrum – they include, for example, healing miracles, visions and prophecies – certain miracles are performed only by men. Only the sanctity of male saints, for example, is divinely foreordained and only males perform miracles of translocation or telekinesis.[39] The numerical and typological difference between male and female miracle-working is significant, for it means that comparatively more male saints are aligned with an active spiritual potency.

Claire Stancliffe's study of Sulpicius Severus' late fourth–early fifth-century life of St Martin provides an extremely useful model for an analysis of Aldhelm's treatment of miracles.[40] As Stancliffe demonstrates, Sulpicius seems to distinguish between those miracles wrought either by divine power or by Martin's own power. Thus in some miracles Martin is a receptor of God's power since either the Holy Spirit inspires his performance of miracles, or the saint invokes God's power through prayer. In these miracles, she suggests, 'one might almost say that he becomes a "medium" for the Holy Spirit'. Alternatively, in other miracles Martin seems to bear his own holy power, or *virtus*, which he uses as he wills.[41] Significantly, if we apply this model to Aldhelm's saints' performance of miracles, whereas the majority of his female saints act merely as a medium for God's power, male saints instead tend to wield their own miracle-working power. Thus, if we plot Aldhelm's use of the word *virtus* throughout his catalogue of saints, he uses the noun proportionately twice as often in his male accounts.[42] Moreover, although Aldhelm exploits the full semantic range of this noun, which comprises many qualities, including virtue, excellence, strength, the power to perform miracles and, moreover, manliness and manhood *per se*, he appears to use it differently in his male and female saints' accounts.[43] When depicting female saints Aldhelm predominantly uses *virtus* to mean good moral conduct; in contrast, in his male accounts he chiefly uses it to refer to their holy power. Whereas women are passive receptors of God's power, men instead actively perform miracles using their own power. Aldhelm's use of *virtus* in his male accounts therefore aligns them with an active spiritual potency which is archetypally male, especially when paired with his female saints' frequent association with the feminine trope of passivity.

A clear male–female distinction in miracle-working is further suggested if we compare those instances in which saints of both sexes perform the same miracle type. Consider, for example, saints' exorcism of astonishingly fearsome dragons, which represent, variously, actual beasts, demons and 'personified vices'.[44] Whilst Victoria is the only female saint to perform this miracle in Aldhelm's double treatise, three male saints accomplish it, namely, the Old Testament prophet Daniel, the pope-saint Silvester and the Palestinian abbot Hilarion. Michael Lapidge has shown that, in order to represent virginity as 'a vigorously aggressive virtue', Aldhelm provided his saints with such potent adversaries as dragons and, in the case of Hilarion, gave this miracle story considerably more prominence than his principal literary source Jerome.[45] Certainly Victoria's dragon is as equally harmful as those exorcized by the men and she eradicates it as fearlessly.[46] In the poetic treatise moreover, she provides a rare example of a female saint who performs this feat using her own *virtus*; by exercising this miracle-working power in an active way Victoria thus parallels Silvester and Daniel, both of whom also use *virtus* to slay their dragons.[47] Nonetheless, despite Victoria's superficial presentation in the same masculine terms as the men, in this particular miracle type she remains distinguished from them in a number of important respects.

Victoria may use *virtus* to eradicate her dragon, but, uniquely, she does so 'relying on the triumph of heaven'.[48] In fact Victoria is the only dragon-expelling saint to directly invoke God's authority, because in his name she implores the beast to abandon the town it has been tormenting.[49] Furthermore, when Victoria journeys to meet her dragon adversary she is 'sustained by the assistance of an angel'.[50] Victoria's reliance on celestial support sets her apart from the male saints. Not only do they combat the beasts alone, but when Hilarion, the only male saint to appeal to heavenly power does so, it is to fight his dragon 'with the weaponry of prayer'.[51] Victoria is presented in a much less overtly masculine way than the males who exorcize these creatures; whilst she is not feminine, nor is she permitted to be as masculine as the male saints are.[52] This male–female distinction in gender is further illuminated in Aldhelm's representation of the saints' successful eradication of the dragons, for whereas his male saints either violently kill or make impotent these adversaries, Victoria does not fight hers physically. Instead, her beast merely flees rapidly from its lair when she orders it to leave 'with her terrifying command'.[53] Although Hilarion's actions resemble those of Victoria, since he also commands his opponent with terrifying words, even so, he does not simply banish the beast from its den. Instead, he compels it to climb a pyre, whereupon it is cremated, so that its ribs and spine are cleaved apart by blazing fireballs.[54] Silvester and Daniel use comparable aggression to overcome their dragon adversaries: Silvester binds his in an inextricable collar and, after Daniel hurls a deadly titbit into his beast's jaws, its entrails burst open.[55] In short, Victoria is a powerful saint, yet she is comparatively much less belligerent and independently powerful than the males who perform this miracle. Recalling Aldhelm's potential audience, perhaps he deliberately intensified his male saints' masculinity in order to compensate for holy men's prohibition from the male heroic status of secular warriorhood.

Aldhelm's decision to align principally male saints with the typically masculine characteristics of power and warrior strength is not isolated to the miracle of dragon fettering. Comparable results are yielded from those miracles in which saints remain unharmed despite their persecutors' fierce efforts to torture them. Since this miracle type is extremely formulaic and is performed by nearly equal numbers of male and female saints, it is particularly useful for gender comparison. Saints of both sexes have extraordinary resolve which enables them to endure the harshest of beatings and floggings. They are bound to rocks or tied up in ropes and then thrown into rivers or the sea, yet they are carried to shore safely. They are roasted on pyres or boiled in vats of water or pitch, yet emerge from these unscathed. Most remarkably, the miraculous rescue of saints is performed repeatedly through God's intercession: he ensures the saints' safety.

Despite Aldhelm's use of the same miracle formula for saints of either sex, his choice of lexicon is gender-specific. Most revealing is his different choice of adjectives to describe the tortured male and female saints, for only male saints are associated with the masculine qualities of strength and invincibility. In significant contrast, female saints are described as comparatively weak and defenseless. The men are thus characterized repeatedly as 'unconquerable', 'uncompromising', 'triumphant' and 'steadfast'.[56] Conversely, female saints are described frequently as 'pretty', 'gentle' or 'delicate', 'feminine' and 'defenceless' or 'unarmed'.[57] Aldhelm's decision to align females with these characteristics is noteworthy when we consider that in the masculinized interior battle against vice he specifically warned men and women that they must not be 'unarmed' (*inermis*) and must not act 'in the manner of a woman' (*muliebriter*). Clearly, Aldhelm's construction of gender differed according to whether acts of holiness were invisible or perceptible. Whereas Aldhelm depicts male and female religious as masculine combatants in their internal spiritual battles, suggesting that he encourages men and women to be masculine in their interior selves, in the palpable act of miracle-working they remained bound to the cultural characteristics of their biological sex. Therefore, Aldhelm treats male and female saints' dragon exorcism and survival of torture differently because in these external acts only the men are presented as truly masculine. In relation to his female audience it is possible that Aldhelm rendered it acceptable for females to imitate masculine qualities in their minds, but did not believe it to be appropriate, or necessary, for them to imitate overtly masculine virtues or male roles. This hypothesis seems to be supported by Aldhelm's treatment of the cross-dressing St Eugenia. Eugenia is the only saint in the double treatise who attempts to disguise her biological gender by dressing in male clothes and by shaving her long hair for a 'short crop of the masculine sex'. Her cross-dressing, Aldhelm remarks, is 'against the laws of nature',[58] a phrase which throughout his corpus of writings refers to acts – especially morally contemptible ones – against the world order which God enshrined at Creation.[59] Visible mimicking of men was clearly inappropriate in Aldhelm's view.

Conclusion

To conclude, two approaches to the theme of masculinity can be adduced in Aldhelm's double treatise on renunciation. First, Aldhelm exhorts all members of his audience to regulate their lives through inward contemplative exercises. In the interior battle against vice both male and female religious assume a shared identity: they are masculinized spiritual combatants. Second, analysis of Aldhelm's lengthy catalogue of saintly *exempla* suggests that in the physical act of miracle performance only male saints are masculinized; in contrast, female saints are aligned with culturally feminine characteristics. These female representations are authoritative but wield less power than men and are less autonomous. It is thus predominately male saints who are *virtus*-empowered miracle-workers. Moreover, in those miracles in which saints remain unharmed during torture, Aldhelm's choice of adjectives associate male saints with power and manliness, females with relative weakness and passivity.

How then are we to interpret the construction of holiness and masculinity in Aldhelm's double treatise? Aldhelm's representation of masculinity would have edified and entertained aristocrats of both sexes, as well as appealed to their literary tastes as they fused Germanic heroic action with Christian holiness.[60] It is also probable that Aldhelm's distinctive ideas on masculinity reflect contemporary cultural circumstances. One reason why he may have associated men with outward acts of holiness was because in early Anglo-Saxon England men had privileged access to holy power through their performance of certain sacramental duties. However, Aldhelm's ideas are perhaps most likely to reflect his attempts to create new identities for adult religious recruits. On the one hand, by providing his audience with a shared invisible spiritual identity heavily indebted to masculinity, Aldhelm perhaps sought to create unity among the disparate members of contemporary double monasteries. On the other hand, Aldhelm's differentiated treatment of men's and women's performance of miracles arguably appreciates their different gendered experiences of religious renunciation. As previously suggested, many female secular roles could still be fulfilled in Anglo-Saxon monasteries. Therefore contemporary female religious did not have to act like men in order to achieve holiness. Male religious, however, made a more significant break with their secular lifestyle because they were released from military service. Might Aldhelm have sought to compensate for this loss by reminding men that they did not have to relinquish completely their masculine association with a warrior idiom, and its associations with strength and triumph? He showed male religious that, whilst women could be masculine in their minds and whilst in double monasteries a woman ordinarily ruled over them, even so, physically, their sex remained stronger and more able. Aldhelm thus reassured men by demonstrating that even as monks they were still masculine and that the spiritual life of the cloister presented an alternative, yet equally authoritative form of masculinity.

Notes

I would like to thank Ross Balzaretti, Gabriella Corona, Katy Cubitt, Chris Fern and Mary Garrison for their helpful advice and encouragement on earlier drafts of this paper.

[1] Bede, *Historia ecclesiastica gentis anglorum*, ed. B. Colgrave and R. A. B. Mynors, *Bede's Ecclesiastical History of the English People* (Oxford, 1969), 3. 18, pp. 268–9; For the phenomenon of the monk-king in the early medieval British Isles, including a discussion of Sigebert's actions, see C. Stancliffe, 'Kings who opted out', in P. Wormald with D. Bullough and R. Collins (eds), *Ideal and Reality in Frankish and Anglo-Saxon Society: Studies Presented to J. M. Wallace-Hadrill* (Oxford, 1983), pp. 154–76.

[2] See, for example, B. Yorke, *Nunneries and the Anglo-Saxon Royal Houses* (London and New York, 2003), pp. 17–46, especially pp. 23–30.

3   For the church's problems distinguishing between aristocratic and secular religious lifestyles in this period see P. Wormald, 'Bede, "Beowulf" and the conversion of the Anglo-Saxon aristocracy', in R. T. Farrell (ed.), *Bede and Anglo-Saxon England*, British Archaeological Reports, British Series, 46 (Oxford, 1978), pp. 32–95.

4   For secular female roles see C. E. Fell, *Women in Anglo-Saxon England* (Bloomington, IN, 1984), pp. 39–40, 50, 67, and A. Hennessey Olsen, 'Gender roles', in R. E. Bjork and J. D. Niles (eds), *A Beowulf Handbook* (Exeter, 1996), pp. 311–24 (pp. 314–18); for the religious life see D. B. Schneider, 'Anglo-Saxon women in the religious life: a study of the status and position of women in an early medieval society' (unpublished Ph.D. thesis, Cambridge University, 1985), pp. 33–6, 72–3, 272–86.

5   For secular male roles see D. Whitelock, *The Beginnings of English Society* (Harmondsworth, 1952), p. 92; for the prohibition of some secular male roles in the religious life see Wormald, 'Bede, "Beowulf" and conversion', p. 51.

6   For the difficulty of reconciling early medieval holiness with aristocratic male values, albeit for lay audiences, see S. Airlie, 'The anxiety of sanctity: St. Gerald of Aurillac and his maker', *Journal of Ecclesiastical History*, 43, 3 (1992), 372–95; J. L. Nelson, 'Monks, secular men and masculinity, c.900', in D. M. Hadley (ed.), *Masculinity in Medieval Europe* (London, 1999), pp. 121–42. The same point is discussed by Edward Christie in the present volume, and by Jacqueline Murray in relation to the twelfth century.

7   These might be translated as the prose 'Concerning Virginity' and 'The Poem/Verse/Song Concerning Virginity' (scholars do not agree as to which term is the most appropriate for the *Carmen*). I use Rudolf Ehwald's Latin edition of Aldhelm's works: *Aldhelmi opera*, Monumenta Germaniae Historica, Auctores Antiquissimi, 15 (Berlin, 1919, repr. Munich, 1984); prose *De virginitate* (hereafter *PdV*), pp. 226–323; *Carmen de virginitate* (hereafter *CdV*), pp. 350–471. For a new edition of the *PdV*, offering a revised version of Ehwald's text, alongside an extremely valuable study of Old English and Latin glosses to the text see *Aldhelmi Malmesbiriensis Prosa de virginitate cum glosa latina atque anglosaxonica*, ed. S. Gwara, Corpus Christianorum Series Latina, 124 and 124A (Turnhout, 2001) (hereafter I cite only vol. 124). Modern English trs of both works are available: for *PdV*, see *Aldhelm: The Prose Works*, ed. M. Lapidge and M. Herren (Ipswich, 1979), pp. 59–132 (hereafter tr. Lapidge); for *CdV*, see J. L. Rosier in *Aldhelm: The Poetic Works*, ed. M. Lapidge and J. L. Rosier (Cambridge, 1985), pp. 102–67 (hereafter tr. Rosier). It is difficult to establish a date for Aldhelm's works on virginity, see *The Prose Works*, ed. Lapidge and Herren, pp. 14–15; but Gwara argues that they should be dated to *c.*700, *Aldhelmi Malmesbiriensis*, pp. 47–55; for the literary form of the *opus geminatum*, its use in Anglo-Saxon England and the differences between Aldhelm's prose and poetic treatises see P. Godman, 'The Anglo-Latin *opus geminatum*: From Aldhelm to Alcuin', in M. Herren (ed.), *Insular Latin Studies* (Toronto, 1981), pp. 115–29 (p. 115).

8 For the difficulties in establishing dates for Aldhelm's life, career and death see *The Prose Works*, ed. Lapidge and Herren, pp. 5–10, and, *Aldhelmi Malmesbiriensis*, ed. Gwara, pp. 19, 23, 26–7, 34, 38–9; generally, his abbacy is thought to date 672/5–705/6, and he is thought to have been appointed bishop in 705/6.

9 See, for example, A. Orchard, *The Poetic Art of Aldhelm*, Cambridge Studies in Anglo-Saxon England, 8 (Cambridge, 1994), pp. 239–60, 284–8; S. Gwara, 'Glosses to Aldhelm's "Prosa de virginitate" and glossaries from the Anglo-Saxon Golden Age, *ca.* 670–800', *Studi Medievali*, 38, 2 (1997), 561–645.

10 For Aldhelm's male saints see *PdV*, chs 20–21, 23–38, pp. 249–91, tr. Lapidge, pp. 76–8, 79–106; *CdV*, ll. 248–1652, pp. 363–422, tr. Rosier, pp. 108–39; for his female saints see *PdV*, chs 40–52, pp. 292–310, tr. Lapidge, pp. 106–21; *CdV*, ll. 1673–2445, pp. 422–52, tr. Rosier, pp. 140–57.

11 *PdV*, ch. 58, p. 317, tr. Lapidge, p. 127, 'ecclesiastici'; *CdV*, ll. 2627, p. 459 tr. Rosier, p. 161, 'fratres'; *PdV*, ch. 10, p. 238, tr. Lapidge, p. 67, 'utroque sexus'.

12 *Aldhelmi Malmesbiriensis*, ed. Gwara, pp. 47–55.

13 For double monasteries see Schneider, 'Anglo-Saxon women in the religious life'; for a recent study of Anglo-Saxon nunneries, with reference to double monasteries, see Yorke, *Nunneries and the Anglo-Saxon Royal Houses*.

14 J. W. Scott, 'Gender: a useful category of historical analysis', *American Historical Review*, 91 (1986), 1053–75 (1056, 1067); for the application of gender as a relational concept with specific reference to medieval masculinities see C. A. Lees (ed.), *Medieval Masculinities: Regarding Men in the Middle Ages* (Minneapolis, 1994).

15 D. M. Hadley, 'Introduction: medieval masculinities', in Hadley, *Masculinity in Medieval Europe*, pp. 1–18 (p. 5).

16 M. Lapidge, 'Introduction to Aldhelm's prose *De virginitate*', in *The Prose Works*, ed. Lapidge and Herren, pp. 51–8; S. O'Sullivan, 'The patristic background to Aldhelm's *De Virginitate*', *Milltown Studies*, 37 (1996), 56–64; S. O'Sullivan, 'Aldhelm's *De Virginitate*: patristic pastiche or innovative exposition?', *Peritia*, 12 (1998), 271–95; G. T. Dempsey, 'Aldhelm of Malmesbury's social theology: the barbaric heroic ideal Christianised', *Peritia*, 15 (2001), 58–80.

17 A point observed by a number of scholars, see, for example, Lapidge, 'Introduction to the prose *De Virginitate*', pp. 56–7; O'Sullivan, 'Aldhelm's *De Virginitate*', 272.

18 Lapidge, 'Introduction'; Ambrose, *De virginibus ad Marcellinam*, ed. I. Cazzaniga, *S. Ambrosii Mediolanensis Episcopi De virginibus libri tres* (Turin, 1948), bk 2, pp. 35–56.

19 This emphasis is also visible within scholarship on medieval saints and their devotees more generally.

20 *Aldhelmi Malmesbiriensis*, ed. Gwara, pp. 56–62.

[21] S. Hollis, *Anglo-Saxon Women and the Church: Sharing a Common Fate* (Woodbridge, 1992), especially pp. 12, 95, 103; O'Sullivan, 'Patristic background', 57–9; O'Sullivan, 'Aldhelm's *De Virginitate*', 277–9; C. A. Lees and G. R. Overing (eds), *Double Agents: Women and Clerical Culture in Anglo-Saxon England* (Philadelphia, 2001), pp. 13, 111–17.

[22] O'Sullivan, 'Patristic background', 57–9; O'Sullivan, 'Aldhelm's *De Virginitate*', 275–9.

[23] Lees and Overing, *Double Agents*, pp. 110–25, 148–9 (p. 149).

[24] *PdV*, ch. 3, p. 230, tr. Lapidge, p. 60, 'hominis . . . interioris gestibus'.

[25] Prudentius' influential allegorical epic *Psychomachia* (405) has been identified by several scholars as a literary model for Aldhelm's spiritual battle, see, for example, S. O'Sullivan, 'Aldhelm's *De virginitate* and the Psychomachian tradition', *Mediaevalia*, 20 (2001), 313–37.

[26] For example, *PdV*, ch. 11, pp. 239–40 and ch. 12, pp. 240–1, tr. Lapidge, pp. 67–9; *CdV*, ll. 2446–2761, pp. 452–65, tr. Rosier, pp. 157–64.

[27] *PdV*, ch. 12, p. 240, tr. Lapidge, p. 68, 'truculentis inimicorum exercitibus'.

[28] *PdV*, ch. 11, p. 240, tr. Lapidge, p. 68, 'lacertosis viribus'; ibid., 'ferocissimas barbarorum legiones'.

[29] Ibid., 'pudicitiae parma' and 'divini macheram verbi et loricam fidei inextricabilem'; Aldhelm borrowed this imagery from Ephesians 6: 11–17.

[30] Ibid., 'inermis'.

[31] *PdV*, ch. 11, p. 240, tr. Lapidge, p. 68, 'bellatores dominici'; Aldhelm's representation of both male and female religious as masculine soldiers of Christ has been discussed by several scholars. See, for example, Hollis, *Anglo-Saxon Women*, pp. 82–98, *passim*; O'Sullivan, 'Patristic background', 57–8.

[32] *PdV*, ch. 10, p. 238, tr. Lapidge, p. 66.

[33] *PdV*, ch. 11, p. 240, tr. Lapidge, p. 68, 'effeminately'; cf. O'Sullivan, 'Patristic background', 57–8; O'Sullivan, 'Aldhelm's *De Virginitate*', 277.

[34] Cf. Hollis, who argues that Aldhelm is encouraging a competitive warrior spirit, *Anglo-Saxon Women*, pp. 83–4; for evidence that the Carolingian church associated women with private interior spirituality, see J. M. H. Smith, 'The problem of female sanctity in Carolingian Europe c.780–920', *Past and Present*, 146 (1995), 3–37 (33–5).

[35] For male saints, see, for example, Aldhelm, *PdV*, ch. 32, p. 274, tr. Lapidge, p. 94; ch. 39, p. 291, tr. Lapidge, p. 106; for female saints, see, for example, *PdV*, ch. 41, p. 293, tr. Lapidge, p. 107; ch. 43, p. 296, tr. Lapidge, p. 110.

[36] For this point with reference to Carolingian hagiography see Smith, 'Problem of female sanctity', pp. 10–12.

[37] See, for example, Dempsey, 'Aldhelm of Malmesbury', 68–9.

[38] Smith, 'Problem of female sanctity', pp. 14–18, 35–7.

[39] A full analysis of the qualitative difference between male and female saints' miracles (including discussion of the problems inherent in this sort of statistical approach) will be available in my Ph.D. (University of York). This is currently in progress and is entitled, 'Aldhelm's *opus geminatum De virginitate* in its early Anglo-Saxon context'.

40 C. Stancliffe, *St Martin and his Hagiographer: History and Miracle in Sulpicius Severus* (Oxford, 1983).
41 Ibid., pp. 244–8, especially; note that Aldhelm drew upon Sulpicius' *Vita S. Martini*, see Ehwald, *Aldhelmi opera*, pp. 261–2, 546.
42 For a list of Aldhelm's uses of the noun *virtus*, found extensively throughout the double treatise, see Ehwald, 'Index verborum', in *Aldhelmi opera*, p. 735; a full discussion of Aldhelm's use of this noun will also be available in my thesis.
43 Stancliffe, *St Martin*, p. 9, for the varied meanings *virtus* takes in Martinian writings.
44 M. E. Goldsmith, *The Mode and Meaning of 'Beowulf'* (London, 1970), pp. 133–5. My use of 'exorcism' to describe this miracle type derives from Christine Rauer, *Beowulf and the Dragon: Parallels and Analogues* (Cambridge, 2000), p. 54.
45 Lapidge, '"Beowulf", Aldhelm, the "Liber Monstrorum" and Wessex', 158–62 (159).
46 *PdV*, ch. 52, p. 309, tr. Lapidge, p. 120.
47 For Victoria see Aldhelm, *CdV*, l. 2404, p. 451, tr. Rosier, p. 156; for Silvester, *CdV*, l. 545, p. 376, tr. Rosier, p. 115; for Daniel, *CdV*, l. 355, p. 368, tr. Rosier, p. 110.
48 *CdV*, l. 2403, p. 451, tr. Rosier, p. 155, *aethrali freta triumpho*.
49 *PdV*, ch. 52, p. 309, tr. Lapidge, p. 120.
50 Ibid., *angeli fulta suffragio*.
51 *PdV*, ch. 29, p. 266, tr. Lapidge, p. 88, *armis orationum*.
52 There are different ways of interpreting Aldhelm's treatment of gender here. Whilst we may read a gender binary into it, since Victoria is presented as relatively passive according to archetypally feminine tropes, even so, she is more active than archetypal female saints, since she wields *virtus*. It may be best to interpret Victoria as masculine, yet to a much lesser degree than her male counterparts.
53 Aldhelm, *CdV*, l. 2407, pp. 450–1, tr. Rosier, p. 156, *verbo terrente*; see also Aldhelm, *PdV*, ch. 52, p. 309, tr. Lapidge, p. 120.
54 *PdV*, ch. 29, pp. 266–7, tr. Lapidge, p. 88; *CdV*, ll. 809–11, p. 387, tr. Rosier, p. 120.
55 *PdV*, ch. 25, p. 258, tr. Lapidge, p. 83; *CdV*, ll. 545–6, 551–2, p. 376, tr. Rosier, p. 115; *CdV*, ll. 356–8, p. 368, tr. Rosier, pp. 110–11.
56 For example, 'invictus', *PdV*, ch. 21, p. 252, tr. Lapidge, p. 78; 'inflexibilis', cf. tr. Lapidge, 'inflexible'; 'triumphalis', *PdV*, ch. 36, p. 283, tr. Lapidge, p. 101; 'durus', *CdV*, l. 1228, p. 404, tr. Rosier, p. 130.
57 For example, 'venusta', *PdV*, ch. 47, p. 301, tr. Lapidge, p. 114; 'tenera', *PdV*, ch. 43, p. 296, tr. Lapidge, p. 110; 'muliebris', *CdV*, l. 2000, p. 435, tr. Rosier, p. 147; 'inermis', *CdV*, l. 2262, p. 446, cf. tr. Rosier, p. 153, 'helpless'.
58 *PdV*, ch. 44, p. 297, tr. Lapidge, p. 110, *tonsura masculini sexus, contra iura naturae*.

[59] See, for example, *PdV*, ch. 52, p. 309, tr. Lapidge, p. 120; for Aldhelm's use of this phrase with reference to same-sex desire in his account of Eugenia, see A. J. Frantzen, *Before the Closet: Same Sex Love from Beowulf to Angels in America* (Chicago and London, 1998), p. 79, and for Anglo-Saxon female 'transvestite saints', pp. 72–89.

[60] For further discussion on the fusion of these themes in contemporary Anglo-Saxon literature see Wormald, 'Bede, "Beowulf" and conversion', *passim*.

3

Masculinizing Religious Life: Sexual Prowess, the Battle for Chastity and Monastic Identity

JACQUELINE MURRAY

The increasing scholarly interest in the meaning of manhood in the Middle Ages is a logical outgrowth of two decades of feminist research into women's roles and lives. Recognizing the incompleteness of a focus solely on one sex or the other, there is now a much more nuanced approach to gender roles and gender definitions. Moreover, our more sophisticated understanding of the social aspects of gender identity, along with a sensitivity to the psychological dimensions of individual subjectivity, has led to a legitimate, if somewhat trendy, recognition of the multiplicities of identities we see reflected in the commonplace of 'medieval masculinities'.[1] As a result of this awareness, scholars tend to take into account social standing and life stage along with cultural context when they approach questions linked to medieval gender.

Medievals did not so much see their world as divided by class or race, as by distinctions based on religion: for example, Christian, Jew, Muslim, pagan or heretic. Among Christian men, 'those who prayed' were distinct and identifiable, to be contrasted with 'those who fought' and 'those who worked'. The extent to which the worldly life of action and the imperatives of religious life were perceived to be at odds is evident in the early life of Gerald of Aurillac. Odo of Cluny reports on Gerald's struggles to pursue sanctity while continuing to exercise secular power and responsibility. These struggles included avoiding a marriage proposed by his feudal overlord, experiencing miraculous psychosomatic blindness when on the verge of fornicating and urging his soldiers to fight with the flat of their swords to avoid drawing blood.[2] In Gerald's case the tension arose from his attempt to bring the values of the cloister into the world.[3] Of considerable interest is the opposite, and more frequent, case of men who left the world to enter the church and become either monks or priests. How did they understand their gender identity as they moved from a secular world that defined masculine behaviour in terms of military prowess and sexual virility to enter a milieu that eschewed both? The tensions that resulted from leaving one world and entering another reveal how men sought to reconcile two coexistent but contradictory belief systems and retain or redefine their identity as men.[4]

In the early Middle Ages, these men, monks and priests, were quite different types. Monks, vowed to chastity and rejecting life in society, lived behind their monastery walls. While pious and respected, for the most part these men remained members of the laity, albeit secluded from society. On the other hand, priests tended to remain active in society, caring for their flocks, earning a living and frequently enjoying marriage and family life. Thus, although ordained, priests were rooted firmly in the world. Even after the eleventh-century reforms and the formal extension of celibacy to all priests, the secular clergy maintained a different mode of life from their monastic brothers, one that frequently continued to include a female companion and their children.[5] In the course of the twelfth and thirteenth centuries, there was another concerted effort to synthesize the values of the cloister and the values of the parish. Jo Ann McNamara has characterized this as precipitating a crisis of masculine identity which she has cleverly termed the *Herrenfrage*.[6] This crisis profoundly destabilized masculine identity in general, but in particular that of monks and clerics who were living through a paradigm shift, a shift that, as McNamara has characterized it, involved the monasticizing of the clergy and the clericalizing of monks. Just as secular priests were being deprived of their wives and irregular families, so there was increasing pressure on monks to receive ordination.[7] Both of these changes occasioned challenges to masculine identity and religious identity.

McNamara posits that monks had hitherto been content with their monastic identity. They had lived comfortably with their vows and with their female counterparts, equally vowed to the monastic life. The privileging of chastity in both men and women, and the concomitant extension and elevation of monasticism as the superior mode of life, had grave implications for society as a whole, however. It threatened to obscure, even erase, gender differences between men and women. Related to this, when secular priests were deprived of their wives, what mechanisms were open to them to prove their manhood in a world that looked for clear and visible markers of gender? The normal avenues by which secular men proved their masculinity – sexual intercourse and engendering children and the exercise of military prowess – were now closed to the clergy.[8]

The whole question of masculinity must have been reasonably traumatic for many men in the church. In a period that experienced the introduction of impartible inheritance practices and primogeniture, there was a sense in which clerical celibacy was more relevant to the aristocracy's economic and political strategies than it was to the clergy themselves. In other words, the aristocracy had a vested interest in ensuring their younger sons remained celibate and did not produce offspring who might upset inheritance strategies by claiming a portion of the patrimony. These younger sons of the aristocracy, reared in households geared for war, absorbing from childhood the values of military and sexual prowess, were, as young men, relegated to an increasingly monastic church which deprived them of the opportunity to deploy the external signs of their masculinity.[9] How these men must have yearned for the good old days when even the upper clergy could have wives or concubines, and when bishops were leaders of men. They had heard the old stories while still youths in their fathers' hall, listening to the minstrels tell tales of greatness and bravery – for example, that of the heroes of Roncesvalles.[10] The figure of Archbishop Turpin would have had a particular resonance for these men.

> Archbishop Turpin is not far away.
> Spurring his horse, he gallops up a hill,
> Summons the French, and speaks these solemn words:
> 'My lords and barons, Charles has left us here,
> And for our king we should in duty die.
> Lend aid now to maintain the Christian faith! . . .
> Say your confessions, for God's mercy pray!
> I will absolve you to secure your souls . . .'[11]

And the poem continues later:

> Archbishop Turpin rides about the field:
> Never has such a cleric sung a mass

> Who did so many deeds of gallantry . . .
> Forward he launches his fine battle-steed
> And strikes [the enemy] square on his Toledo shield
> To hurl him lifeless down on the green grass.[12]

Turpin was very much the priest when he absolved Roland's band of heroes from horseback and he was very much the man when he fought to a glorious hero's death. Archbishop Turpin could be seen as the epitome of ecclesiastical masculinity – the complete integration of spiritual and secular values: saving souls and granting absolution, all the while exhibiting the physical prowess that gained one admission to the ranks of the epic heroes.

Turpin deployed a secular virility for which the reluctant clerics of the twelfth and early thirteenth centuries could only yearn.[13] Nor was this necessarily an idle yearning. Many twelfth-century churchmen came from the ranks of the military aristocracy. And even those who embraced the church willingly and voluntarily carried with them the values and the language of their warrior-class upbringing. For these men, the challenge was to maintain their masculine gender identity, socially and sexually, while remaining in the church and adhering to its admonitions against drawing blood or emitting semen.[14] Two related strategies for achieving this synthesis can be identified. The first involved the careful deployment of the myth of uncontrollable male lust. Celibate men came to redefine masculinity in such a way that they could *be* masculine without having *to act* masculine. Lust was a sign of manhood: real men experience sexual desire and, by extension, have sexual prowess. But this lust was also a threat to manhood: real men are not dominated by lust and physical desire; they overcome it.[15] The assumption of ungovernable male sexuality, then, allowed the clergy to possess the sexual prowess that defined secular manhood without engaging in sex acts. The second strategy, the transformation of the chaste life into the 'battle for chastity', allowed men to overcome an enemy and deploy the language of military prowess without wielding a weapon or shedding blood.[16]

The military values of the warrior class were visible at many levels of the church. For example, Peter Abelard's father was a soldier and Peter himself was the first-born son of a military family. Abelard reported that in pursing scholarship he was 'giving up . . . the pomp of military glory . . . I preferred the armour of logic . . . I exchanged all other arms for it and chose contests of disputation above the trophies of war'.[17]

Thus, by turning the schools into a battlefield and dialectic into a weapon, Abelard asserted his masculinity.[18] Abelard's nemesis, Bernard of Clairvaux, was also born into a military family. William of St Thierry, one of Bernard's biographers, wrote that he had a well-proportioned body and that many careers in the world were open to him. Given that Bernard's brothers were knights, presumably he, too, could have aspired to the military life. Not only did Bernard turn his back on this, but he convinced his brothers to join him in the cloister.[19] One brother, Gerard, considered this flirtation with monasticism to be a passing phase, suggesting he perceived a dissonance between military and monastic values. It took being wounded and captured by his enemies, as foretold by Bernard, to change Gerard's mind about embracing monastic life.[20]

Given the volatility of medieval society, arms had a practical role to play in daily life, protecting people from danger, especially that posed by the robbers and thieves who roamed at night. Caesarius of Heisterbach recorded the story of a priest whom he characterized as 'a very religious man for his class', suggesting that those who knew arms did indeed have difficulty leaving behind worldly military values.[21] This priest was rushing alone from one church to another before daylight. He did not have a servant to accompany him and protect him so he 'carried with him a sword in fear of the dangers of the road'. Suddenly, the priest was struck with fear and saw a terrifying man at the side of the road. This was, of course, the Devil who proceeded to chase the priest all the way to town. When the poor priest related his misadventure to a lay brother of a nearby monastery – a truly pious man according to Caesarius – the brother informed him that 'the Church would tell you that, if in going to the Divine Office you had taken a psalm into your mouth instead of a sword into your hand, these things would not have happened on the road. That terror of yours was the penalty of sin; for in truth the devil fears a psalm, not a sword.'[22] This story presents a useful perspective on the tension between secular and religious values. First, the secular priest was tainted by his class. He was 'very religious *for his class*', Caesarius might have said in spite of it.[23] The sword clearly signals his secular social position. By comparison, the monastic was superior in piety although, given his status as a lay brother, he was no doubt of inferior social standing to the priest. The story contains the message that men should not bring the trappings of their secular status into their religious lives. Moreover, there is a clear implication that those in monastic life, even lay brothers, were superior to their clerical colleagues who remained in the world. This perspective is reinforced by another of Caesarius' stories, this one about a knight named Walewan, who sought to enter the Cistercians.[24] He arrived

> arrayed in all his armour and riding upon his charger, and thus armed entered the convent . . . [H]e went . . . down the middle of the choir to the altar of the Blessed Virgin and there, with all the convent looking on, he laid down his arms and took up the monk's dress. It seemed to him fitting and proper that he should lay down the warlike trappings of the world there, where he proposed to assume the garments of a soldier of Christ.[25]

Walewan, then, acted out the process of conversion from secular to monastic, physically shedding one identity and assuming the other. Yet, he remained very much a soldier, certain, despite his vow of chastity, that his masculinity remained firmly intact. The use of military language to express religious experience was more than an ancient metaphor or commonplace; it could be reified through individual performance and thus give meaning to individual lives.

The moral literature of the period also provides indications that weapons and women were linked conceptually. Both were the markers of manhood and, for religious men, both remained an enduring temptation. For example, Caesarius recorded another story about some young Bavarian scholars studying in Toledo. Eager to learn about necromancy, they begged their teacher to reveal his secrets to them. Reluctantly, the master called forward some demons:

> Immediately [the demons] showed themselves under the appearance of well-armed soldiers, practising their military games around the youths. At one time they would pretend to fall, at another they would stretch out their lances and swords against them, trying in every way to induce them to leave the [protective] circle. When they found that this was to no avail, they changed themselves into very beautiful girls, and danced about them, inviting the young men with every kind of alluring movement.[26]

This story, then, suggests that, for young men, even though they were scholars and clerics, the practice of arms continued to exercise an attraction.[27] Moreover, it was only after the students had resisted the temptations of sword and lance that the demons transformed themselves into alluring women and invoked the temptations of the flesh. While conventionally the latter was perhaps the stronger of the two desires, arms were nevertheless considered to be sufficiently tempting that the demons employed them first in their attempt to seduce the men.

The link between the twin desires of physical prowess and sexual control is also found in the *vita* of Hugh of Avalon, bishop of Lincoln. Hugh entered religious life as a youth, when his father decided to abandon the world. Hugh's father William was 'a nobleman and flower of knighthood'. We are told that '[h]e laid aside the burden of earthly soldiering for heavenly . . . He donned armour against the flesh, soldiered against himself, and himself overcame himself, both conqueror and conquered in one and the same conflict.'[28] This description summarizes the manner in which military language was appropriated by religious men and redirected to their spiritual struggles. Religious though they were, monks and clerics still had a stake in self-identification with the twin secular values of military and sexual prowess. Now, however, both the language and the physical prowess was directed inward, at their own human sexual desires and their own bodies. The monk was at once his own champion and his own worst enemy, as he 'soldiered against himself'.[29]

This monastic appropriation of the language of masculine virility reveals deep conflicts between the ongoing need for men to be men according to secular values and the religious requirement that they repress their sexual selves and deny their sexed bodies. The 'myth of men's uncontrollable lust', then, was a double-edged sword in the inherently contradictory battle for chastity and masculinity. The cloister was supposed to provide monks with respite from worldly temptations, yet the clang of armour and the shouts of warfare are found throughout monastic literature focusing on the control of the flesh. The act of denying the male body came to be one of the profound ways in which celibate men could assert and reaffirm their masculinity. This was how celibates could *be* men without *acting* like men.

Ecclesiastical writers record a number of ways by which monks demonstrated and reaffirmed their physical courage and masculinity compared to their brothers in the world. Caesarius of Heisterbach told the story of a knight, renowned for his bravery and ability with arms, who did not want to join the Cistercians because he was afraid of the lice that infested their robes. Ultimately, the knight overcame his squeamishness and joined the order. Caesarius used this example to edify his monastic brethren, observing, 'You see how great bravery he gained, who before his conversion had been so timorous.'[30] Other mundane monastic activities could be given a masculine spin as well. For example, Walter Daniel reported that Aelred of Rievaulx happily engaged in manual labour and 'manfully wielded with his fingers the rough tools'.[31] Aelred, himself, in his *Mirror of Charity*, described another monk as 'that most valiant athlete . . . who chastizes his body and subdues it'.[32] Thus, the physical disciplines and discomforts associated with monastic life were presented as standing up well in comparison to the physical demands of secular masculinity.

For all of this, however, monks were still liable to the temptations and trappings of worldly masculinity. Caesarius of Heisterbach is again a useful source. He recorded a story that deliberately casts the Benedictines in a poor light and reveals how worldly values could continue to exercise their attractions. A certain monastery needed to send a representative to the king to defend some of their privileges. The community selected a young man of noble birth because he was familiar with courtly protocol and would know how to present their case to the king. While the monk indeed made the case successfully, the king quizzed him on his birth and family connections, eventually conceding his nobility of birth and status. The king, however, took the opportunity to chastize his tight leggings, which he did not consider to be suitable attire for a monk.[33] In other words, the monk had no business affecting stylish dress, even though he was at court and among men of the world.[34]

Horsemanship, too, could be a continuing temptation for monks, especially for those who had been raised to ride and to take pleasure in it. Caesarius discussed the case of an abbot who, more from naivety than pride, rode a too-spirited horse and consequently scandalized the laity.[35] While in this particular case, the abbot was not motivated by worldly concerns, Caesarius took the opportunity to highlight the importance of monks avoiding causing scandal by engaging in acts of secular pride and virility. Monks were expected to ride docile palfreys, not the high-spirited destriers preferred by knights. By demonstrating his equestrian skills and his ability to control and dominate a powerful horse, a man was also, by extension, exhibiting his military prowess and his ability to control and rule over men.[36]

The imperative to reject the trappings of worldly masculinity left monks vulnerable to allegations of effeminacy. For example, Walter Daniel characterized Aelred of Rievaulx as an adolescent who 'even when of tender years had the makings of a fine man, save that he had greater virtue, and the vices of manhood were not possible in him'.[37] While Walter was trying to provide Aelred with that youthful spark of religious fervour that would foreshadow his sanctity in adulthood, this passage also leaves open the possibility that Aelred was incapable of sexual sins; that he was effeminate and lacked masculine virility. There may be a logic to this, given the by now generally accepted view that Aelred's desires were homoaffective if not actually homoerotic.[38] Nevertheless, as if trying to reassure his readers of the saint's masculinity, Walter chose to present Aelred as virile in his administration of Rievaulx. Aelred was a good businessman and under his leadership the community expanded and its wealth increased. These were signs of worldly success and Walter summarized these accomplishments by observing that Aelred 'was not sterile'.[39] Aelred himself, in his *Mirror of Charity,* criticized the presence of 'effeminate amusements' within monastery walls.[40] Moreover, according to Gerald of Wales, men who could not or would not control their lust were effeminate, revealing the endurance of Stoicism in definitions of masculinity.[41]

Other writers, too, reveal monastic anxiety in the face of allegations of effeminacy. For example, Caesarius of Heisterbach described the case of a monk who, on his deathbed, was suddenly slapped on the head by the Virgin Mary. The monk, although 'pure in body' nevertheless was worldly and dainty, especially in his dress.[42] Here, as with the knight who feared lice, care in dress and grooming appears to be both worldly and unmanly, a subtle means of eliding the secular with the effeminate. Elsewhere, Caesarius discussed the case of an apostate monk who, prior to entering the order, had disguised himself as a woman and entered a community of nuns, some of whom he had corrupted sexually.[43] Initially, such a monk might be considered to be hyper-masculine, conforming to the conventional understanding of male transvestism as a means to gain illicit access to women.[44] However, this was not the case. This monk's true unmanly nature was reflected in his assumption of female clothing. The reader, thus, is able to anticipate the monk's ultimate effeminate abandonment of masculine monastic life in his earlier adoption of female clothing.

There was, indeed, a connection in the minds of monks between bodies and clothes. St Bernard was reported to have told novices that 'before you enter [the monastery] you must leave outside the bodies which you have brought from the world, for only hearts and minds may come in, since the flesh will not help you'.[45] Bernard's hagiographer observed that:

Some novices used to be frighted at these unusual words, but [Bernard] showed that he understood their difficulty by explaining what he meant, and he used to tell them how they must leave off the desires and inclinations of the flesh just as they left off the clothes that marked them as men of the world.[46]

This link between clothing, the body and desire encapsulates the masculinity inherent in worldly fashion and style, while implying its inferiority to the harsh simplicity of monastic dress. It also reveals that male physical and emotional identity was linked to dress, something that could be put on, taken off or changed, something that could accentuate or disguise the physical attributes it covered. Yet, for men entering the cloister, there were mixed messages regarding the body and its sexual attributes.

The reception of the sacrament of orders was believed to change a man in a profound and enduring manner. The effects of ordination endured even if a priest were deposed or degraded. Ordination, however, did not seem to have the same effect as monastic vows. According to Bernard, when a man entered a monastery, the old body, the body that experienced lust and secular life, should be checked at the door and the body of chastity assumed. Priestly ordination, however, was not equivalent to monastic vows, although *The Golden Legend* did portray the secular priesthood as conferring something of the same grace. Jacobus de Voragine described the effect of episcopal anointing on Thomas Becket: 'At once the dignity of his office made of him a new, and absolutely perfect man'.[47] Yet, Hugh of Lincoln apparently had quite a different view of ordination to the priesthood. Gerald of Wales reported that, in a moment of wit, having been approached by a woman complaining of her husband's impotence, Hugh quipped 'If you want, let us make him a priest and the power will immediately be restored to him. Then he would, without doubt, be potent.'[48] Hidden beneath this risqué, clichéd joke is something of the tension between monks and clerics during the period of synthesis of the two modes of religious life. The secular cleric did not engage, fully armed, in the battle for chastity. Indeed, the rubric to the chapter containing this jest makes this point even more clearly: 'That turbulence disturbs priests and others in holy orders more seriously.'[49]

The monastic discourse of chastity was directed as much against the behaviour of married or sexually active secular clergy as it was against the temptations of lustful women. Caesarius of Heisterbach warned that priests who were fornicators or adulterers – which at this time would include any priest in a stable domestic relationship since marriage was forbidden to them – could rightly expect death if they handled or, much worse, consumed the sacrament when so foully polluted.[50] In this context, we must consider whether the characterization of priests' wives as concubines or whores was directed so much at the women as at their clerical husbands. It stripped married priests of the honourable secular status of husband and father and relegated them to the ranks of fornicators and lascivious – that is, effeminate – johns.[51]

Another of Caesarius' stories reveals even more clearly the tension between monastic and secular clergy. He recorded the tale of a monk, clearly a man who should have known better, who 'by persuasion of the evil one, laid aside his gown and undertook the government of a certain parish, for he was a priest'.[52] The man is described as 'a deserter from the Order [who] fell into the further vice of lust. He took a concubine to live with him, as is the custom of many, by whom he also begat children.'[53] Eventually, the errant man repented of his decision to leave the monastery. He planned to return, but died before he was able to do so. The man's former abbot, who had approved of his plan to resume the monastic habit,

> ordered that the tomb should be opened; and when they asked him why, he replied, 'I wish to see whether it is a monk or a clerk that lies there'. 'It is a clerk', they said, 'whom we buried in secular dress'. The earth was thrown aside, and he appeared to all not in the secular dress in which he was buried, but in the tonsure and habit of a monk.[54]

The abandonment of the religious habit was recognized in the Middle Ages as a clear sign that one had rejected religious life and re-entered the world.[55] Thus, when the exhumed corpse was found clothed in a monastic habit, this signalled the sincerity of the man's repudiation of the world and his intention to re-enter religious life. His story is presented as a miracle of contrition. Caesarius' novice interlocutor, however, outraged by the whole incident, exclaims, 'The man was an apostate, was a fornicator and, what I count far worse, did not scruple to handle daily with his polluted hands the most sacred mysteries of Christ.'[56] This, then, is another example of the tension that could endure between monk and priest, monastic and secular clergy. It is significant that the novice's denunciation of the priest verges on the heretical, indicating how fraught the monasticizing of the clergy was as late as the early thirteenth century. The other significant point, however, is that a polluted priest was once again transformed into a chaste monk because of the depth of his contrition for having embraced the worldly enticements of parish, wife and children. Gerald of Wales summarized the changing values: '[F]or our priests (who seek spiritual perfection, not carnal progeny), who are supposed to be present daily at the altar, perpetual chastity has been introduced. Therefore, they ought to shun [be prevented from] not only concubinage but also cohabitation with women (*muliercularum*)'.[57] Thus, not only sexual activity, but innocent daily contact with any woman, including a mother or sister, was transformed into a threat to the weaker secular priest.

The challenge for the monk was to remain in control of his body and its desires in a real and meaningful way. True chastity should not come too easily or naturally. For example, in a rare medieval example of personal revelation, Robert Grosseteste observed that, because his own nature was cold, the absence of seminal emissions did not indicate he had reached a higher spiritual plane than men who continued to experience nocturnal emissions.[58] There was no virtue associated with a low libido or a cold complexion that made it easier to give the appearance of controlling the flesh. Similarly, Gerald of Wales criticized men who delayed their monastic conversion until old age had put out their fires and cooled their flesh. 'For no crown is given unless the struggle of a fierce battle has taken place. It is highly praiseworthy if they restrained themselves in the heat of passion and youth.'[59] The conversion of the elderly, then, was scarcely conversion at all because physical decrepitude lowered the stakes.

As a result of this perspective, the fact that it was public knowledge that Aelred of Rievaulx was not a virgin actually enhanced the value of his monastic chastity rather than detracting from his sanctity. This circumstance was considered sufficiently important that some friends took to task Aelred's biographer, Walter Daniel, for attempting to suppress the saint's youthful sexual experience. Walter said he was criticized 'because in that same period of his life Ailred [sic] occasionally deflowered his chastity I ought not have compared a man of that sort to a monk'.[60] It was this kind of sexual experience, however, that elevated Aelred's subsequent bodily disciplines, including frequent immersions in freezing water to 'quench the heat in him of every vice'.[61] Indeed, this mode of physical discipline was an archetype of monastic sanctity. Aelred was but one of dozens of male saints who reportedly cooled their lust with an icy dip. Other near contemporaries included Wilfrid, Goderic, Dogmael and the austere Bernard himself.[62]

Thus, monks were able to transform their chastity into something inherently masculine. It was not an easy gift but a hard-won reward. Gerald of Wales warned: 'Be watchful therefore, my brothers, and beware because the attacks of temptation press more strongly on priests, monks, hermits, and those dedicated to the service of Christ than other men.'[63] The celibate's ability to control and conquer his flesh immediately enhanced his masculinity. Laymen, married and given over to the flesh, were diminished in the face of the monk's heroic battle for chastity.

And a battle it was. Over and over, with predictable regularity, the literature employs the language of war, battle and struggle. Hugh of Lincoln described to Adam of Eynsham the temptations he faced upon entering the Carthusians:

> The tempter direct[ed] all the ancient weapons of his infernal armoury against a new recruit to this holy warfare, and in particular, as if from a very powerful crossbow, he shot bolts which, he hoped I could not resist, since they were part of myself. I mean that he aroused my carnal lusts.[64]

Later, Adam reported that when assailed by lust Hugh 'the valiant warrior, now being fiercely attacked, . . . defended himself . . . winning a magnificent victory'.[65] Perhaps most telling of all, however, is the manner in which Adam used the language of hand-to-hand combat to describe Hugh's battle for chastity:

> [T]he angel of darkness fought with him to deliver him into the dark night of evil consent. Not content with resisting this one, he [Hugh] also strove with another angel till dawn, when he triumphed . . . One man struggled against the two, pleading with the latter and repulsing the former, resisting the first and imploring aid from the second, endeavouring with all his might to win the blessing which would free him from the attacks of the other. The lists for combat in which he fought so manfully was his cell.[66]

Nor was Hugh's military valour relegated to his sexual dream life alone. He was a brave man by any measure, as befitted the son of 'a nobleman and flower of knighthood'.[67] Adam recounted how 'in order to restrain the violence of angry men, [Hugh] bravely and intrepidly often advanced unarmed into the midst of an armed band, and stood calm, undaunted and bareheaded amongst the naked brandished swords and clenched fists'.[68] What greater example of bravery and military prowess was there than standing alone and unarmed in the midst of an angry armed mob? This surely was bravery worthy of the heroic Archbishop Turpin.

Thus, we see in Hugh of Lincoln the epitome of monastic masculinity: a monk who achieved chastity after fierce battle, and a man who exhibited bravery beyond the grasp of secular warriors. An anonymous life characterized him as someone who 'was not afraid to declare war on all forms of evil. The steed on which he charged into battle was his own body, while for armour he had the shield of integrity.'[69] This description was one that would have comforted and reassured men as they entered into a mode of life in which the boundaries between monk and clerk were becoming increasingly blurred. It would also have reassured those younger sons of the warrior class that they were not being deprived of their masculinity when they were required to forgo wives and warfare.[70] Here was a language and here were the role models who reaffirmed to celibate men that they were not a third gender nor were they effeminate or emasculinized. A monk could be certain he was profoundly different from his virile sisters, who transcended their gender and their bodies and through virginity became virile and manly. A monk's battle for chastity proved not only his spiritual prowess but also his masculinity. The monk had the sexual virility that was a marker of manhood but he transcended and conquered lust in a way that enhanced his masculinity. A priest no longer needed his worldly attachments to wife and family and property, the aspects of life that he shared with the laymen of his flock. These were effeminate considerations, appropriate for the inferior laity but unworthy of a soldier of Christ. Indeed, the reassuring nature of this new, virile, monastic masculinity, embraced by monks and clerics alike, is perhaps best demonstrated by the opening lines of the *Metrical Life of Saint Hugh of Lincoln*. In order to underscore the epic quality of Hugh's deeds and the heroic nature of his spirituality, the poet appropriated the opening line of the *Aeneid*: 'Arms and the man I sing . . .'[71] The celibate man, monk or clerk, had no need to feel diminished by the memory of the virile Archbishop Turpin. Here was a new kind of hero, one who integrated masculine identity and religious identity: a man's man for a new age, a hero whose sexual prowess was reaffirmed by the temptations of the flesh and whose military prowess was demonstrated in the battle for chastity.

Notes

I would like to acknowledge with gratitude the Social Sciences and Humanities Research Council of Canada which supported the research and writing of this article.

1 See, for example, the introduction to Clare A. Lees (ed.), *Medieval Masculinities: Regarding Men in the Middle Ages* (Minneapolis, 1994), pp. xv–xxv.
2 See Odo of Cluny, *Vita s. Geraldi Comitis Aurillac*, PL 133, 1. 8, cols 646–7; 1. 9, cols 647–9; 1. 34, cols 662–3.
3 A useful discussion of the tension between the cloister and the world is found in Stuart Airlie, 'The anxiety of sanctity: St Gerald of Aurillac and his maker', *Journal of Ecclesiastical History*, 43 (1992), 372–95.
4 The tensions between the twin pillars of secular masculinity and religious values have been explored, for an earlier period, in J. L. Nelson, 'Monks, secular men and masculinity, c.900', in D. M. Hadley (ed.), *Masculinity in Medieval Europe* (London, 1999), pp. 121–42.
5 The process began c.1050 when married priests were prohibited from serving at the altar. It was extended and rendered more rigorous when the Second Lateran Council (1139) rejected the legitimacy of clerical marriage. Nevertheless, clerics continued to form enduring domestic relationships with women well into the thirteenth century. See the important work by Anne Llewellyn Barstow, *Married Priests and the Reforming Papacy: The Eleventh-Century Debates* (Lewiston, NY, 1982). The masculinity of secular clergy at the end of the Middle Ages is discussed in P. H. Cullum, 'Clergy, masculinity and transgression in late medieval England', in Hadley (ed.), *Masculinity in Medieval Europe*, pp. 178–96.
6 Jo Ann McNamara, 'The *Herrenfrage*: the restructuring of the gender system, 1050–1150', in Lees (ed.), *Medieval Masculinities*, pp. 3–29.
7 See the discussion of this process in Jo Ann McNamara, 'Canossa and the ungendering of the public man', in S. P. Ramet and D. W. Treadgold (eds), *Render unto Caesar: The Religious Sphere in World Politics* (Washington, DC, 1995), pp. 131–50.
8 R. N. Swanson has argued that the clergy were trying to establish two genders for the male sex: masculinity for laymen and emasculinity for celibate clergy. His overview does not distinguish between monastic and secular clergy, arguably the meeting point of the *Herrenfrage* and, thus, a useful focus for examining masculine gender identity. Swanson's point, however, that a sex and gender binary should not be presumed and perpetuated without examination, is well taken. R. N. Swanson, 'Angels incarnate: clergy and masculinity from Gregorian Reform to Reformation', in Hadley (ed.), *Masculinity in Medieval Europe*, pp. 160–77.
9 Georges Duby credited the increasing importance of the secular clergy at the expense of monastics, especially in twelfth-century court society, to the entry of aristocratic sons into the church. This process, he argued, saw the

development of two distinct cultural models, the knight and the clerk, each similarly ambitious and competitive in their distinct arenas. Duby suggested, but did not explore, the implications of the introduction of knightly values into clerical culture. Georges Duby, *The Chivalrous Society*, tr. Cynthia Poston (London, 1977), pp. 171–7. For an overview of masculinity and its characteristics for this social group, see M. Bennett, 'Military masculinity in England and northern France c.1050–c.1225', in Hadley (ed.), *Masculinity in Medieval Europe*, pp. 71–99.

[10] See the discussion of the songs and stories of Roland as 'social property' in Andrew Taylor, 'Was there a Song of Roland?', *Speculum*, 76, 1 (2001), 28–65.

[11] *The Song of Roland*, tr. D. D. R. Owen (Woodbridge, 1990), p. 74.

[12] Ibid., p. 87.

[13] It is no coincidence that it was during this same period that the monastic fighting orders such as the Templars and Hospitallers emerged. Their explicit integration of military and monastic values met the needs of many unmarried aristocratic younger sons. My concern here is how men who were not members of the military orders might have made their accommodation with the two conflicting value systems.

[14] Not only was sexual intercourse forbidden, but nocturnal emissions were a particular concern for monks. See the discussions in Dyan Elliott, 'Pollution, illusion and masculine disarray: nocturnal emissions and the sexuality of the clergy', in eadem, *Fallen Bodies: Pollution, Sexuality and Demonology in the Middle Ages* (Philadelphia, 1999), pp. 14–34, and Jacqueline Murray, 'Men's bodies, men's minds: seminal emissions and sexual anxiety in the Middle Ages', *Annual Review of Sex Research*, 8 (1997), 1–26.

[15] McNamara, 'Canossa and ungendering'.

[16] While Michel Foucault used this metaphor to describe the asceticism of Cassian and other desert fathers, the term was less metaphorical in the Middle Ages. This was in part due to the eliding of the concepts of spiritual and bodily chastity over time. Michel Foucault, 'The battle for chastity', in P. Ariès and A. Béjin (eds), *Western Sexuality: Practice and Precept in Past and Present Times* (Oxford, 1985), pp. 14–25.

[17] Pierre Abélard, *Historia Calamitatum*, ed. J. Monfrin (Paris, 1959), pp. 63–4; tr. J. T. Muckle, *The Story of Abelard's Adversities* (Toronto, 1964), p. 11.

[18] See the discussion in Andrew Taylor, 'A second Ajax: Peter Abelard and the violence of dialectic', in David Townsend and Andrew Taylor (eds), *The Tongue of the Fathers: Gender and Ideology in Twelfth-Century Latin* (Philadelphia, 1998), pp. 14–34.

[19] *St Bernard of Clairvaux Vita primi Bernardi*, tr. Geoffrey Webb and Adrian Walker (Westminster, MD, 1960), pp. 13, 23–7.

[20] Ibid., p. 27.

[21] For a discussion of the centrality of saints' lives, sermon *exempla* and

miracle stories such as those by Caesarius as a means to understand popular ideas and the mental universe of medieval society, see Aron Gurevich, *Medieval Popular Culture: Problems of Belief and Perception*, tr. Jànos M. Bak and Paul A. Hollingsworth (Cambridge, 1988), pp. 1–38.

[22] Caesarius of Heisterbach, *Dialogus miraculorum: textum ad quatuor codicum manuscriptorum editionisque . . .* , ed. Joseph Strange (Cologne, 1851), 5. 55, vol. 1, pp. 281–2; tr. H. von E. Scott and C. C. Swinton Bland, *The Dialogue on Miracles* (London, 1929), vol. 1, pp. 388–9. Unless otherwise indicated, for the reader's ease of access, I have cited the admittedly dated tr. by Scott and Bland.

[23] The italics have been added.

[24] It would not appear to be coincidental that so many of the surviving stories involve knights who had entered the Cistercians. Constance Berman has noted that knights may have preferred to enter the Cistercians because they preferred the balance of physical labour and prayer offered by life at Cîteaux and Clairvaux compared to the more sedentary life of contemplative orders. Constance Hoffman Berman, *The Cistercian Evolution: The Invention of a Religious Order in Twelfth-Century Europe* (Philadelphia, 2000), p. 167.

[25] *Dialogus miraculorum*, 1. 37, ed. Strange, vol. 1, pp. 45–6; tr. Scott and Bland, vol. 1, p. 49.

[26] *Dialogus miraculorum*, 5. 4, ed. Strange, vol. 1, pp. 279–81; tr. Scott and Bland, vol. 1, pp. 318–19.

[27] Ruth Mazo Karras has noted the enduring attraction of weapons for medieval students, despite the proscription against students bearing arms. 'Sharing wine, women, and song: masculine identity formation in the medieval European universities', in Jeffrey Jerome Cohen and Bonnie Wheeler (eds), *Becoming Male in the Middle Ages* (New York, 1997), pp. 187–202 (p. 190).

[28] *The Metrical Life of Saint Hugh of Lincoln*, ed. and tr. Charles Garton (Lincoln, 1986), p. 15.

[29] John Arnold argues that, for religious men, chastity and virginity were distinguished by interiority or exteriority. Desire was both within the man but also could be triggered by external stimuli. At risk for masculinity was the power of the will over the body. John H. Arnold, 'The labour of continence: masculinity and virginity in the twelfth and thirteenth centuries', in Anke Bernau, Ruth Evans and Sarah Salih (eds), *Medieval Virginities* (Cardiff, 2003), pp. 102–18.

[30] *Dialogus miraculorum*, 4. 48, ed. Strange, vol. 1, pp. 214–15; tr. Scott and Bland, vol. 1, pp. 244–5.

[31] Walter Daniel, *The Life of Ailred of Rievaulx*, tr. F. M. Powicke (London, 1950), p. 22.

[32] Aelred of Rievaulx, *The Mirror of Charity*, tr. Elizabeth Connor (Kalamazoo, MI, 1990), p. 170.

[33] *Dialogus miraculorum*, 4. 12, ed. Strange, vol. 1, pp. 183–4; tr. Scott and Bland, vol. 1, pp. 207–8.

[34] Rachel Dressler discusses the importance of a well-muscled leg in noble society whereas the legs of churchmen remained hidden under their loose robes. 'Steel corpse: imaging the knight in death', in Jacqueline Murray (ed.), *Conflicted Identities and Multiple Masculinities: Men in the Medieval West* (New York, 1999), pp. 135–68 (pp. 151–2).

[35] *Dialogus miraculorum*, 4. 14, ed. Strange, vol. 1, p. 185; tr. Scott and Bland, vol. 1, pp. 209–10.

[36] Joyce Salisbury has observed that 'a nobleman was set apart and above commoners by the horse beneath him'. The same might be said of religious men. For a discussion of the importance of horses, especially high-spirited warhorses, to the nobleman's identity see the discussion in Joyce E. Salisbury, *The Beast Within: Animals in the Middle Ages* (New York, 1994), pp. 28–31.

[37] Daniel, *Life of Ailred*, p. 2.

[38] See Brian Patrick McGuire, 'Sexual awareness and identity in Aelred of Rievaulx (1110–67)', *American Benedictine Review*, 45, 2 (1994), 184–226.

[39] Daniel, *Life of Ailred*, p. 29.

[40] Aelred, *Mirror of Charity*, p. 212.

[41] Giraldi Cambrensis, *Gemma ecclesiastica*, 2. 9 in *Opera*, vol. 2, ed. J. S. Brewer, Rolls Series, 21 (London, 1862), p. 211; tr. John J. Hagen, *The Jewel of the Church* (Leiden, 1979), p. 162. For the enduring legacy of Stoicism see James A. Brundage, ' "Allas! That evere love was synne": sex and medieval canon law', *Catholic Historical Review*, 72 (1986), 1–13 (5–8).

[42] *Dialogus miraculorum*, 7. 55, ed. Strange, vol. 2, pp. 74–5; tr. Scott and Bland, vol. 1, pp. 540–1.

[43] *Dialogus miraculorum*, 4. 91, ed. Strange, vol. 1, pp. 257–8; tr. Scott and Bland, vol. 1, pp. 293–4.

[44] Vern L. Bullough and Bonnie Bullough, *Cross Dressing, Sex, and Gender* (Philadelphia, 1993), p. 51.

[45] *St Bernard*, tr. Webb and Walker, p. 37.

[46] Ibid.

[47] *The Golden Legend of Jacobus de Voragine*, tr. Granger Ryan and Helmut Ripperger (New York, 1941), p. 68.

[48] *Gemma ecclesiastica*, 2. 18, ed. Brewer, p. 250; tr. Hagen, p. 190.

[49] 'Quod sacerdotes et divino cultui datos gravior molestat inquietatio'. *Gemma ecclesiastica*, 2. 18, ed. Brewer, p. 249. Both J. S. Brewer, the editor of the Rolls Series edition, and John J. Hagen (p. 189), the translator, understand the word *inquietatio* as temptation. It would seem, however, that turbulence or disturbance would better capture the sense of gnawing sexual desire that Gerald seems to describe. See Charlton T. Lewis and Charles Short, *A Latin Dictionary* (Oxford, 1879; repr. 1975), p. 960, and R. E. Latham, *Revised Medieval Latin Word-List From British and Irish Sources* (London, 1965), p. 251.

[50] *Dialogus miraculorum*, 9. 53, ed. Strange, vol. 2, pp. 207–8; tr. Scott and Bland, vol. 2, pp. 157–8.

51 Since the time of Jerome, it had been conventional to associate women with lust and weakness of the flesh. By extension, when men were prey to lust, whether in marriage or at the brothel, they were by definition giving in to their bodily desires and behaving in an effeminate manner.
52 *Dialogus miraculorum*, 2. 3, ed. Strange, vol. 1, pp. 62–4; tr. Scott and Bland, vol. 1, pp. 67–9.
53 Ibid.
54 Strange, p. 63; tr. Scott and Bland, p. 69.
55 Donald Logan, *Runaway Religious in Medieval England, c. 1240–1540* (Cambridge, 1996), pp. 25–6.
56 Strange, p. 63; tr. Scott and Bland, p. 69.
57 *Gemma ecclesiastica*, 2. 7, ed. Brewer, p. 196; tr. Hagen, p. 151. The Latin term *muliercularum* might not imply all women but rather women of ill-repute or prostitutes. See *Novum glossarium mediae latinitatis*, ed. Franz Blatt (Hafniae, 1959–69), *v. muliercula*, vol. M–N, col. 895. The third definition explicitly identifies the term to be pejorative.
58 Joseph Goering and Frank A. C. Mantello, 'The "*Perambulauit Iudas* . . ." (*Speculum confessionis*) Attributed to Robert Grosseteste', *Revue Bénédictine*, 96 (1986), 125–68 (149–50).
59 *Gemma ecclesiastica*, 2. 8, ed. Brewer, p. 199; tr. Hagen, p. 153.
60 Daniel, *Life of Ailred*, p. 76.
61 Ibid., p. 25.
62 For Godric and Dogmael, see *Gemma ecclesiastica*, 2. 10, ed. Brewer, pp. 214–16; tr. Hagen, pp. 164–5. For Wilfrid, see Edmer, *The Life of Saint Wilfrid by Edmer*, ed. and tr. Bernard J. Muir and Andrew J. Turner (Exeter, 1998), p. 87. For Bernard, see *Bernard of Clairvaux Vita primi*, p. 20.
63 *Gemma ecclesiastica*, 2. 18, ed. Brewer, p. 249; tr. Hagen, pp. 189–90.
64 Adam of Eynsham, *Magna Vita Sancti Hugonis. The Life of St Hugh of Lincoln*, ed. and tr. Decima L. Douie and Hugh Farmer, 2 vols (London, 1961), vol. 1, p. 28.
65 Ibid., vol. 1, p. 50.
66 Ibid., vol. 1, pp. 50–1.
67 *Metrical Life of Saint Hugh*, p. 15.
68 Adam of Eynsham, *Magna Vita*, vol. 2, p. 17.
69 *Metrical Life of Saint Hugh*, p. 9.
70 Emma Pettit and Edward Christie's essays in the present volume discuss the same issue in relation to Anglo-Saxon England.
71 Ibid.

4

Matronly Monks: Theodoret of Cyrrhus' Sexual Imagery in the *Historia Religiosa*

CHRISTOPHER C. CRAUN

Holiness in Christian late antiquity often seems to be intrinsically linked with masculinity. Hagiographical accounts of male anchorites frequently portray their subjects as spiritual athletes, warriors of God who, while celibate, remain extremely virile, capable of facing the extremes of the desert and the attacks of demons.[1] At the other end of the gender spectrum, female ascetics were marvels for overcoming their stereotypical weaker nature. Their example could shame their male counterparts, goading them towards greater efforts. Paradoxically, however, the hagiographies of female ascetics have provided our clearest image of the masculine nature of Christian holiness during late antiquity, as frequently these women are portrayed in a process of 'becoming male', either figuratively, or literally (through cross-dressing), as a means of increasing their sanctity.[2] In contrast to what has become the norm, my paper will step back from these understandings of holy masculinity. Instead, I will examine how, during the fifth century, Theodoret of Cyrrhus portrayed Syrian holy men not in masculine terms, but in feminine ones, as Brides of Christ and Matrons of God, who bear spiritual children from this relationship. Using his *Historia religiosa* as a source it will become clear that Theodoret's conception of asceticism results in a description of male holiness that apparently only reaches its apex in femininity.

In order to interpret this imagery, we need to consider Theodoret's background and the historical and theological context in which he was writing. Theodoret (393–466) was a native of Antioch and had been dedicated to God by his parents at birth. He spent his childhood visiting the holy men who lived around Antioch. After the death of his parents he became a monk and entered a house at Nicerte, where he became well known as a writer. He was made bishop of Cyrrhus in northern Syria in 423.[3] He penned his *Historia religiosa* (Religious History) at some point between 437 and 448, in the midst of the Nestorian controversy that had effectively split the Eastern Church.[4] Nestorius was living as a priest and monk in Antioch when he was chosen by the Emperor Theodosius II to be patriarch of Constantinople. He was consecrated in 428, but within a year had begun to speak out against the Virgin Mary's title of *Theotokos* (God Bearer), arguing that although God begot Christ as divine, Mary was his mother only with respect to his humanity. The Council of Ephesus was convened to settle the dispute in 431 and it condemned Nestorius, giving official affirmation to the *Theotokos* and pronouncing that Christ had two distinct natures in one person; both human and divine. Nestorius was deposed and disgraced. Theodoret had a personal stake in this controversy for he was a friend of Nestorius', and begged him not to reject the *Theotokos* before the Council of Ephesus, although Theodoret continued to support his friend despite Nestorius' refusal to back down. In addition, like Nestorius, Theodoret had received his early ecclesiastical training within the heartland of what came to be known as Antiochene theology. Unlike Egyptian Alexandrian theology, which emphasized the deity of Christ, Antiochene theology placed much more importance on Christ's humanity. Antiochene theology will be discussed in more detail below, as it informs Theodoret's writings and use of gendered language.

Theodoret witnessed at first hand the Byzantine Empire's powerful ecclesiastical factions and their rabid antipathy for Antiochene reformers. For example, he had seen the great patriarch of Constantinople, John Chrystostom, suffer deposition and exile, in spite of the enormous public support he enjoyed among the masses.[5] Not only had Chrystostom also come from the ranks of the Antioch church, he had studied under Diodore, one of the fathers of Antiochene theology. All the signs indicated that the Antiochene traditions so dear to Theodoret were under attack. Thus it is not surprising that, shortly after Nestorius' fall, Theodoret can be seen instigating a riot in the city of Chalcedon, on the Bosphorous, by preaching to a large crowd of Nestorian supporters.[6] Emperor Theodosius' response, if not exactly swift, was eventually harsh. In 435, perhaps under pressure from pro-Alexandrian monks within Constantinople, he forbade the Nestorians from calling themselves Christians and ordered that their books be burnt.[7] Thus, the Antiochene church and its beliefs were in dire need of a champion. Theodoret's growing reputation as a skilled exegete and writer soon thrust him into the role. The burden of defending his Antiochene heritage and its doctrine would sit heavily upon Theodoret's shoulders, however, for he would pay a high price for his efforts. Theodoret sacrificed what had promised to be an impressive career within the Orthodox Church to suffer temporary expulsion from his diocese of Cyrrhus in 449, while facing accusations that his doctrine was heretical.[8] It is within this highly charged atmosphere of personal risk and conviction that Theodoret wrote his *Historia religiosa*, a collection of the biographies of thirty famous ascetics and hermits, which has been described as 'our principal source for early Syrian monasticism, a movement as preeminent in its anchorites as was Egypt in coenobitic monasticism'.[9] Theodoret used these exemplary narratives to justify the Antiochene theological tradition by an appeal to the past, and to the activities of twenty-seven Syrian holy men and three women. The first twenty chapters are devoted to monks already deceased, beginning with James of Mesopotamia (d. 337/8) and ending with Maris of Cyrrhus (d. 430). The next seven chapters tell of monks who were still alive when Theodoret was writing, and it is only in the last two that we are given the lives of three female ascetics, Marana, Cyra and Domnina, who were also still alive at the time.

Unfortunately, since the audience of the *Historia religiosa* remains uncertain, we can say little about the specific goals of Theodoret's text, although the prologue makes it clear that he intended the lives to be didactic and exemplary, writing: 'How fine it is to behold the contests of excellent men, the athletes of virtue, and to draw benefit with the eyes; when witnessed, the objects of our praise appear enviable and become desirable, and impel the beholder to attain them.'[10] Here he introduces his subjects in archetypal masculine religious terms, using the metaphor of the strong, accomplished athlete. But within the individual lives of some of these men he uses very different and much more feminine and sexual language to describe their conduct and spirituality. For our purposes it is highly significant that Theodoret's use of feminine, sexual imagery is much more predominant within the first third of his work; the chapters that portray Syria's earliest ascetic masters. As will be seen, a gradual tapering towards less provocative metaphors is demonstrable throughout the text. Chapter 9, the account of Peter of Mt Silpius who died *c.*403, contains the last openly erotic references to male ascetic desire for God.

It is important to place Theodoret's work within the context of writings about and historical practices of Syrian asceticism as this may help us to understand why he restricted the use of sexual imagery within the *Historia religiosa* to his depictions of fourth-century ascetics and did not use similar language to describe the holy men who appear later in the collection. The writings of Aphrahat the Persian (d. 345) and Ephraim the Syrian (d. 373) have provided some of our earliest evidence for the ascetic practices of the early Syrian church.[11] Theodoret's treatises on doctrine are written staunchly, if not slavishly, within the same Antiochene tradition which governed their works. One fascinating insight which emerges from these is the role of a group of select, celibate Christians within the early Syrian church. The particular make-up, purpose and goals of these individuals, whose name translates as 'Singles', remain highly contentious.[12] However, it is enough to observe that both Aphrahat and Ephraim discuss these ritually separated men and women in terms that emphasize their celibate lifestyle, single-minded dedication to God and public imitation of Christ – as both examples for, and, perhaps, representatives of, the Christian community.[13]

These are also precisely the same characteristics which Ephraim praises in the newly developed anchorite movement that blossomed in Syria near the end of his life. He states how, in this new asceticism, 'Jesus was ever depicted. Because he (the ascetic) had seen the glory of the One, he too became a One.'[14] The Syrian word for 'One' in this sentence is the same form for 'Single' or 'One' as that used to describe the ritual celibates of the early Syrian church. Ephraim is pointing out how the anchorites are fulfilling an established role, one that was probably readily recognizable to his fourth-century audience. In this depiction, the anchorite is drawn to the glory of the divine One, the Beloved, and becomes celibate, dedicated to the things of God and elevated to a special position because of the resulting relationship with God. The similarity between Theodoret's imagery in the *Historia religiosa* and Ephraim's praise of the anchorites is too precise to be coincidental. The 'Singles' movement seems to have died out within decades of Ephraim's comments, and it may be that they were made redundant by the more dramatic and, if Ephraim is to be believed, more successful anchoritic movement. Moreover, whereas both men and women were among the 'Singles', Theodoret's *Historia religiosa*, as we have seen, is given over almost entirely to male ascetics, despite the fact that Theodoret explicitly intended these examples to be relevant to both men and women. In particular, no female examples are provided among the models of early Syrian Christian endeavour and it may be for this reason that Theodoret decided to use archetypally female/feminine language to describe some of his earlier male subjects instead, as a way of exploring and justifying the Antiochene emphasis on an emotional response to the divine.

Having considered the historical and ideological background, we need now to consider the Antiochene christology and hermeneutics which underlie Theodoret's ascetic ideal. In his own words, Theodoret intended the *Historia religiosa* to relate 'the way of life of the men who have loved God . . . who in a mortal and passable body have displayed impassability and emulated bodiless beings'.[15] While stating that his subjects, through their ascetic way of life, have 'won so radiant a crown of victory as to rout their adversaries', Theodoret assures his readers that these individuals were not created naturally superior to the normal Christian.[16] 'It is not their nature that afforded them victory', he says, 'for it is mortal and full of innumerable passions', rather, it is 'their resolve, attracting divine grace'.[17] In this way Theodoret's subjects can be of exemplary relevance to readers who do not directly emulate their extreme way of life. This statement also introduces one of the defining tenents of Antiochene theology. The Antiochene father, Theodore of Mopsuestia, had taught that the prelapsarian condition of man was akin to an image of God, as mentioned in Genesis 1.[18] According to Theodore, the successful fulfilment of humankind's purpose is only possible for individuals who have been assumed by the divine character or nature. For ascetics to succeed in regaining a prelapsarian state (which was the goal of their practices), their natures had to become one with God. They should imitate Christ in their fusion of human and divine natures. Therefore, christology provides an important way of understanding this process. Just as Antiochene christology emphasized the complete separation between Christ's earthly nature and that of his divinity, so a strict separation between the ascetic's final holiness and his fleshly nature, full of innumerable and unruly passions, must be maintained.[19]

This parallel continues into Theodoret's explanation of the mechanism enabling this union of earthly ascetic with divine virtue. The ascetic's 'resolve, attracting divine grace' is an act of the human will, but it is this divine grace which enables the ascetic to transcend human boundaries: God is the protagonist. This relationship refers to the role played by Christ's human nature within Nestorius' conception of the incarnation. Significantly, the assertion that asceticism rises within normal Christians through divine grace stands rather sharply opposed to contemporary trends in Egyptian monasticism, which was beginning to elevate its predecessors such as Antony and Pachomius to a level of spirituality masculinity which was unattainable by contemporary ascetics.[20] Moreover, Theodoret's assertion that the ability of Syrian ascetics to withstand extreme hardship was derived from God and not from man's own strength also served to justify the notoriously severe asceticism practised by them. God, he argued, 'is wont to measure the gifts of the All-Holy Spirit by the resolve of the Pious and give greater gifts to those with more perfect resolve'.[21] For Theodoret, resolve is the required sanctifying principle of all ascetics. The increasingly harsh ascetic disciplines are themselves the physical symptoms of God's reciprocal and empowering gift of the Holy Spirit, awarded in direct correlation to the ascetic's desire. The hermit's works of *askesis* served to subdue the urges of his flesh and to cleanse his mind of competing worldly distractions. Theodoret is commonly credited with supporting ascetic moderation, but it may be that, with the descriptions of the extreme asceticism practised by his subjects, he is here subtly pricking at the more regulated and subdued asceticism of Egypt. If Syrian ascetics were capable of enduring sterner practices than their Egyptian brethren, he seems to argue, what does this say about their comparative levels of commitment and masculinity? Certainly, in many respects the *Historia religiosa* holds its subjects up as prime examples of both holiness and masculinity, emphasizing their status as spiritual athletes able to turn away from the temptations of the world and devote themselves to a life of hardship and deprivation instead. Moreover, these are qualities also shared by the three female ascetics with whom Theodoret ends his collection, in keeping with the commonplace practice, noted at the outset, of emphasizing the holy woman's ability to rise above her natural disadvantages and become spiritually masculine.[22]

But, in the earlier chapters, when Theodoret comes to describe the early ascetics' personal relationship with God he writes in a different register. This relationship is explained as one of love: 'The more a man devotes himself to the things of God, the more does he kindle the fire of love.'²³ This quotation is taken from the epilogue to the *Historia religiosa*, which is entirely given over to discussion of this issue, being entitled 'On divine love'. It is for the expression of this love between ascetic and God that Theodoret uses feminine rather than masculine imagery to describe these men. This love carries the hermit into an ever-building spiral of physical rejection and spiritual ecstasy. In accordance with Plato and his patristic Christian interpreters, Theodoret pictures the successful ascetic as 'united in contemplation with the eternal divine beauty'.²⁴ Since God was considered the ultimate masculine being, this suggests that despite the masculine nature of the ascetics' physical struggles against the World and the Flesh, in their relationship and union with God it was far more appropriate to present them as spiritually feminine; indeed, contemporary ascetics were encouraged to perceive themselves in these terms.²⁵ It is for this reason that Theodoret presents these male ascetics as Brides to God's Bridegroom.²⁶

Acknowledging the desirability of this spiritually feminine state, the Bride and Bridegroom motif provides a readily accessible metaphor for Theodoret's *Historia religiosa* – illustrating the interaction of desire, fulfilment and gracious response by the one fulfilled, that continues to provoke renewed passion. Theodoret's ascetics choose to seek God and become entangled by his beauty. He describes this passionate desire of Lover for Husband, commending the true ascetics who: 'as fervent lovers of the beauty of God, choosing to do and to suffer all things gladly on behalf of the Beloved . . . bore nobly the revolt of the passions and were steadfast in shaking off the showers of the Devil's darts'.²⁷ Theodoret heightens the feminine nature of the ascetics' response here by emphasizing its emotional intensity. As other scholars have noted, in this respect Theodoret's writings diverge from many Western Christian equivalents, with their distaste for the passions. An emotional response (*apathea*) is portrayed as an ascetic goal in the *Historia religiosa*; Theodoret urged his readers to enkindle their emotions to a fever pitch, provided that these emotions were aimed towards the proper object.²⁸ The ascetics are feminized by their status as God's Bride, but also by the fervent nature of their love for him. This point is amply illustrated by the individual biographies contained within the *Historia religiosa*. In the second chapter the hermit Julian Saba most clearly displays Theodoret's image of this marriage with God where God is masculine and hermit feminine. Julian Saba (d. 367) was originally a solitary recluse, but eventually became the centre of a large monastic community which sought to follow his example. In Theodoret's biography Julian's resolve is mentioned first – Julian travelled to the extremities of the desert and beyond the point of turning back. There in the Eden of the wilderness, he resided in the prelapsarian home prepared not by human hands, but by God's own. Because of God's involvement in its preparation, Julian 'was glad to settle in that place, thinking it of more value than palaces shining with gold and silver' (2. 23). Julian remained there, living a simple life in God's household. Alone with his Beloved, God, Julian completed the daily tasks of preparing food, mending clothing and caring for his surroundings. In other words, he kept house for his husband and undertook typically female chores.

Theodoret, however, quickly focuses upon Julian's most important duty. 'As his luxury, his indulgence, and elaborate banquet he had the hymnody of David and perpetual intercourse (*homilea*) with God' (2. 23–4). *Homilea* possesses the same double connotation as the English word intercourse and it seems that Theodoret intentionally utilized these shared meanings, for here in Julian's cell, the inner room of his Master's desert, Julian's union between his soul as Bride and God as Bridegroom became extremely intimate, Theodoret describing it in markedly sexual language. This sexual symbolism is made more evident by the pleasure which Julian experiences during *homilea*. Theodoret states that Julian's 'enjoyment of this was insatiable, he refused to experience repletion; instead he was always taking his fill and crying out' (2. 24). Here Julian's insatiability identifies him very clearly as the female partner in his intercourse with God.[29] Throughout his long life, Julian's relationship with God remains passionate. Theodoret characterizes it as such 'a firebrand of longing that he was intoxicated with desire, and while seeing nothing of earthly things dreamt only of the Beloved at night and thought only of Him by day'.[30] Even after a community has grown up around his hermitage, Julian, 'separating himself from all human company and turning into himself enjoyed solitary intercourse with God . . . that divine and inexpressible beauty' (2. 25).

Similar sexual imagery occurs in the account of the hermit, Marcianus (d. 385), who also 'transferred all his love to God and the things of God' (3. 37). Like Julian, he too experiences the female sexual role in his relationship with God, 'in his constant enjoyment of such delight [he] refused to experience satiety' (3. 38). The ascetic cannot achieve satiety with God because of the Bridegroom's infinite nature, as God can never be completely known. In the Epilogue to the *Historia religiosa* Theodoret notes that satiety is something that only results from physical intercourse, whereas 'divine desire does not admit the laws of satiety'.[31] The point is clear: by avoiding physical fulfilment, the spiritual version may be experienced forever, and the language and image of the insatiable female sexual partner provides Theodoret with the most vivid and appropriate way of illustrating the experience of the hermits in this respect. Nor are Julian and Marcianus the only examples of such representation within the *Historia religiosa*. In his chapter on Peter of Mt Silpius, Theodoret refers directly to the Song of Solomon when he states that Peter did 'nothing unreasonable when he fell in love with the same Bridegroom and used the words of the Bride: I am wounded with love'.[32]

The sexual metaphor continues, for after this prolonged intercourse with the Divine One both Julian and Marcianus conceive. This is no mere play on words. Union and its natural product conception were common Syrian understandings of the soul's salvation.[33] A particularly clear example of this saving union may be found in the Syrian text, the *Odes of Solomon*. The third Ode states, 'I have been united to Him because the Lover has found the Beloved. Because I love Him that is the Son, I shall become a Son. Indeed he who is joined to Him who is immortal, truly shall be immortal.'[34] The union of the individual with Christ changes him from spouse into offspring and signals his rebirth into salvation. Thus, after perpetual intercourse with God, Julian's spiritual body gives birth to ascetic works which 'became conspicuous to all and drew to [Julian] . . . the lovers of the good' (2. 29). Just as God's beauty seduces the ascetic, those of lesser resolve may be seduced by the ascetic's beautiful disciplines, which will eventually inflame these observers with a greater desire for God. In due time, Julian's fruitful asceticism drew others to his side and they became his spiritual progeny. Thus Theodoret, when discussing the growth of monastic foundations, points both to God and to the individual ascetic founders. The one who 'provided . . . seed could fairly be called the cause of the good plants', by which he means ascetic followers (3. 39). Taking the masculine procreative role again God provided the seed, but receptive souls were needed for the feminine role of incubating the seed and allowing it to grow. Eventually these plants would grow to spiritual puberty, and be capable of similar reproduction themselves, in a cycle of procreation. The later ascetics whom Theodoret describes can thus be seen as the offspring of the earlier ones, but the emphasis in their lives is on physical hardship, self-abnegation and pastoral endeavours. None of them are described in either bridal or matronal terms. The fact that Theodoret does include three actual women at the end of his collection may partially explain why none of the later men are described as brides. Theodoret has real women instead to illustrate the feminine and emotional response to God, and Marana and Cyra are described in exactly the same language as the earlier men, kindling 'the firebrand of their love for God', and prepared to undergo various hardships, for 'to such a degree has divine yearning driven them to a frenzy, so much has divine love for the Bridegroom driven them mad' (29. 185). However, the life of the other female ascetic, Domnina, does not describe her in these terms, recounting instead how she imitated the male ascetic Maron (d. 410), whose life Theodoret had already recounted, in the harshness of her daily regime. In her life Theodoret goes on to remark that

> From the time when Christ the Master honored virginity by being born of a virgin, nature has sprouted meadows of virginity and offered these fragrant and unfading flowers to the Creator, not separating virtue into male and female, nor dividing philosophy into two categories. For the difference is one of bodies, not of souls. (30. 187)

Theodoret then emphasizes that he has offered both male and female models 'that men old and young, and women too, may have models of philosophy' (30. 188). It was noted at the outset that female saints were frequently used as models of holy masculinity, demonstrating an understanding that, although their bodies may be different to men, their souls were capable of the same endeavours. Indeed, at the beginning of the lives of Marana and Cyra Theodoret noted:

> After recording the way of life of the heroic men, I think it useful to treat also of women who have contended no less if not more; for they are worthy of still greater praise, when, despite having a weaker nature, they display the same zeal as the men and free their sex from its ancestral disgrace.[35]

However, as noted earlier, the vast majority of lives which Theodoret included in the *Historia religiosa* are of men rather than women. Moreover, although this representation of female saints leaving the disadvantages of a female body and feminine attributes behind to become holy fits into a wider trope within contemporary hagiography, it is much more unusual to find male saints being used as models of holy femininity within this context. This is perhaps because, whereas the woman who sought to become masculine was rising above her nature, the man who sought to become feminine was seen to betray his.[36] It may be that in rendering the earlier male ascetics more feminine the intention was, in part, to provide more material to which Theodoret's projected female readers could relate. Given that he does not describe any of the more recent or contemporary men responding to God in such feminized and sexual terms it may be that these were not qualities which he expected or wished the men around him to imitate.[37]

This could also link back to the political and theological environment within which he was writing. Considering his situation, a subtle promotion of the Antiochene doctrine which underpins his analysis may have been safer for Theodoret than an outspoken treatise. Thus his more extreme descriptions of spirituality, drawing on the Antiochene emphasis on humanity and an emotional response to the divine, were safely located in the past, exemplified by dead men and not practised by those who were still alive. It may be that, in order not to appear too radical (he did not entirely share Nestorius' beliefs, as we have seen) and perhaps to achieve compromise with those who opposed Antiochene theology, Theodoret deliberately chose to adopt a more straightforwardly masculine presentation of the men who had lived more recently, or who were still alive.

In summation, the cumulative effect of Theodoret's Bride and Bridegroom motif is the establishment of an ascetic ideal. However, he also makes it clear throughout his *Historia religiosa* that this ideal is applicable to all Christians. Theodoret posits an intimacy, indeed a co-identity, with the divine as a believer's true goal. The individual's wilful desire for correct alignment with God produces a feminine condition in the soul, enabling a containment and implantation of the Holy Spirit, which eventually results in spiritual reproduction. After this conception, the believer gives birth to physical manifestations of holiness and virtue which, when seen by others, produce spiritual children.[38] Therefore spiritual femininity was something to which both men and women could aspire. These physical manifestations are more present in ascetics than in other figures because, through their asceticism, they have succeeded in attracting more divine grace. As public images of Christ, as well as his Bride, ascetics display heavenly virtues and produce spiritual children by the voluntary submission of their human natures to the divine. The fact that their submission is voluntary is crucial, because it is this which prevents the early ascetics from being completely feminized. In Theodoret's system, the individual's will is paramount. The ascetic may dissociate from God at any time, and continued intimacy is achieved by recurring acts of will. This emphasis is linked to the Antiochene understanding of sin as an act of the rational will in denial of the known good.[39] Sin is not tied merely to the flesh, but its most dangerous forms lie in the rejection by man's soul of God's spiritually obvious truth.[40] Satan's role is that of a tester, placing temptations before our physical senses and our rational consciousness. Theodoret observes that 'the Devil uses our own limbs as weapons against us; for if the eyes are not enticed nor the hearing bewitched nor touch titillated nor mind receptive of evil intentions, the zeal of those plotting is in vain'.[41] Sin is voluntary, a turning away from one's first love. A perfect lover of true philosophy then is marked by 'the soul's resistance to its [the flesh's] appetites through the knowledge of its relation to its [the soul's] own desires and their objects', knowing intimately the One which the created soul was designed to love: the Creator.[42] If the ascetic's relationship with God is a product of will, he retains the important masculine quality of self-mastery. He has become feminine not as a natural product of his physical condition, or through any other compulsion, but through choice; it is a self-willed submission that does not compromise his innate masculinity. Theodoret's earlier ascetics are still masculine while languishing in the feminine role of God's insatiable lover, because, unlike real women, they still possessed the will, if they wished, to choose to stop and to turn away from God instead.

Notes

This paper is heavily indebted to the comments and support of Dr Lynda Coon, University of Arkansas, Fayetteville, and Drs Katherine Lewis and P. H. Cullum. I am very grateful for their suggestions. Any remaining weaknesses are totally my own, despite their efforts.

[1] See Athanasius, *The Life of Antony*, ed. and tr. Robert Gregg, *The Life of Antony and the Letter to Marcellinus*, in the Classics of Western Spirituality series, ed. Kevin Lynch *et al.* (New York, 1980), specifically pp. 77–94 for examples of ascetic exorcism. See also the manifold examples in

Apophthegmata Patrum, ed. J. B. Cotelier, *PG* vol. 65, cols 71–440; for an English tr. see B. Ward, *The Sayings of the Desert Fathers* (Oxford, 1975).

[2] See Susanna Elm, *Virgins of God. The Making of Asceticism in Late Antiquity* (New York, 1994), pp. 253–69, for a discussion of the female desert ascetic and the various ways of representing her, including a hagiographical instance where a male ascetic is pushed to greater endeavour by observing saintly females. For discussion of the cross-dressing or 'transvestite' saints, see Vern L. Bullough, 'Cross dressing and gender role change in the Middle Ages', in Vern L. Bullough and James A. Brundage (eds), *Handbook of Medieval Sexuality* (New York and London, 1996), pp. 223–42 (pp. 228–31).

[3] For a more detailed account of Theodoret's childhood and subsequent career see: R. M. Price, *A History of the Monks of Syria* (Kalamazoo, MI, 1985), pp. xi–xiii.

[4] Theodoret of Cyrrhus, *Histoire des moines de Syrie*, in P. Canivet and A. Leroy-Molinghen (ed.), *Sources chrétiennes*, vols. 234 and 257 (Paris, 1977 and 1979). Price, *History of Monks of Syria* provides an English tr. and all quotations will be taken from this. Hereafter citation will be to chapter number and page number.

[5] For a provocative look at the events surrounding the depositions of both Chrystostom and Nestorius, see T. Gregory, *Vox Populi: Popular Opinion and Violence in the Religious Controversies of the Fifth Century AD* (Columbus, OH, 1979).

[6] *Acta Conciliorum Oecumenicorum*, ed. Eduard Schwartz (Berlin, 1927), tomus 1, vol. 1, p. 80, for mention of these events in a letter to Alexander of Heliopolis. See also Gregory, *Vox Populi*.

[7] *Codex Theodosianus*, ed. Theodore Mommsen and Paul Mayer (Berlin, 1905), vol. 1, pp. 879–80.

[8] D. S. Wallace-Hadrill, *Christian Antioch: A Study of Early Christian Thought in the East* (Cambridge, 1982), pp. 134–41. Finally in 451 Theodoret was persuaded to renounce Nestorius and was recognized as orthodox at the Council of Chalcedon, which effectively marked the end of his activities as the champion of Antiochene theology.

[9] Price, *History of Monks of Syria*, p. x.

[10] Prologue, 1.

[11] See Sidney Griffith, 'Asceticism in the church of Syria: the hermeneutics of early Syrian asceticism', in V. Wimbush and R. Valantasis (eds), *Asceticism* (Oxford, 1995), pp. 220–45.

[12] Ibid., p. 224, contains a bibliographical outline of the lively and ongoing debate over the role and demographics of this group.

[13] Ibid. Robert Murray, 'The characteristics of the earliest Syriac Christianity', *Dumbarton Oaks Symposium,* 1980 (Washington, DC, 1982), pp. 3–16.

[14] E. Beck, *Des heiligen Ephraem des Syrers: Hymnen auf Abraham Kidunaya und Julianaus Saba,* Corpus Scriptorum Christianorum Orientalium, 322

(Louvain, 1972), 2. 13, p. 41. The English tr. quoted here is from Griffith, 'Asceticism', p. 228.
[15] Prologue, 4.
[16] Prologue, 5. For the angelic character of asceticism, see Prologue, 3–4; 3. 44; 4. 53–4; 21. 134; 36. 170.
[17] Prologue, 5.
[18] See R. A. Norris, *Manhood and Christ: A Study in the Christology of Theodore of Mopsuestia* (Oxford, 1963), pp. 140–4, for a synopsis of the Antiochene view represented in Theodore's *Homilies on the Catechism* and his exegesis of Genesis.
[19] See J. F. Bethune-Baker, *Nestorius and his Teachings: A Fresh Examination of the Evidence* (Cambridge, 1908; repr. New York, 1969), pp. 171–89; Jaroslav Pelikan, *The Christian Tradition: A History of the Development of Doctrine*, 1, *The Emergence of the Catholic Tradition 100–600* (Chicago, 1971), pp. 230–56.
[20] The role of the ascetic master as it developed in Egypt during the fourth and fifth centuries has been outlined by Philip Rousseau, *Ascetics, Authority and the Church in the Age of Jerome and Cassian* (Oxford, 1978).
[21] Prologue, 8.
[22] Chs 29 and 30.
[23] Epilogue, 193.
[24] Ibid.
[25] Verna Harrison, 'The allegorization of gender: Plato and Philo on spiritual childbearing', in Wimbush and Valantasis, *Asceticism*, pp. 520–34 (pp. 524, 526–7). I believe that Theodoret is closer to Gregory of Nyssa and Maximus the Confessor than Philo.
[26] Representations of the religious man or his soul as bride of Christ can be found throughout the Middle Ages, see for example Caroline Walker Bynum, *Jesus as Mother: Studies in the Spirituality of the Middle Ages* (Berkeley, CA, and London, 1982), p. 161, and the examples discussed by Carolyn Diskant Muir in the present volume. For the possibility of applying queer readings to such representations see the essay by Karma Lochrie cited in n. 37 below.
[27] Prologue, 5.
[28] As argued by Kallistos Ware, 'The way of the ascetics: negative or affirmative', in Wimbush and Valantasis, *Asceticism*, pp. 3–13 (pp. 11–12).
[29] See, for example, Joyce E. Salisbury, 'Gendered sexuality', in Bullough and Brundage, *Handbook of Medieval Sexuality*, pp. 81–102 (p. 92).
[30] 2. 24. The motif of the Fire of Love was a common means of expressing union with God in later mystical writings, such as those of Richard Rolle in the fourteenth century.
[31] Epilogue, 193.
[32] 9. 82, with the Song of Solomon 5: 8.
[33] H. W. Drijvers, 'East of Antioch: forces and structures in the development of early Syriac theology', *East of Antioch: Studies in Early Syriac*

Christianity (London, 1984), pp. 1–27, observes that 'The tenor of all stories about the heavenly wedding and the entering of the heavenly bridal chamber is the same, it is a poetical phrasing based on the biblical parallels of the union of soul and spirit' (p. 10).

34 *The Odes of Solomon*, ed. and tr. J. B. Charlesworth (Oxford, 1973), Ode 3, p. 19, ll. 7–9.

35 19. 183. This passage is also discussed in S. A. Harvey, 'Women in early Byzantine hagiography: reversing the story', in L. L. Coon, K. J. Haldane and E. W. Sommer (eds), *That Gentle Strength: Historical Perspectives on Women in Christianity* (Charlottesville, VA, and London, 1990), pp. 36–59 (p. 40).

36 As noted, for example, in Bullough, 'Cross dressing and gender role', p. 225.

37 To draw on Karma Lochrie's contention, it may also be that Theodoret's restriction of feminine imagery to dead ascetics is due to the unnamed problem of homosexuality in representing men (albeit feminized ones) engaging in intercourse with a male deity: Karma Lochrie, 'Mystical acts, queer tendencies', in Karma Lochrie, Peggy McCracken and James Schulz (eds), *Constructing Medieval Sexuality* (Minneapolis, 1997), pp. 180–200 (p. 187).

38 See also 9. 50–1.

39 Norris, *Manhood and Christ*, pp. 157–8.

40 See Wallace-Hadrill, *Christian Antioch*, pp. 117–31, for a discussion of this concept and its importance for the christological questions.

41 Prologue, 5–6.

42 Edith Wyschogrod, 'The howl of Oedipus, the cry of Heloise: from asceticism to postmodern ethics', *Asceticism*, pp. 16–30 (pp. 21–2).

5

Bride or Bridegroom? Masculine Identity in Mystic Marriages

CAROLYN DISKANT MUIR

Mystic marriages are well-known phenomena among medieval women. From the virgin martyr St Catherine of Alexandria to later mystics like Hadewijch of Brabant, Mechthild of Magdeburg and St Catherine of Siena, women often experienced that supreme state of union with the divine. Yet, what about such experiences among medieval men? The collection of information about male mystic marriages reveals two striking features. First, no matter the period, from medieval to modern, many more women than men experienced a mystic marriage, by a factor of roughly three to one.[1] Second, for women, the holy spouse is always Christ. Men, however, wed various figures – Christ, the Virgin Mary, Wisdom or Poverty.

The concept of a mystic marriage with Christ is not difficult to understand as it applies to women. The most detailed and influential biblical text on the subject, the Song of Songs, inspired allegorical interpretations by many later writers. While all commentators saw the bridegroom as Christ, medieval writers differed in their interpretation of the bride as the church, the Virgin Mary or the individual soul.[2] This last interpretation had a great impact on mystics in their experience with divine union. During the thirteenth and fourteenth centuries in particular, there was a great surge of mystical writing by women, in which they refer to Christ as their beloved or spouse.[3] This self-identification by women as the bride of Christ poses no challenge to any notion of what it means to be female. After all, the bride in the Song of Songs is female, the Virgin Mary is female and the soul is feminine. The ceremony for becoming a nun involves the donning of a veil and ring, as all nuns become 'brides of Christ'.[4]

By the period of the high Middle Ages, the thirteenth to fifteenth centuries, the mystic marriage was a well-established theological concept. Men as well as women in their writings on the Song of Songs refer to the bride as the soul, normally using the feminine pronoun in such references.[5] Another striking feature of this time period is the nature of the saints themselves. Weinstein and Bell have demonstrated that at this time a distinctive type of saint emerged that they term 'androgynous'. Both male and female saints engaged in a more affective type of religious experience, comprising private prayer and mystical communion with God.[6] Given these facts, plus the clear dominance in numbers of male saints over female, one might expect to find larger numbers of men experiencing a mystic marriage at this time. Yet this is not the case.[7] This relative paucity of male examples makes their specifics worth examining more closely, in order to try to understand why this might be so, and what a mystic marriage might have meant to a medieval man. Under what circumstances did they have them? Whom did they marry? With whom did they identify in such a marriage? What light can representations of male mystic marriage shed on perceptions of holiness and masculinity in the Middle Ages? The examples of two such men, the Blessed Henry Suso and St Hermann-Joseph, both of Germany, make interesting case studies that can be used in order to explore some of the complexities of this issue.

Heinrich Seuse, or Henry Suso, is often cited by scholars as an unusual male figure for the period. Caroline Walker Bynum, for instance, sees him as one of the men of his time whose piety could be characterized as most 'feminine', which she uses to mean affective, exuberant, lyrical and filled with images.[8] Born *c*.1295 in Constance, Suso entered the Dominican house there at the age of 13. During his years of study, he was deeply affected by the Dominican theologian Meister Eckhart, with whom he studied in Cologne.[9] Returning to Constance in 1326 or 1327, he remained there for the next twenty years. One of his main duties from the mid-1330s was as spiritual adviser to Dominican nuns. Around 1348, Suso was transferred to the Dominican house in Ulm, where he remained until his death in 1366, in all likelihood continuing the same type of pastoral duties as in Constance.[10]

This *cura monialium* (care of religious women) was not only an important duty for Suso, it is thought to have provided the impetus for his most important vernacular writings, which scholars see as having functioned as spiritual guides for the women in his care.[11] His four principal German works are contained in the compendium known as the *Exemplar*. Edited and compiled in Ulm between 1362 and 1363, two of these works, the *Leben* (Life) and the *Büchlein der Wahrheit* (Little Book of Eternal Wisdom), are relevant to considerations of Suso's mystic marriage. This latter book was later expanded and published in Latin as the *Horologium sapientiae* (Clock of Wisdom), and widely disseminated throughout Europe with a largely monastic readership, as indicated by the provenance of existing manuscripts. With the Latin edition, therefore, the audience for Suso's work underwent a dramatic shift from a more limited to a wider readership, and from a female to a male audience.[12] Vernacular editions of this Latin text then followed, in French, Dutch, Italian, English, Swedish, Danish, Polish and Czech, expanding the audience for Suso's work still further.[13]

Suso's efforts to win the love of Eternal Wisdom are described in detail in chapter 3 of his *Leben*, entitled, 'How he entered into a spiritual marriage with Eternal Wisdom'. It begins with a statement of the emphasis he placed in a 'constant effort to achieve intense awareness of loving union with eternal Wisdom'.[14] This desire was prompted by his listening to readings from the Wisdom of Solomon. Convinced that Wisdom must be his love and he her servant, Suso longs to see and talk with her, and to win her love. Once he has confirmed his decision to devote himself to her, she appears to him in the following way: 'She was suspended high above him on a throne of clouds. She shone as the morning star and dazzled as the glittering sun. Her crown was eternity, her attire blessedness, her words sweetness, and her embrace the surcease of all desire.'[15] Smiling at him, she then asks him for his heart. He describes how, afterwards, he frequently thinks of her, sees her and embraces her. The figure of Eternal Wisdom reappears throughout the *Leben*, and Suso composed the *Büchlein der Wahrheit* in the form of a dialogue between Wisdom and her servant, that is, Suso. While this latter book contains many references to the servant as the beloved or bride, it does not contain a section explicitly presenting a spiritual marriage, nor does the *Leben*. However, the *Horologium sapientae* stresses even more strongly his marriage to Wisdom.[16] Chapter 7 of book 2 is entitled, 'How numbers of the faithful may marry Divine Sapientia, and how through daily good works they should renew themselves continually in that love.' The chapter then begins with the disciple's spiritual marriage to Wisdom.[17]

The personification of Wisdom, or Sophia, can be traced back to early Jewish texts. Wisdom first appears in the book of Proverbs and more fully in the apocryphal books of Ecclesiasticus and the Wisdom of Solomon. In these writings, she is clearly a female figure, and is highly exalted, being presented as the creator, governor of the cosmos, the spirit of God. She is also viewed as a bride, a concept that can be seen in the writings of Philo and in the Wisdom of Solomon.[18] Though spoken of as female in the Wisdom of Solomon, Sophia takes on both masculine and feminine roles in Philo.[19]

Sophia's identification with Jesus goes back to Christ's own teachings. According to Luke, Christ saw himself as a prophet of Sophia, and, according to Matthew, as Sophia herself. Paul then makes this identification explicit in his first letter to the Corinthians.[20] Medieval writers, therefore, had a tradition that understood Christ as analogous to the feminine Sophia. These early writers were not concerned with the fact of Wisdom's shifting and ambiguous gender.[21] However, Suso himself is rather ambiguous about the gender of the figure whom he sees and marries. Early in chapter 3 of the *Leben*, he refers to Eternal Wisdom as being presented in the Bible as a woman.[22] But when he vows to become her servant, he asks: 'What must my beloved look like if she has so many delightful things hidden within her! Is she divine or human, man or woman, art or knowledge or what?'[23] In describing how she would appear to him, he writes, 'The minute he thought her to be a beautiful young lady, he immediately found a proud young man before him.'[24]

Although Suso sometimes treats Wisdom as female, and in some cases as an ambiguous figure, in other instances, Wisdom is clearly identified with the male Christ.[25] Suso's understanding of the true nature of his spouse is clearly manifest in his statement in the *Büchlein der Wahrheit*, chapter 5: 'The heavenly Father had adorned me more beautifully than all other corporeal creatures and had chosen me for his tender and lovely bride.'[26] Suso's description of himself in these terms shows a clear self-imagining as female, ready to join in union with the male God the Father.[27]

This ambiguity as to the gender of Wisdom, as well as to Suso's role in the spiritual marriage, is particularly evident when one considers pictorial representations of Suso used to illustrate his writings. Ambiguities over the spouse's gender that may be glossed over in textual form become especially obvious when an artist must make decisions as to the representation of a visual image of the spouse. Illustrations of

Suso and Wisdom can be found in manuscripts of the *Exemplar*, early printed editions of the same work, manuscripts of the French *Horloge de sapience*, as well as single woodcuts from printed versions of Suso's writings.[28] While Suso is usually depicted as clearly masculine, in some cases, he is feminized. Even more common are variations in the presentation of Wisdom, who is shown in some instances as feminine, in others as masculine and occasionally as androgynous. I shall now examine some examples of these representations in more detail.

Of the various manuscripts of the *Exemplar*, six are illustrated, with the earliest one dating from *c*.1371, and the remainder from the fifteenth century.[29] The illustrations to the earliest manuscript of the *Exemplar* (Bibliothèque Nationale et Universitaire de Strasbourg, MS 2929) are especially intriguing, and have been studied by Jeffrey Hamburger, who has asserted the importance of the images in Suso's works and their essential relationship to the text. The high value that Suso placed on artistic images can be further attested by the frequent references throughout his writings to works of art, and his commissioning of an artist to make an image of Eternal Wisdom to take with him to Cologne, an image now unfortunately lost. Hamburger has also argued that the original illustrations in the Strasbourg manuscript were devised by Suso himself, then repeated, and in some cases varied, by artists illustrating manuscripts produced at a later date.[30] In these early illustrations, both Eternal Wisdom and Suso exhibit changeable genders, with Suso acting as both the bride of Christ and the bridegroom of Eternal Wisdom.

Folio 28^v (Figure 5.1) from the manuscript shows Suso with an angel and friars, as they appear in a vision to Anna, one of his followers, depicted with an angel below. Suso, crowned with a rose garland, exhibits the typical swaying pose of female figures in Gothic manuscripts. The curve of his robe accentuates the S-shape of his body. Moreover, the placement of his arms, with one crossing his chest and the other covering his pubic region, imitates the well-known Venus Pudica (modest Venus) pose of ancient art, which was a common model for female figures in post-antique periods of Western art.[31] Suso is clearly shown according to visual conventions in a feminized form, in his role as the bride of Christ. Hamburger comments that Suso is often represented in this manuscript in a feminine form, in particular wearing a chaplet of red and white roses to show his purity and patience.[32]

In contrast, a clear example of Suso's portrayal with a masculine appearance can be found in a woodcut produced in Ulm a century

Figure 5.1. *The Exemplar*, MS 2.929, fo. 28ᵛ. Photo and collection of the Bibliothèque Nationale et Universitaire de Strasbourg

later, c.1470–80 (Figure 5.2). Here he kneels before a half-length figure of Eternal Wisdom. The rose garland is depicted as surrounding his halo. His robes fall heavily to the ground, revealing little of his body, unlike the more tightly wrapped garments in the Strasbourg manuscript.[33] Neither his face nor his body exhibits any feminine qualities, the result being an image that is more typical of the depiction of Suso than that shown in the Strasbourg manuscript's illumination (Figure 5.1).

This more masculine image may in part result from a simple change in style. By the late fifteenth century, the Gothic sway used in the Strasbourg manuscript was long out of fashion, even for female figures. A further reason for this more conventional imagery, however,

Figure 5.2. 'Heinrich Seuse with the Vision of Eternal Wisdom', woodcut, c.1470–80. Nuremberg, Germanisches Nationalmuseum

may be found in the nature and use of the woodcut as an artistic medium. Late fifteenth-century single-sheet woodcuts were intended for wide circulation and popular consumption. Religious images such as this one were often produced by monasteries for their members, as well as for sale to pilgrims.[34] Whether this was true in the case of this print cannot be confirmed; however, it was undoubtedly produced as a devotional image to be circulated, making a clear-cut, unambiguous rendering of Suso more desirable. In contrast, the limited, private circulation of a handwritten manuscript allowed for a more idiosyncratic, unconventional imagery.

Eternal Wisdom's varied appearance is particularly interesting. The woodcut mentioned above presents a clearly feminine form of Eternal Wisdom, which is also the case in the illuminations of the French *Horloge de sapience* by the Rolin Master, now in the Bibliothèque Royale in Brussels (M^s IV, 111). The figure of Wisdom consistently appears as feminine in all the miniatures, as in the final illumination in the manuscript, that of 'The Spiritual Marriage of Sapientia and the Disciple' (folio 127^v) (Figure 5.3). This scene, illustrating the text of book 2, chapter 7, depicts Suso being married to a female Wisdom by a high priest in a church. Yet, the priest's triple tiara identifies him as God the Father, Wisdom's cruciform halo reveals her as Christ, and the hovering dove between them completes the Holy Trinity. In the background is shown an event that occurred soon after the marriage, when Suso fell asleep in the arms of his bride, who gave him the new name of *Frater Amandus* (Loving Brother).[35]

A very different conception of Wisdom, however, occurs in a printed edition of the *Exemplar*, produced by Anton Sorg in Augsburg in 1482, which includes a group of illustrations that derive from the earlier ones in the Strasbourg manuscript, yet with certain crucial differences. Especially interesting is the consistent representation of Eternal Wisdom as obviously masculine (Figure 5.4). In this example, Suso and several other figures shelter under the cloak of Wisdom, who is depicted as God the Father, holding the orb and sceptre usual to representations of Him. Yet the identifying scroll clearly indicates the figure to be Eternal Wisdom.[36] A more androgynous depiction of Eternal Wisdom appears in the Strasbourg manuscript, on folio 1^v (Figure 5.5). Here, the figure of Wisdom, though showing the familiar swaying posture of the female type, is bearded, indicating her masculine nature as well.[37] The inscription at the top of the page reads: 'These pictures show the spiritual marriage of Eternal Wisdom with the

Figure 5.3. 'The Spiritual Marriage of Sapientia and the Disciple',
Horloge de sapience, MS IV, 111, fo. 127ᵛ. Copyright Bibliothèque Royale
de Belgique, Brussels

soul.'[38] The contrast with the same subject shown in the Brussels manuscript is striking.

This variation in the imagery of Eternal Wisdom is less surprising than that of Suso himself, given the multiple gender identities that Wisdom embodies, both in long-standing tradition and for Suso. The more feminized presentation of Suso in the first manuscript of the

BRIDE OR BRIDEGROOM? 67

Figure 5.4. *The Exemplar*, Anton Sorg, Augsburg, 1482,
Inc. 447, fo. 89ʳ. Einsiedeln, Stiftsbibliothek

Exemplar is more striking, especially in the light of Hamburger's argument that these images reflect Suso's self-perception. Hamburger relates this to Suso's purpose in writing the *Exemplar* as a model of religious life, designed for a female audience, the nuns under his spiritual care. He stresses that Suso's aim, in text and image, was to facilitate his spiritual daughters' sense of identification with him, which accounts for his self-presentation in the female role, as the bride of Christ.[39] This distinctly female audience was specific to the images from this manuscript, for the audience for other images of Suso was not necessarily female, as has been noted in the earlier discussion of the Ulm woodcut.

Yet perhaps Suso's self-imagining as female was also in part intended to facilitate his own conception of a personal marriage with

Figure 5.5. *The Exemplar*, MS 2.929, fo. 1ᵛ. Photo and collection of the Bibliothèque Nationale et Universitaire de Strasbourg

Christ. After all, while nuns were clearly identified as the 'brides of Christ', priests were essentially Christ's surrogates, his physical embodiments on earth (one of the reasons why only men could be priests of course). The existence of this clearly defined role with regard to Christ may have added a layer of complexity for a priest wishing to unite his soul with the Lord in a mystical union. Perhaps this very fact may help to account for the scarcity of men in this position, with Suso's enthusiastic embracing of the feminine role a striking anomaly.[40]

In contrast, the implications for a man having a mystic marriage with the Virgin Mary, the other primary figure of devotion in the Middle Ages, were rather different. A general rise in Marian devotion in twelfth- and thirteenth-century Europe, combined with the flourishing of courtly love poetry, resulted in Mary becoming the ideal figure of the beloved. Poems by writers such as Gautier de Coincy speak of her specifically in nuptial terms. Various legends and plays of the fourteenth century also take this theme. Several late medieval texts repeat, with variations, a story of a young canon who had promised to serve Mary forever, having placed a ring on the finger of her statue, but is forced by his family to marry. On his wedding night, Mary appears and scolds him for leaving her for another woman. The groom then abandons his bride and joins Mary in heaven.[41]

Despite the prevalence of this general devotion to the Virgin, it is rare to find cases of specific men who experience a mystical union with her, and the stories of those few that occur are similar in nature to the 'ring on the finger' story just mentioned. For example, the pregnant mother of St Robert of Molesmes (d. 1111), founder of the Cistercians, received a vision of the Virgin Mary, who presented her with a ring to give to her unborn son. The case of St Edmund of Abingdon (d. 1240) is similar to the story of the young man and a statue. Like them, Edmund placed a ring on the finger of a sculpted Virgin, proclaiming himself wed to her.[42] A very different circumstance, however, befalls St Hermann-Joseph, the second example of medieval male mystic marriage to be considered here. Hermann, as he was known for the first part of his life, was born in Cologne around 1150 and died in Hoven in 1241. His biography was first written by Razo Bonvisnus, a contemporary and the prior at the monastery of Steinfeld, not far from Cologne, where Hermann-Joseph lived for most of life and where his cult was centred.

Known for his great devotion to the Virgin even as a child, stories abound attesting to Hermann's close relationship with her and the young Christ, with whom he would sometimes play.[43] Entering the Premonstratensian monastery at Steinfeld at the age of 12, he maintained frequent contact with Mary in the years that followed, hearing her voice, smelling the scent of roses and occasionally seeing her.[44] The relationship that developed between them lasted throughout Hermann's life, and was one in which Mary served as his inspiration and adviser. Because of this, Hermann's fellow monks started to call him Joseph, indicating their early recognition of the quasi-marital relationship between Hermann and Mary, even before his actual mystic marriage. However, Hermann disliked carrying such an illustrious name and found it annoying.[45]

The intensity of Hermann's devotion is certainly not unique. But what is unusual is the culmination of this devotion – his mystic marriage with Mary. As he later described the scene to his biographer, Hermann was praying alone, when the choir suddenly lit up and angels appeared to prepare a throne. Mary then took her place on the throne, assisted by two angels, with others forming a choir on either side. One of the angels then said to another: 'To whom shall we marry this virgin?' The other answered, 'To whom shall we marry her, if not to the Brother here present?' Some angels then flew to Hermann, took him by the hand, and brought him to kneel at Mary's feet. One angel then said to Hermann: 'It is fitting that this most beautiful girl be married to you.' Hermann was dumbfounded and at first did not reply. But, after a glance at Mary, and assurance from the angel that Mary had agreed, Hermann expressed his own agreement and joy. The angel then took his right hand, joined it to the hand of Mary, and performed the marriage, saying: 'Behold, I give this Virgin to you as a wife, even as she was married to Joseph; and you shall take the name of Joseph together with the wife.' The entire choir of angels then sang 'Amen' and 'Long live Hermann-Joseph, the second spouse of the Queen.'[46]

Hermann from this moment was known as Hermann-Joseph, formalizing the name by which he had become increasingly known among his peers, and the Virgin intensified her role as his adviser, friend, confidante and partner. They shared an affectionate and companionable relationship in which she sometimes allowed him to hold the Christ child, as had Joseph himself.[47] She concerned herself with many aspects of his life, from worries about his health to his spiritual formation.[48] Although Hermann-Joseph's experience bears similarities to the general type, in poem and legend, of medieval men whose beloved is Mary, his situation diverges from theirs. For Mary chooses him, rather than he choosing her, the two go through a formal marriage ceremony and he is specifically associated with Joseph.[49]

This last point, the identification as a second Joseph, might seem a very logical way to interpret a marriage to Mary, particularly as Mary and Joseph's union was the best-known example of virginal marriage.[50] Yet marriage to Mary and affinity with Joseph does not seem to have been common in the cases of other such men. Perhaps this was in part because devotion to Joseph was not widespread during the Middle Ages, with Joseph only being canonized in 1621. Hermann-Joseph, in fact, was one of the first to advocate Joseph's cult. He wished to establish a feast in Joseph's honour in the whole church, even composing an office for the feast and refuting objections that had been made to the establishment of Joseph's cult.[51]

In order to better understand the meaning of Hermann-Joseph's marriage to Mary, it may be useful to consider some of his writings. Beginning to write after his ordination, he continued to do so throughout his life. Those writings that are identified with him include two poems to St Ursula (a favorite saint in Cologne, where Hermann had studied), two to the Virgin Mary and three prayers to Christ.[52] Late in life, he also wrote a commentary on the Song of Songs, written, as he said, at the express instruction of the Virgin herself. Unfortunately, this work is lost.[53] The dates of his writings are not known, nor when they occur with respect to his mystic marriage, although André comments that his first verses were for Mary.[54] Throughout the longer of his two poems to her, Hermann-Joseph continually calls Mary his 'Rose', thus further cementing the link between the conventions of courtly love and Marian devotion common at the time. This image of a rose as the beloved was common in the Middle Ages.[55]

Of his two hymns to Christ, one focuses on the suffering heart of Christ, while the other is a prayer to Christ the bridegroom. In this latter hymn, a long love poem of twenty-six stanzas, the author incorporates imagery and references from the Song of Songs. As in the Song of Songs, Hermann-Joseph casts himself as the bride trying to find the bridegroom.[56] The first three stanzas are:

> O Jesus sweet and beautiful!
> O rose smelling in a wondrous way!
> O my loving bridegroom,
> Magnificent beyond measure!
> O my most handsome beloved!

Where, I ask, do you stay?
What place do you want, that you would carefully search for?
Where do you sleep or rest,
Why are you so fragrant and sweet,
O dear flavour of the soul?

Draw me to you, O my beloved!
Turn my mind towards you,
That I may run after your scent,
I who am worn out because of love.
Give me your hand, saying: Follow me.[57]

Several modern writers on Hermann-Joseph have concluded that his mystical union with Mary was linked to his desire for an ultimate union with Christ, and that she was the path for him to achieve this.[58] The saint himself wrote to Mary, 'O my beloved, purify my heart so that we can live together with Jesus in an ardent and sincere love.'[59] Hermann-Joseph thus experienced, or at least desired, an uncommon double marital relationship – as a bridegroom with Mary and a bride with Christ. Moreover, his relationship with Christ was multifaceted. He was a playful companion of the Christ child, a surrogate foster-father (the second Joseph), and ultimately, a loving bride in search of his bridegroom. This complexity of relationships reveals the multiple and many-layered gender identities of the male devotee who forges such a relationship with Mary. And in this complexity, one can see parallels with the case of Suso.[60]

While the experiences of Hermann-Joseph and Henry Suso are obviously different in many aspects, certain parallels emerge. Both Eternal Wisdom and Mary choose their spouses rather than the other way round. In chapter 1 of the original German *Büchlein der Wahrheit*, Wisdom says, 'It is I, eternal Wisdom, who chose you for myself in eternity with the embrace of my eternal providence', while Mary's appearance to Hermann makes it clear that it is she who initiates the marriage.[61] In both relationships, the dominance of the heavenly spouse is stressed, either in the text or the visual imagery.[62] The Brussels manuscript of the *Horloge de sapience* shows a kneeling Suso, posed in submission before his bride. So too is Hermann brought by the angels to kneel at his bride's feet. Finally, in both cases, with the marriage comes a new name. Eternal Wisdom gave Suso the name *Frater Amandus*, and the Virgin Mary honoured Hermann by joining his name to that of her first spouse, Joseph. In both instances, one may speak of the transforming effect of the new name, which marks the beginning of a new stage in life for the one so honoured, and, with the clearly masculine names, is a reaffirmation of their masculine identities.

These examples of Hermann-Joseph and Henry Suso provide intriguing information about male experience of mystic marriage during the Middle Ages, an experience that was more varied and rare than it was for women. Unlike women who always perceived themselves as the feminine bride of a masculine Christ, these men were not restricted to one gender role in their union with divine figures, but could move fluidly between feminine and masculine identities, occupying different roles and positions that were not necessarily predicated on their biological sex. These men were both holy and masculine, but they could also be holy and feminine, without apparent contradiction, depending on the contexts in which they envisaged themselves.

Notes

[1] I have collected so far references to fifty women from the fourth to twentieth centuries, and only nineteen such men. In the period from the eleventh to fifteenth centuries, the figures are twenty-eight women and nine men.

[2] Early church writers such as Jerome, Ambrose and Origen identified the bride as the church or the individual soul. See Marina Warner, *Alone of All her Sex: The Myth and the Cult of the Virgin Mary* (New York, 1983), pp. 126–7. Several twelfth-century writers, chief among them Rupert of Deutz and Bernard of Clairvaux, saw her as the Virgin Mary. See Penny Shine Gold, *The Lady and the Virgin: Image, Attitude, and Experience in Twelfth-Century France* (Chicago, 1985), p. 57.

[3] Caroline Walker Bynum, *Fragmentation and Redemption: Essays on Gender and the Human Body in Medieval Religion* (New York, 1991), pp. 124, 169; Elizabeth Alvilda Petroff, *Medieval Women's Visionary Literature* (New York, 1986), p. 34.

[4] The designation of Christian virgins as brides of Christ can be traced to Tertullian in the third century and was in common use by the fourth century. See Kate Lowe, 'Secular brides and convent brides: wedding ceremonies in Italy during the Renaissance and Counter-Reformation', in Trevor Dean and K. J. P. Lowe (eds), *Marriage in Italy, 1300–1650* (Cambridge, 1998), pp. 41–65, especially pp. 41, 43, and 46; J. Bugge, *Virginitas: An Essay in the History of a Medieval Ideal* (The Hague, 1975), pp. 58, 66. This is not to imply that medieval women's relationships with Christ were not also complex and multivalent. It has been well studied, especially by Bynum, that Christ could function as mother, child and

bridegroom to many of these devout women. My point, however, is that there is nothing inherently problematic about the notion of a mystic marriage of a female figure with a male deity. In that aspect of their relationship, the question of gender is quite straightforward.

5 Nelson Pike, *Mystic Union: An Essay in the Phenomenology of Mysticism* (Ithaca, NY, 1992), p. 69; Caroline Walker Bynum, *Jesus as Mother: Studies in the Spirituality of the High Middle Ages* (Berkeley, CA, 1982), p. 138.
6 Donald Weinstein and Rudolph M. Bell, *Saints and Society: The Two Worlds of Western Christendom, 1000–1700* (Chicago, 1982), pp. 236–7.
7 Bynum, *Jesus*, pp. 140–1, alludes to this phenomenon in her comment that bridal imagery is more common in the writings of women than men in the thirteenth and fourteenth centuries. Other examples, besides the ones to be considered here, of medieval men for whom texts and/or images refer to a spousal relationship with Christ are St John the Evangelist, John of Fécamp, St Bernard of Clairvaux, Jacopone da Todi and Friedrich Sunder.
8 Caroline Walker Bynum, *Holy Feast and Holy Fast: The Religious Significance of Food to Medieval Women* (Berkeley, CA, 1987), pp. 102–3, 105. She also notes that he often saw himself in female images. Barbara Newman, 'Some mediaeval theologians and the Sophia tradition', *Downside Review*, 108 (1990), 111–30 (122), calls Suso perhaps the most 'female-identified' of all male spiritual writers. Barbara Newman's article, 'Henry Suso and the medieval devotion to Christ the Goddess', *Spiritus*, 2 (2002), 1–14, only came to my attention after this essay was completed. In this work, and in her recent book, *God and the Goddess: Vision, Poetry, and Belief in the Middle Ages* (Philadelphia, 2003), Newman considers some of the same issues that I here address regarding Suso's relationship with Eternal Wisdom.
9 Johannes Eckhart (*c*.1260–1327/8) was an active preacher, writer, teacher of theology, and supervisor of women's convents. The idea for which he is best known – the possibility of a union between man and God – permeates his writings and influenced his closest followers. Steven Fanning, *Mystics of the Christian Tradition* (London, 2001), pp. 102–3.
10 Frank Tobin (ed.), *Henry Suso: The Exemplar, with Two German Sermons* (New York, 1989), pp. 19–26, for biographical details. Tobin comments that little is known of the details of his years in Ulm.
11 See, for example, Jeffrey Hamburger, *The Visual and the Visionary: Art and Female Spirituality in Late Medieval Germany* (New York, 1998), pp. 233, 243. See also Meri Heinonen's essay in the present volume, for her comments on this point, and her reference to Walter Blank's work in n. 9.
12 Ibid., p. 206.
13 Peter Rolfe Monks, *The Brussels Horloge de Sapience: Iconography and Text of Brussels, Bibliotheque Royale, MS. IV 111* (Leiden, 1990), p. 31.
14 Tobin, *Suso*, p. 67.
15 Ibid., p. 69.
16 Ibid., p. 35.

17 Monks, *Horloge*, p. 123, with Latin original as well.
18 Newman, 'Sophia tradition', 112–14 and Richard A. Horsley, 'Spiritual marriage with Sophia', *Vigiliae Christianae*, 33 (1979), 30–54 (31–2).
19 Horsley, 'Spiritual marriage', 34.
20 Ibid., pp. 51–2 and Newman, 'Sophia tradition', 114–15.
21 Newman, 'Sophia tradition', 114–15.
22 Tobin, *Suso*, p. 67.
23 Ibid., p. 69.
24 Ibid.
25 Newman, 'Sophia tradition', 123–4. Newman notes that, as Suso matured, he discarded the feminine imagery of Wisdom in favour of the masculine Christ. This coincides with Suso's own imitation of the sufferings of Christ in the form of self-mutilation, fasting and other forms of endurance. For examples of references to Wisdom as Christ, see Tobin, *Suso*, pp. 77, 165 of the *Leben*. It is especially explicit throughout the *Büchlein der Wahrheit*.
26 Tobin, *Suso*, p. 219.
27 The same is true of the Syrian male ascetics whom Christopher C. Craun discusses in the present volume.
28 The imagery of Suso may well be richer than the examples cited here. A complete study remains to be done of the illuminations in the Latin and vernacular renderings of the *Horologium sapientiae*, as well as all the German manuscripts and printed versions of the *Exemplar*. Those images here discussed are meant by way of example, and are not intended to be comprehensive.
29 Hamburger, *Visual and the Visionary*, p. 236.
30 Ibid., pp. 234–7. See also Newman, 'Sophia tradition', 123.
31 These observations are made by Hamburger, *Visual and Visionary*, p. 243, who compares the scene to an Annunciation image and Suso to the Virgin Mary. P. P. Bober and R. O. Rubenstein, *Renaissance Artists and Antique Sculpture* (London, 1987), p. 59, state that the Venus Pudica image was known throughout the medieval and Renaissance periods. An example of the original Venus pose is the Hellenistic Medici Venus, while Botticelli's *Birth of Venus*, c.1485, is a well-known Renaissance instance of its use. Both works are in the Uffizi Gallery, Florence.
32 Hamburger, *Visual and Visionary*, p. 243.
33 For discussion of this woodcut, see *Spiegel der Seligkeit: Privates Bild und Frömmigkeit im Spätmittelalter* (Nuremberg, 2000), pp. 210–11.
34 David Landau and Peter Parshall, *The Renaissance Print, 1470–1550* (New Haven, 1994), p. 347. The *Spiegel* catalogue entry in the previous note also mentions this possibility with regard to the Ulm woodcut.
35 See Monks, *Horloge*, for a detailed discussion of the manuscript, especially pp. 123–4 for comments on this image.
36 The Strasbourg manuscript uses a female figure in this illustration (see Hamburger, *Visual and Visionary*, p. 264), while a later manuscript of the *Exemplar* reproduced in Karl Bihlmeyer, *Heinrich Seuse: Deutsche Schriften*

(Stuttgart, 1907), p. 154, uses a male bearded figure, as in the Sorg print. Hamburger, *Visual and Visionary*, p. 249, comments that later illustrated copies of the *Exemplar* all stress Wisdom as being Christ and having masculine features.

[37] See Hamburger, *Visual and Visionary*, pp. 246, 249, for more discussion.

[38] Translation of inscription, ibid., p. 249.

[39] Ibid., pp. 244 and 245.

[40] E. Ann Matter, 'Mystical marriage', in L. Scaraffia and G. Zarri (eds), *Women and Faith: Catholic Religious Life in Italy from Late Antiquity to the Present* (Cambridge, MA, 1999), pp. 31–41 (p. 35), also discusses mystic marriage as most common in medieval women's religious communities, observing that it is not as common among men. She further observes that medieval nuns could see themselves as spouses of Christ without a change of gender. Karma Lochrie has argued that descriptions of male mystics marrying a male Christ may also have been problematic because of the implicit 'problem' of homosexuality that such accounts entailed: 'Mystical acts, queer tendencies', in Karma Lochrie, Peggy McCracken and James Schulz (eds), *Constructing Medieval Sexuality* (Minneapolis, 1997), pp. 180–200 (p. 187).

[41] For discussion of this motif, see Warner, *Alone of All her Sex*, pp. 156–9 and Frederic C. Tubach, *Index Exemplorum: A Handbook of Medieval Religious Tales* (Helsinki, 1969), p. 389.

[42] See James Morris, *Oxford* (London, 1965), p. 178, and Louis Réau, *Iconographie de l'art chrétien* (Paris, 1959), vol. 3/3, p. 1154. A somewhat different story is that of the post-medieval saint John Eudes (d. 1680), who, in his great love for Mary, chose her as his spouse by placing a ring on the finger of her statue. Years later, he wrote out a marriage contract which he signed in blood and had buried with him. See Pierre Herambourg, *Saint John Eudes: A Spiritual Portrait* (Dublin, 1960), pp. 125–32, for details. Interestingly, although Suso did not engage in a marriage with the Virgin, in his *Leben* he does mention his early devotion to her, using the term 'spiritual beloved', and describes how he would crown her statue with a wreath of flowers. See Tobin, *Suso*, pp. 142–3.

[43] For details of these encounters, see J. André, *Le Chapelain de Notre-Dame. S. Hermann-Joseph, Chanoine Prémontré* (Taracon-sur-Rhône, 1955), pp. 17, 19, 20.

[44] Ibid., pp. 34–8. Other studies devoted to Hermann-Joseph include I. Engels, *Maria's Kapelaan, Herman Jozef* (Antwerp, 1943), Karl Koch and Eduard Hegel, *Die Vita des Praemonstratensers Hermann Joseph von Steinfeld* (Cologne, 1958) and H. J. Kugler, *Hermann Josef von Steinfeld (um 1160–1241) im Kontext christlicher Mystik* (St Ottilien, 1992).

[45] André, *Chapelain*, pp. 38–9.

[46] Joannes Chrysostomus vander Sterre, *Lilium inter spinas: Vita b. Joseph presbyteri et canonici Steinveldensis ordinis praeminstratensis* (Antwerp, 1627), chs 22, 70–1 (tr. for me by Ethel Olaer). See also David Herlihy,

47 André, *Chapelain*, p. 42.
48 Ibid., p. 38.
49 Jacques Coret, in his *Le second Joseph et le second époux de Marie Herman Joseph, réligieux du tres-celebre et tres S. ordre de Prémonstré, representé sous la qualité de favori des anges, de Marie, et Jesus* (Liege, 1685), p. 168, writes that Mary took him as her spouse because of his beautiful relationship with Joseph, and that Hermann saw Joseph as possessing many virtues that he tried to follow. In his version of the mystic marriage, one angel comments that Hermann was so chaste that the brothers already called him Joseph (p. 162), and that all the brothers were aware that Mary caressed him so visibly that she seemed as familiar with Hermann as with Joseph himself (p. 168).
50 See Dyan Elliott, *Spiritual Marriage: Sexual Abstinence in Medieval Wedlock* (Princeton, 1993), pp. 176–81, for discussion of the Virgin Mary as a model of imitation.
51 C. C. Wilson, 'Francesco Vecellio's *Presepio* for San Giuseppe, Belluno: aspects and overview of the cult and iconography of St Joseph in pre-Tridentine Art', *Venezia Cinquecento*, 6 (1996), 49–57 (43, 68); J. Dusserre, 'Les origines de la dévotion à Saint Joseph', *Cahiers de Josephologie*, 1–3 (1953), 1–32; 33–60; 61–86 (1/2, 39–41).
52 For the Latin texts of these poems and German trs, see Josef Brosch, *Hymnen und Gebete des seligen Hermann Josef* (Aachen, 1950). André, *Chapelain*, pp. 145–60, gives a French tr. of one of the poems to Christ.
53 André, *Chapelain*, pp. 112 and 122.
54 Ibid., p. 34.
55 Kugler, *Hermann Josef*, pp. 90, 92.
56 Ibid., pp. 74–81, for discussion of the poem, and Brosch, *Hymnen und Gebete*, pp. 11–15 for the Latin text and a German tr.
57 Tr. for me from the Latin by Ethel Olaer.
58 See André, *Chapelain*, pp. 136–7, 220, 219; Kugler, *Hermann Josef*, pp. 100–6.
59 André, *Chapelain*, p. 136, quotes Hermann-Joseph, although he does not give the source of the quote.
60 Kugler, *Hermann Josef*, pp. 99–100, suggests that many of Hermann-Joseph's ideas find their later expression in the writings of Suso. A parallel with Suso's life lies in Hermann's own pastoral duties with regards to the nuns at Hoven; however, it has not been suggested that his writings were meant for his spiritual daughters, as has been proposed for Suso. This multiplicity of Hermann-Joseph's roles with respect to Mary parallels as well the situation for medieval women and their many-sided relationships with Christ, who could function as their child, spouse and mother.
61 Tobin, *Suso*, p. 212.
62 This dominance of the heavenly spouse is also true in the case of St John

Eudes, mentioned in n. 42. His marriage contract with the Virgin departs from contemporary marriage contracts in its rephrasing of certain clauses to indicate clearly that the Virgin is the dominant partner in the marriage.

6

Henry Suso and the Divine Knighthood

MERI HEINONEN

Over the last twenty-five years the study of medieval mysticism has paid increasingly more attention to the specific historical contexts for different forms of the religious life as well as factors such as social status, education and gender.[1] This trend in research has opened up new perspectives onto medieval life. It has also, however, sometimes led to undue generalization, especially with respect to issues of gender. Many scholars have tended to interpret women's mysticism as affective and visionary while men have generally been held to produce more intellectual forms of mystical writing.[2] This kind of polarization has distorted the study of both gender and mysticism in medieval religious cultures, because, as Amy Hollywood has argued, these differences do not occur simply between male- as opposed to female-authored texts, but within them both.[3] Some female mystics, such as Beatrix of Nazareth and Marguerite Porete, are deemed to describe their visions in speculative masculine terms, whereas the work of Caroline Walker Bynum has famously explored instances of male mystics whose piety and modes of expression she identifies as feminine.[4] She uses the writings of the Dominican friar Henry Suso (1295/6–1366) as an important example within her argument, citing passages like the following:

> You should do as a young girl does who is picking roses. When she breaks off one rose from the bush, she is not satisfied, but takes it into her head to pick one more of them. You should do the same. Prepare yourself

beforehand. When the present suffering comes to an end, you will soon encounter another one.[5]

This is taken from Suso's German *Leben* (Life) written while living at the Dominican convent in Ulm, in the early 1360s.[6] This quotation and others like it have led Bynum to suggest that Suso particularly identified himself with women, children and female piety.[7] Nor is she the only scholar to consider Suso's spirituality as feminine and his writing similar to texts written by women. Ursula Peters, for instance, has pointed out that Henry Suso's *Leben*, together with Friedrich Sunder's (1254–1328) *Gnadenleben* (Life of Godly Grace), is comparable to female rather than to male visionary literature because it shares the same premises. It resembles in many aspects the visionary or 'autohagiographic' literature that is often considered typical for women, as Jeffery Hamburger has also noted.[8]

It is often argued that the *Life* was written chiefly as a didactic guide designed especially for the female religious with whom Suso worked.[9] *Cura monialium* (the care of religious women) was a central aspect of Suso's life and most of his spiritual children were women. In addition the *Life* has also been characterized either as an autobiography or as autohagiography.[10] Werner Williams-Krapp has argued that, though *Life* was a didactic text, which contained some fairly derivative tropes from various literary models (for example, the lives of the desert fathers), its conception and content was closely connected to the personality of Suso and his work among the religious women, thus lending it a unique aspect as well.[11] Given its intended purpose and didactic nature we cannot read the *Life* simplistically as a direct portrayal of Suso's own life, but some parts of it are clearly based on his own experiences. We also know that many contemporaries as well as readers one hundred years later did interpret it directly as a 'true life' of Suso: in most of the medieval manuscripts the *Life* is subtitled explicitly as being 'of Suso' (der Seuse).[12] The Servant of Eternal Wisdom was seen by contemporaries not just as the representation of a good friar, but as a representation of Henry Suso himself and the *Life* was subsequently taken to be a direct account of his own holy life, even if this is not what Suso actually intended.[13]

The focus of this essay and its analysis will be not the feminine aspects of the *Life*, but the masculine ones, which have received much less attention. Despite Bynum's identification of Suso's piety as feminine I shall argue that the potential way to holiness (even sanctity) described in the *Life* is in fact a specifically masculine one and moreover one that is explicitly held to be appropriate only to men and not to women. It will be seen that Suso uses the text's central character, the Servant of Eternal Wisdom, to outline a life governed by masculine forms of piety, and a subsidiary female character, the Servant's Spiritual Daughter, to establish the correct way of life for women. Of course there are elements of the Servant's spiritual path that were necessary for the proper conduct of the religious life for all people, whether male or female. In theory the premises of holiness were the same for both men and women. However, in practice there were great differences between the ways in which these ought to be expressed in real life, and these dissimilarities are reflected in the *Life*. As we shall see, the text firmly delineates certain aspects of the Servant's religious conduct that were not to be imitated by women. Through including the figure of the Servant's Spiritual Daughter, the *Life* encourages women to be content with a more passive and traditionally feminine role, as the Spiritual Daughter is seen to be.[14] As already noted, scholarship on the *Life* has tended to emphasize the female component of its audience. But the nature of the text suggests that Suso may have intended it to be of use to men as well as women. Perhaps it was aimed, in part, at other men who, like him, were responsible for looking after religious women, in order that such men might learn how to inculcate a proper gender identity in their charges, and ensure that their piety was expressed in feminine not masculine ways.

As a starting point, let us consider the ways in which Suso emphasizes the purely masculine nature of the Servant's religiosity by making extensive use of the theme of knighthood within the *Life*. The Servant is presented as a young nobleman whose parents sent him into a Dominican convent at the age of 13. However, he is not interested in the religious life until he has worn the habit for five years.[15] At this point he experiences a religious conversion which completely changed his empty and restless life, and Suso depicts this conversion as a love story. The Servant has been looking for a lady to love, and finally he meets her in the shape of Wisdom. In fact the Servant's conversion resembles a sexual seduction: 'Now eternal Wisdom presented itself in sacred scripture as lovable as an agreeable beloved who gets herself up in finery to please male inclinations, speaking softly, as a woman does, so that she might attract all hearts to her.'[16] Suso presents the Servant's subsequent religious career in chivalric terms, describing the ways in which the Servant, like a young, inexperienced knight, seeks to endure and survive trials for his lady, Wisdom.[17] The Servant's relationship with Wisdom is described in highly sexualized terms, as is common in accounts of mystical marriage more widely.[18] But unlike male mystics who depicted themselves or their souls as the feminine bride of the masculine bridegroom Christ, here the Servant is the knightly bridegroom, marrying a lady.[19] If the Servant had not joined the Dominicans he would have been an earthly knight, but Suso shows that he becomes something more superior: a heavenly knight. Suso combines the old Christian idea of a *miles Christi* (soldier of Christ) with the image of a strong, invulnerable and morally upright knight from chivalrous literature.[20] He compared the Servant to earthly knights and argued that, although they can undergo almost inhuman trials, heavenly knights are capable of enduring much more difficult trials.[21] One of the most significant trials that the Servant has to undertake is that of self-control.

As a Dominican friar, sexual activities of any kind were forbidden to the Servant. Thus Suso depicts the various devices the Servant uses to control his body: he wears a hairshirt and iron chain, as well as an undergarment of hair for his lower body closed with thongs by 150 nails. Furthermore, he locks up his hands at night, and wears leather gloves with pointed brass tacks all over them.[22] As several scholars have noted, the intrinsic connection between manliness, sex and procreation was frequently drawn in the Middle Ages.[23] Being unable to father a child meant that a man was not a real man and this could give rise to anxieties for men in religious orders who had committed themselves to chastity and could not, therefore, prove their masculinity in this way.[24] However, the sort of heroic struggle against lust which Suso shows the young Servant experiencing provided an alternative for religious men because stressing that their sexual abstinence was not self-evident and easy, provided them with an alternative means of proving their masculinity. Suso's account emphasizes that the Servant is a real man in that he feels sexual drives, but the implication which should be drawn from it is that the Servant is so masculine that he does not give in to these.[25] This point is further strengthened in Suso's *Life* by the inclusion of examples of religious women, including the Servant's sister, who had failed to keep their vow of chastity.[26] This story about his sister is very long and one of the most dramatic ones in the *Life*. It was surely meant as a warning for the religious women in the audience and also served to underline the superiority of men over women in this respect. Moreover, in several other passages of the *Life* women are depicted as incapable of controlling themselves unless they were locked behind the cloister walls. Suso greatly criticized open monasteries that allowed religious women to be in contact with other people, especially men.[27] In Suso's opinion only strong, rational men like the Servant (and presumably himself) could live surrounded by women and still restrain sexual temptations by concentrating on heavenly things. In the Servant's case, his heroic chastity proved his holiness as well as his masculinity, and this issue of self-control is further elaborated on in the *Life* in relation to other bodily desires. The Servant is also extremely abstemious in his eating and drinking for instance.[28]

To help him command his bodily urges, the Servant sets the desert fathers as direct models for himself. He follows them in chastisement, moderation and silence, and often his practices are physical and painful.[29] Servant tortures his body and Suso used pages to describe these exercises, clearly identifying them as masculine; for when the Servant gives in to weeping at the harshness of his regime he sees himself acting in an 'unmanly' way.[30] By contrasting womanly weeping and manly boldness Suso emphasizes the difference between heroic men and feeble women. And this is something that God himself underlines when he criticizes the Servant in these terms: 'You miserable creature! Are you going to weep like a woman? You are disgracing yourself at the court of heaven. Wipe your eyes and act cheerfully so that neither God nor man notice you have wept because of your suffering.'[31]

The endurance of these ultimate physical exercises was not only typical to men, but also presented as appropriate to them alone. The Servant explicitly forbids his Spiritual Daughter to imitate him and the desert fathers in bodily sufferings, because she was a weak woman.[32] Servant wrote to her: 'Dear daughter, if you intend to order your spiritual life according to my teachings, as you had requested of me, then put aside such exaggerated severity because it is out of keeping with your weakness as a woman and your physical well-being.'[33] For Suso, to be God's knight entailed strength and masculinity, qualities that women did not have and which they could not attain. However, we know that many religious women did practice extreme asceticism; indeed, in many recent studies asceticism has been seen as particularly significant for women. Corporeality has been represented as a unique way for medieval women to participate actively in religious life and appropriate their own symbols.[34] Williams-Krapp has noted that in German-speaking areas the church's representatives were worried about women's extreme mystical experiences that often included harsh ascetic practices together with bodily expressions. They considered these practices as a possible threat to the church's authority and teaching. As a result some churchmen tried to control women's overblown corporeality.[35] It could be argued that in the *Leben* Suso was himself trying, in part, to control and modify the more excessive practices of the women around him by emphasizing that extreme asceticism was, or should be, a masculine, not a feminine practice.

Enduring physical and other forms of suffering was thus part of Suso's conception of the knight of God. These practices were not, however, only connected to controlling desires, but they were important forms of *imitatio Christi*, which was central to Suso's spirituality, as it was for later medieval religious people in general.[36] Therefore at least part of the pain and hardship of the aforementioned practices were intended to be understood as a way of imitating the Passion of Christ. In addition to these the Servant also imitated Christ's suffering much more directly. The Servant, for instance, bore on his bare back a wooden cross that had thirty sharp iron nails upon it, which pierced his flesh. Furthermore he did special disciplines with this cross while meditating on the Passion, trying to echo the sufferings of Christ in detail.[37] The use of an actual cross is significant here; bearing a cross was seen as the ultimate form of *imitatio Christi*.[38]

After over twenty years of torture and bodily sufferings the Servant was allowed to give up the practices described above. God told him that these sufferings had been a good start and a means for breaking the undisciplined man within him. Suso wrote that the Servant thought he could at last enjoy life, but instead of that God sent him a new kind of arrows. Being God's knight now called for other heroic endeavours. As an angel pointed out, the Servant had only been a squire and it was now time him to get into the boots and clothes of a true knight.[39] If God had freed him from austere practices, there were others to come. These new sufferings were not physical, but mental ones and they were mainly attacks on his mind and reputation. This is presumably, in part, because he was now an older man. Suso stressed that the temptations of lust had mainly come to the Servant when he was younger; as an older man he would not be expected to be bothered by these to such an extent so there would be less merit in any measures he took to control his body.[40] Thus he needed to face a new kind of trial, of a different nature and administered not by himself, but by others. These future trials were rationalized by God as follows:

First, until now you have been punishing yourself with your own hand and if you felt pity for yourself, you stopped whenever you wanted. Now I will take you away from yourself and hand you over defenceless to be dealt with at the hands of others. Then you will have to accept the public destruction of your reputation in the estimation of some blind men. The blow will strike you harder than the suffering you endured from the pointed cross on the wounds of your back. Your earlier exercises caused you to be highly esteemed by people, but now you shall be beaten low and must be utterly ruined. The second suffering is this. However often you have inflected bitter and deathly agony upon yourself, by a determination of God you have kept your tender, loving nature. It is going to happen that in those places where you especially look for love and loyalty you shall experience deceit, much suffering and hardship. The suffering will be so manifold that those people who have a special loyalty toward you will have to suffer along with you out of pity. The third suffering is this. Until now you have been a baby and pampered sissy and have moved about divine sweetness like a fish in the sea. This I shall now take from you and will let you wither and go ruin. You shall be abandoned both by God and the whole world and shall be persecuted publicly by friends and enemies. In short, everything that you undertake out of joy or to be consoled will go awry and whatever is suffering or repulsive to you will prosper.[41]

God's words make it quite clear that the masculine goals of the heavenly knight were not yet achieved. Even though the Servant had suffered he had still, in some respects, been feminine – tender, loving and sissy (*zart*, *liebsuchende* and *zertling*) – and was therefore going to have to gain his real knighthood in future contests. From this moment on the *Leben* introduces a vast list of different kinds of mental sufferings and attacks. The Servant was accused of robbing wax from a shrine, of poisoning wells with the Jews, fabricating a miracle, fathering a child and spreading heretical thoughts. Furious townsmen chased him, angry knights were after him and even friends and fellow friars abandoned him.[42]

The vivid depictions of life in urban communities, and the problems the Servant had to try to solve within them, give a colourful picture of late medieval towns and the meaning of reputation. In these oral communities the fame a person gained was often literally a matter of life and death.[43] The Servant even asked God for corporeal sufferings instead of these that were bad for his reputation. But within the *Leben* the Servant's difficulties here are obviously to be understood as another form of *imitatio Christi* as they present the Servant as suffering badly but blamelessly. Like Christ he is accused by other people, even his friends and fellow friars, of crimes that he has not committed. The positioning of this episode in the text indicates that to be despised by other men and scorned even by one's own friends was the ultimate way to be one with Christ in his sufferings. The physical pains were not enough, even though they were central for spiritual growth. The most important thing in Christian life was to accept humbly the sufferings God had sent.[44] As the Servant himself puts it: 'God often prepares what is best for his friends through his friends.'[45] The miracle of Christ's death was not the physical suffering itself, but the fact that an innocent man freely let himself be crucified for the wrongdoings of others. Therefore the most Godlike man was the one who was meek and subservient. In this Suso was the follower of his teacher Meister Eckhart who had described the ultimate state of mystical experience as complete detachment (*Gelassenheit*).[46]

On one level this is a message that was appropriate to all Christians, but following its dictates was not the same thing for men and women in practice. For only men, especially mendicants, could work actively in the world and thus have the chance to experience, like the Servant, other people's mocking and scorn, as well as their admiration. This option was not open to nuns and other religious women. The Council of Vienne (1312) had forbidden the beguines' way of life with its ethos of following a pseudo-mendicant vocation in the world, and particularly in Germany many former beguinages had been turned into Dominican convents.[47] This meant that the former beguines had become cloistered nuns, not allowed to leave their buildings and live among other townspeople. Similarly the attempts of St Clare and other early mendicant women to live in the world had been completely curtailed by the church and by their orders. The thirteenth-century beguine writers like Hadewijch and Mechthild of Magdeburg are comparable to Suso in their perception of the true nature of Christ and the best way to imitate him. These beguines also emphasized the experience of Jesus as being present in sufferings caused by other people, especially the other religious, who doubted their experiences or otherwise accused them.[48] However, during Suso's lifetime religious women had been shut into cloisters and the *Leben* and other evidence indicates that Suso was keen to promote this development himself. Women could not go out into the world to face shame and humiliation as the Servant did, so Suso uses the Spiritual Daughter to give them a more appropriate model of feminine suffering: they are to be proudly and patiently ill within the confines of the cloister instead.

When his Spiritual Daughter, who had been told not to do severe ascetic practices, becomes extremely ill, Suso writes that the Servant was sorry and disappointed, because she had helped him so much with his books. He even tried to question God about her illness by abandoning his special morning prayers, but finally decided that her sickness was for the best as it was the cross which God had sent for her.[49] The Servant encouraged his Spiritual Daughter to follow Christ in his sufferings by enduring her malady with fortitude, which was a common trope among medieval religious women at the time.[50] As Jo Ann McNamara has pointed out, women even used their illnesses as a means for helping souls in purgatory, indicating that they were perceived of by them as directly analogous to Christ's sacrifice.[51] In this way sickness becomes a gender-specific form of suffering which men did not need, because they were able to show their commitment in other ways.

Suso's *Leben* has been considered as an example of a text where a spiritual teacher gives an account of his life and then of his follower's life. However, the differences between the experiences of teacher and follower are gendered markedly. As a man and a friar the Servant (like Suso) was able to live a much more public and challenging life than his Spiritual Daughter. Women were to choose Christ as their spouse and enter a cloister. They were to live apart from other people and conquer their body only with minimal exercises and work. They should then humbly wait for the cross God intended them to bear, but rather than this taking the form of a physical cross, like the Servant's, or any self-inflicted form of suffering, God would send them some kind of sickness instead, which they should bear patiently. Men could be active and aggressive in their *imitatio Christi*, but women should be passive and reserved.

Thus men and women were expected to go through the same phases in spiritual growth but were supposed to experience them differently. Further evidence of these dissimilarities is to be found in the account of the monogram IHS which the Servant pierced onto his breast with a stylus. It was an extreme and painful way for him to show his devotion to Christ, and according to the *Leben* he secretly bore this mark for the rest of his life.[52] The Spiritual Daughter, on the other hand, was not permitted to do anything like this. Instead, she embroidered the same letters onto a piece of red silk and asked the Servant to place it on his engraved breast. Afterwards she placed the cloth on her own breast and used it as an object of devotion. She also made new ones, which the

Servant similarly 'blessed' by placing them in contact with his physical wound. The Spiritual Daughter then sent them away to other religious, presumably other nuns, to be used similarly by them.[53] She was expected to follow the Servant's example, but in a feminine way; embroidering the monogram rather than scratching it on to her body, an act that was permissible only for a man.

Suso's *Leben* expresses overall the idea that both men and women should reach for the same goal in Christian perfection. At the same time, however, it also demonstrates the importance of context and gender ideology to the ways in which this idea was played out in practice. In a more mystical treatise, such as for instance Suso's *Büchlein der ewigen Weisheit* (Little Book of Eternal Wisdom), it was easier to transgress gender lines than it was in primarily didactic texts, which explicitly set out to present practical models of conduct for the audience to follow in their everyday lives. Therefore the *Leben* represented the Servant as an orthodox and ideal friar, who could become a heavenly knight by physical and mental suffering, thus presenting an ideal of holy masculinity to male readers. On the other hand the Spiritual Daughter presented a much more passive and restrained model for religious women to imitate and one which is predicated on normative femininity. However, it is significant that Suso felt the need to present such an oppositional binary between the activities of the Servant and his Spiritual Daughter, and also that he shows a man reprimanding a woman for attempting more masculine demonstrations of piety. This rather suggests, of course, that many women, perhaps even some of those for whom Suso was responsible, were not content with what holy femininity had to offer and were more interested in imitating holy masculinity, otherwise he would not have needed to present such admonishments in the *Leben*. The *Leben* also indicates that, rather than seeing extreme manifestations of piety and intense identification with Christ as intrinsically female or feminine experiences, we need to consider the possibility that the reason these activities were often deemed problematic for women is because it led them to transgress gender norms and display masculine qualities – something which they, as mere women, should not have been capable of achieving. The clear message which Suso's *Leben* gives to its readers is that only men could be true knights of God.

Notes

[1] The tendency to use mystical texts as sources that can shed light on historical, social and cultural contexts can also be seen as an aspect of the study of saints, for example, Bernard McGinn, *Presence of God: History of Western Christian Mysticism* (New York, 1992–).

[2] For a discussion of perceived differences between women's and men's mystical experiences see Rosalynn Voaden, *God's Words, Women's Voices: The Discernment of Spirits in the Writing of Late-Medieval Women Visionaries* (Woodbridge, 1999).

[3] Amy Hollywood, *The Soul as Virgin Wife: Mechthild of Magdeburg, Marguerite Porete and Meister Eckhart* (Notre Dame, IN, and London, 1995), p. 16; see also Gabriele L. Strauch, 'Mechthild von Magdeburg and the category of Frauenmystik', in Albrecht Classen (ed.), *Women as Protagonists and Poets in the German Middle Ages: An Anthology of Feminist Approaches to Middle High German Literature* (Göppingen, 1991), pp. 171–86. The fact that most female visionaries had their texts physically written by men complicates this issue further.

[4] Ursula Peters, 'Frauenliteratur im Mittelalter? Überlegungen zur Trobairitzpoesie, zur Frauenmystik und zur feministischen Literaturbetrachtung', *Germanisch-Romanische Monatsschrift*, NF 38 (1988), 35–56 (46–7); Caroline Walker Bynum, *Holy Feast and Holy Fast: The Religious Significance of Food to Medieval Women* (Berkeley and Los Angeles, 1987), esp. pp. 102–5.

[5] Heinrich Seuse, *Leben*, in Karl Bihlmayer (ed.), *Deutsche Schriften. Auftrag der Württembergischen Komission für Landesgeschichte* (Frankfurt am Main, 1961), 20. 58–9; Frank Tobin (ed. and tr.), *Henry Suso: The Exemplar, with Two German Sermons* (New York, 1989), 102. All the references to Suso's *Leben* are to Bihlmayer's edition (hereafter *Leben*), I shall give the chapter number and page reference. The English quotes are from Tobin's tr. (hereafter Tobin, *Suso*). Bynum refers to this passage in *Holy Feast and Holy Fast*, p. 103.

[6] For discussion of Suso's background and life see Bihlmayer, *Deutsche Schriften*, pp. 61 ff.; Tobin, *Suso*, pp. 19–26, and also Kurt Ruh, *Geschichte der abendländischen Mystik*, vol. 3, *Die Mystik des deutschen Predigerordens und ihre Grundlegung durch die Hochscholastik* (Munich, 1996), pp. 417–20. The *Leben* was originally published as the first part of Suso's compilation of his German books called *Exemplar*, though it later circulated as an individual book as well as part of the entity. For the manuscript tradition of Suso's *Leben* and his other works see Bihlmayer, *Deutsche Schriften*, pp. 3–29. See also Carolyn Diskant Muir's essay in the present volume.

[7] Bynum, *Holy Feast and Holy Fast*, p. 103. The admiration Suso felt for his mother and the clearly expressed dislike towards his father has also been seen as a proof of Suso's femininity. See, for instance, *Leben*, 6 22 4, 42. 142.

[8] Peters, 'Frauenliteratur im Mittelalter?', 46–7; Jeffrey F. Hamburger, *The*

Visual and the Visionary: Art and Female Spirituality in Late Medieval Germany (New York, 1998), pp. 238–55.
9 See, for instance, Walter Blank, 'Heinrich Seuses "Vita": Literarische Gestaltung und pastorale Funktion seines Schriftums', *Zeitschrift für deutsches Altertum und deutsche Literatur*, 122 (1991), 285–311; Hamburger, *Visual and Visionary*, pp. 276–8.
10 For example, Julius Schwietering, 'Zur Autorschaft von Seuses *Vita*', in Kurt Ruh (ed.), *Altdeutsche und altniederländische Mystik* (Darmstadt, 1964; orig. published 1960), pp. 309–23; Richard Kieckhefer, *Unquiet Souls: Fourteenth-Century Saints and their Religious Milieu* (Chicago and London, 1987), p. 6; see also Tobin, *Suso*, p. 41; Frank Tobin, 'Henry Suso and Elsbeth Stagel: was the *Vita* a cooperative effort?', in Catherine M. Mooney (ed.), *Gendered Voices: Medieval Saints and their Interpreters* (Philadelphia, 1999), pp. 118–35 (pp. 126, 236, n. 33).
11 Werner Williams-Krapp, 'Heinrich Suso's *Vita* between mystagogy and hagiography', in Anneke B. Mulder-Bakker (ed.), *Transmission of Knowledge and the Problems of Gender* (Turnhout, 2003). I am grateful to Professor Williams-Krapp for an advance copy of this essay and for discussions on the nature of Suso's *Life*. See also Werner Williams-Krapp, '"Nucleus totius perfectionis" Die Altväterspiritualität in der "Vita" Heinrich Seuses', in Paul Sappler, Frieder Schanze and Hans-Joachim Ziegeler (eds), *Festschrift für Walter Haug und Burghart Wachinger* (Tübingen, 1992), pp. 405–21.
12 For readers' approach to Suso's *Life* in the late fifteenth century in relation to illustrations of the text see *Spiegel der Seligkeit: Privates Bild und Frömmigkeit im Spätmittelalter*, Katalog zur Ausstellung 'Spiegel der Seligkeit. Sakrale Kunst im Spätmittelalter', Germanisches Nationalmuseum Nürnberg 31. Mai bis 8. Oktober 2000 (Nuremberg 2000), p. 210; Bihlmayer, *Deutsche Schriften*, p. 7; Williams-Krapp, 'Heinrich Suso's *Vita*', p. 218, n. 27. Muir's essay in the present volume also discusses these images as representations of Suso himself.
13 I prefer to maintain a distinction between the historical Henry Suso, the writer of the *Life* and the Servant who is its central character, rather than writing of the Servant as if he is a direct representation of Suso as Bynum does, for example.
14 The name of the Spiritual Daughter is never given and the usual explanation is that the Dominican nun Elsbeth Stagel from the convent of Töss was Suso's model for this figure.
15 *Leben*, prologus, p. 18.
16 *Leben*, 3. 11; Tobin, *Suso*, p. 67.
17 For a discussion of Suso's use of the chivalric language and motifs of secular poetry see Gisela Baldus, 'Die Gestalt des "dieners" im Werke Heinrich Seuses' (Inaugural-Dissertation zur Erlangung des Doktorgrades der Philosophischen Fakultät der Universität zu Köln, 1966), pp. 75–7.
18 See, for example, Diane L. Mockridge, 'Marital imagery in six late twelfth- and early thirteenth-century vitae of female saints', in Lynda L. Coon,

Katherine J. Haldane and Elisabeth W. Sommer (eds), *That Gentle Strength: Historical Perspectives on Women in Christianity* (Charlottesville, VA, and London, 1990), pp. 60–78 (pp. 61–3).

[19] See for instance, *Leben*, 8. 26–7; 44. 151–2, and the examples cited by Muir.

[20] Walter Blank, 'Heinrich Seuses "Vita": literarische Gestaltung und pastorale Funktion seines Schriftums', *Zeitschrift für deutsches Altertum und deutsche Literatur* 122 (1991), 299–307. See also Baldus, 'Die Gestalt des "dieners"', pp. 87–8. In general, for the similarities between secular and religious literature in medieval Germany, see Grete Lüers, *Die Sprache der deutschen Mystik des Mittelalters im Werke der Mechthild von Magdeburg* (Darmstadt, 1966; orig. publ. 1906).

[21] *Leben*, 44. 149–52.

[22] *Leben*, 15. 39–40; 17. 44–5.

[23] Joan Cadden, *Meanings of Sex Difference in the Middle Ages: Medicine, Science and Culture* (Cambridge and New York, 1993), p. 220; Vern L. Bullough, 'On being male in the Middle Ages', in Clare A. Lees (ed.), *Medieval Masculinities: Regarding Men in the Middle Ages* (Minneapolis and London, 1994), pp. 31–46 (pp. 34, 39–43).

[24] P. H. Cullum, 'Clergy, masculinity and transgression in late medieval England', in D. M. Hadley (ed.), *Masculinity in Medieval Europe* (London, 1999), pp. 178–96.

[25] A point also made by Jacqueline Murray in the present volume.

[26] *Leben*, 24. 70–4.

[27] See *Leben*, 41. 135–7; 37. 115.

[28] *Leben*, 18. 46–50.

[29] See, for instance, *Leben*, 14. 37–8; 15. 39–40; 17. 44–6; 18. 46–53. Christopher C. Craun's essay in the present volume discusses representations of the Syrian desert fathers.

[30] *Leben*, 16. 41.

[31] Ibid., 44. 152.

[32] Ibid., 35. 107–8.

[33] Ibid., 35. 107; Tobin, *Suso*, 139–40.

[34] Bynum's work has been particularly influential in this respect of course; Bynum, *Holy Feast*. See also Elizabeth Avilda Petroff, *Body and Soul: Essays on Medieval Women and Mysticism* (New York, 1994).

[35] Williams-Krapp, 'Heinrich Suso's *Vita*', pp. 206–7. Williams-Krapp has furthermore interpreted the *Life* as an opposition to harsh bodily asceticism among women. According to him, Suso is trying to lead the reader to understand that true mystical spirituality is not to be found in the images attained through askesis, but rather in imageless intellectual union, as Eckhart also stated, Williams-Krapp, ' "Nucleus totius perfectionis" ', pp. 405–21.

[36] Giles Constable, 'The ideal of the imitation of Christ', in Giles Constable, *Three Studies in Medieval Religious and Social Thought* (Cambridge, 1995), pp. 143–248; Ulrich Köpf, 'Die Passion Christi in der lateinischen religiösen und theologischen Literatur des Spätmittelalters', in Walter Haug und

Burghart Wachinger (eds), *Die Passion Christi in Literatur und Kunst des Spätmittelalters* (Tübingen, 1993), pp. 25–56.
37 *Leben*, 16. 41–2.
38 For the meaningfulness of the cross see Sarah Beckwith, *Christ's Body: Identity, Culture and Society in Late Medieval Writings* (London and New York, 1993); David Aers, 'Figuring forth the body of Christ: devotion and politics', *Essays in Medieval Studies*, 11 (1994), 1–14.
39 *Leben*, 20. 55.
40 For differing perceptions of the masculinity of a young as opposed to an old man see also Fiona S. Dunlop's chapter below.
41 *Leben*, 20. 57; Tobin, *Suso*, pp. 100–1.
42 These events are depicted in *Leben* from chapter 23 onwards.
43 For the meaning of good and ill repute and the different kind of social and cultural networks see Barbara A. Hanawalt, *'Of Good and Ill Repute': Gender and Social Control in Medieval England* (New York, 1998), especially pp. 5–8.
44 Ellen M. Ross has argued that this kind of spiritual path can also be found in the writings of Margery Kempe and Julian of Norwich. See Ellen M. Ross, ' "She wept and cried right loud for sorrow and for pain": suffering, the spiritual journey and women's experience in late medieval mysticism', in Ulrike Wiethaus (ed.), *Maps of Flesh and Light: The Religious Experience of Medieval Women Mystics* (Syracuse, NY, 1993), pp. 45–59 (pp. 49–51).
45 *Leben*, 38. 125; Tobin, *Suso*, p. 154.
46 On Meister Eckhart see, for instance, Bernard McGinn, *The Mystical Thought of Meister Eckhart: The Man from Whom God Hid Nothing* (New York, 2001).
47 Ernst McDonnel, *The Beguines and Beghards in Medieval Culture: With Special Emphasis on the Belgian Scene* (New Brunswick, NJ, 1954), pp. 187–93. In addition to this the Dominican penitents' way of life was becoming stricter and more institutionalized in the course of the fourteenth century; see Maiju Lehmijoki-Gardner, *Worldly Saint: Social Interaction of Dominican Penitent Women in Italy, 1200–1500* (Helsinki, 1999).
48 On Hadewijch see M. Ortmanns-Cornet (ed.), *Brieven* (Bruges, 1986), pp. 50–2; J. van Mierlo (ed.), *De Visioenen van Hadewych* (Leuven, 1924), p. 131. On Mechthild see Hans Neumann (ed.), *Das fliessende Licht der Gottheit*, Nach der einsiedler Handschrift in kritischem Vergleich mit der gesamten Überlieferung (Munich, 1990), pp. 240, 242–3.
49 *Leben*, 35. 109.
50 Donald Weinstein and Rudolf Bell, *Saints and Society: The Two Worlds of Western Christendom, 1000–1700* (Chicago and London, 1982), pp. 233–5. This is something also discussed by Bynum, *Holy Feast*, *passim*.
51 Jo Ann McNamara, 'The need to give: suffering and female sanctity in the Middle Ages', in Renate Blumenfeld-Kosinski and Timea Szell (eds), *Images of Sainthood in Medieval Europe* (Ithaca, NY, and London), pp. 199–221 (pp. 214–18).
52 *Leben*, 4. 15–16.
53 Ibid., 45. 154–5.

7

Holy Eunuchs! Masculinity and Eunuch Saints in Byzantium

SHAUN TOUGHER

Introduction: Byzantine eunuchs

In the year 2000 Pauline Stafford and A. B. Mulder-Bakker observed that the historical study of men and masculinity was at 'the relatively early stage of development'.[1] One group of Byzantine men that has recently received much attention is eunuchs.[2] Eunuchs were a fact of life in Byzantium for its entire existence.[3] They were most notable for their roles at the imperial court, an aspect of eunuch history stretching back to ancient Assyria and China, and bequeathed to Byzantium by the later Roman Empire. Eunuchs in Byzantium were employed as servants of the imperial family, from lowly chamberlain to the heady heights of *praipositos* (grand chamberlain) or *parakoimomenos* (chief eunuch). They could also attain posts in the imperial administration; for instance, they are found as treasurers (*sakellarioi*) and generals (*strategoi*). But eunuchs in Byzantium were not just secular attendants or officials; spiritual roles were also open to them. They are found as clergy, bishops, and monks. They could be recognized for their holiness, and some were honoured with sainthood.

From the point of view of gender, eunuchs are obviously an especially interesting group to consider, given the contradictions they embody.[4] Mathew Kuefler has recently made the observations that 'the eunuch provides a focus for . . . self-conscious reflections on masculinity' and the 'ambiguous quality of . . . eunuchs . . . makes them . . . a useful means of studying men'.[5] Eunuchs were born male, but castration (usually before puberty) altered their physical development. Their voices did not break, remaining high-pitched; the growth of body hair was impeded, and in particular it is noted that eunuchs could not grow beards; body-shape tended to follow a female pattern; they were infertile, unable to father children. Essentially eunuchs could be seen as feminized men. As such they were attributed with female behavioural characteristics. Like women, they were 'carnal, irrational, voluptuous, fickle, manipulative, and deceitful'.[6] They were thought of as passive sexual partners. Their possible role as attendants on women could also contribute to their perceived feminization; a feminization that was not necessarily believed to be inherent, but which was acquired by spending too much time in the company of women.[7] In other ways eunuchs were still clearly part of the male world. They could hold public office, exercise official power, even command armies. It was thought that they could be sexual partners of women too. A further, alternative, view of eunuchs also existed: they could be seen as neither male nor female but something else, a third sex, a third gender.[8]

In this chapter I will focus my attention on a particular subset of eunuchs: eunuch saints. This group is intriguing to consider further since they highlight some sharp contradictions. As noted, eunuchs can be associated with women, and like women they could be seen as a threat to holiness. For instance it is well known that 'beardless men – eunuchs and young boys – merely because they resembled women were also a source of grave concern, and were sometimes banned [from monasteries]'.[9] How then could some become holy themselves? The answer to this question raises another paradox about the identity of eunuchs, for they could also be seen as pure and chaste.[10] (This conflicting identity has resonance with that of women, who were polarized between Eve and Mary.) The term 'eunuch' could even be metaphorical for Christians who were not literally castrated, but simply celibate: this is famously illustrated by Jesus' own reference to eunuchs for the kingdom of heaven (Matthew 19:12), and is underscored by the existence of so-called 'mystical castration', where holy men dreamt of being castrated by angels.[11] Thus the existence of eunuch saints need not necessarily be problematic. However, a different complication then presents itself, a complication that raises the question of gender identity again.[12] As Martha Vinson puts it: 'Since eunuchs had no manly passions to control, abstinence required no special effort on their part and thus did not merit the name of virtue.'[13] My interest is to examine how hagiographers of eunuch saints deal with these issues of sanctity and gender, if in fact they do at all. My discussion will centre on one particular example of a eunuch saint, Ignatios the Younger, twice patriarch of Constantinople in the ninth century (847–58, 867–78). I shall however include comment on other lives of eunuch saints too.[14]

Masculinity and holiness

Before exploring eunuch saints and masculinity, it is necessary to consider whether masculinity is an issue when it comes to holiness. The image of the early saint suggests that it is relevant.[15] The martyrs are depicted as soldiers and athletes, very stereotypical masculine roles. These roles were maintained by monks and holy men in their ascetical practices.[16] It has been observed that sanctity was 'normally achieved' by asceticism and renunciation.[17] Kuefler comments that 'it was . . . in the waging of this war . . . that the monk proved his manliness'.[18] The archetype was, of course, St Antony, whose *Life* was 'the model for all subsequent hagiography'.[19] Vinson, considering the Life of Antony the Younger (a ninth-century saint) in a rare discussion of middle Byzantine hagiography and gender, has suggested that the quality of masculinity still has relevance for sanctity in this period. She asserts: 'Here, the primary objective is to combat the perception that male religious are inherently effeminate.'[20] Antony is masculinized, endowed with 'the traditional attributes of manly virtue' – 'physical strength, public service, and decisive leadership'. She notes the 'literal athleticism' of Antony's spiritual father John, a rather Rambo-esque figure.[21] John and Antony emerge as 'muscular Christians of the ninth century'. Antony also serves as a soldier, though always in defence of the state; Vinson observes: 'Manly courage, in the person of Antony, thus occupies the middle ground between effeminate cowardice and wanton aggression.' The sexual conduct of Antony is also addressed by the Life; it is noted that he did not touch either a woman or a man.[22] It is also a familiar idea that holy women tended to attain sanctity by becoming masculinized.[23] The issue of masculinity is stressed by Coon, Haldane and Sommer in *That Gentle Strength*. They assert:

> The lurking presence of Eve . . . contributed to other less positive female traits such as weak flesh, moral depravity, quarrelsomeness, and ostentation. Masculine qualities, in contrast to the feminine, included

intellectual talent, strength in action, and the ability to exercise public power. Yet in late antiquity masculine and feminine were not synonymous with male and female since female martyrs, penitents, pilgrims, and ascetics were often venerated for their manly strength.[24]

Some women even cross-dressed as monks, the infamous transvestite nuns (for example, Anna the Younger, Matrona (the 'eunuch' Babylas), Thekla).[25] Harvey, discussing especially Pelagia and Eugenia, notes that the message which emerges from the lives of transvestite nuns is: 'Men were worthier than women, monks were holier than nuns.'[26]

But is this picture too simplistic? Harvey is keen to stress that ultimately the transvestite nuns 'were canonized as women'.[27] Their femaleness is not denied. Another nuance is added by Delierneux. Considering the identification of transvestite nuns with eunuchs and angels, she raises the possibility that what is at issue in holiness is asexuality, lack of gender.[28] She observes:

> The transvestites manifest their 'asexualisation' by the progressive disappearance of all that characterises them physically as women . . . Despite their habits and their male name, the transvestites remain always beardless; they thus pass naturally for eunuchs . . . When the saints arrive at a monastery proclaiming themselves 'eunuchs', they announce at the same time their chastity, perfect in its virility, which gives the kingdom of heaven, that God had promised to virgins and to eunuchs as to angels . . . Established amongst the monks . . . the transvestites, perfect virgins, perfect eunuchs, perfectly virile and vanquishers of sexuality, are triply heirs of the heavenly kingdom and assemble in themselves all the criteria of the true angelic life.

The identification of eunuchs with angels was common enough in Byzantium; as Kazhdan comments: 'Angels had no sex; in visionary dreams they resemble eunuchs. And the monastic community, an ideal of hagiography, was an angelic, that is, epicene society.'[29] Thus angels were the model for the entire community of the holy, not just eunuchs. This issue of angels and alternative gender identity also finds reflection in a recent article on the clergy of the medieval West by Robert Swanson. He suggests that priests could be considered a third gender, akin to angels.[30] Further, it has been noted generally by Stafford and Mulder-Bakker that 'asceticism retained its ability to subvert simple gender divisions. It produced other categorisations which did not easily map on to those of gender.'[31] Thus the hagiographers of eunuch saints might find mileage in the potential alternative gender status of their subjects.

Eunuch saints

Turning now to the eunuch saints themselves, it can be observed that several holy eunuchs are encountered in early hagiography, especially in Passions.[32] However my interest lies with those who have full-blown *Bioi*. These emerge in the middle Byzantine period, and include:

1. Niketas the patrician (761/2–836), a Paphlagonian, and an iconophile.[33] The Life survives only in part, supplemented by short notices. The Life is missing in particular the early chapters, including sections on Niketas' youth, his secular career and his decision to be a monk. For these episodes we have to depend mainly on Synaxarion A, a summary of the Life. He was castrated for a palace career by his parents.[34] He received the title of *patrikios* (patrician), and became *strategos* (general) of Sicily. On his return he dreamed of becoming a monk, and did so under Michael I (811–13).
2. Nikephoros, bishop of Miletos in the tenth century, under Nikephoros II Phokas (963–9). His Life was written up shortly after his death.[35] He was castrated for a church career by his parents.
3. John the Faster, founder of the Petra monastery in Constantinople in the late eleventh/early twelfth century. His twelfth-century Life is lost, but we have a fourteenth-century encomium by Nikephoros Kallistos.[36] He was an involuntary eunuch from Cappadocia, castrated as he had an incurable illness in his genitals.
4. John, bishop of Heraclea. He lived *c.*1250–1328. His Life was written in the fourteenth century by the famous Nikephoros Gregoras, his nephew.[37] He was castrated as a child due to illness.

Other middle Byzantine holy eunuchs exist, though not all have *Bioi*.[38] It is possible that there are also some saints who could be added to the list. For instance, it is often suspected that Symeon the New Theologian (*c.*949–1022) was a eunuch, given his early palace career before he became a monk, but if so his Life by his disciple Niketas Stethatos does not make this clear.[39]

The Life of Ignatios

The example I will concentrate on however is the tenth-century Life of Ignatios. Ignatios is perhaps the most famous eunuch saint.[40] He had a varied and dramatic life in the ninth century. He was of an elite family that became imperial, since his father Michael married Prokopia, the daughter of future emperor Nikephoros I (802–11). Michael became emperor himself in 811, but in 813 was forced to resign and take up the monastic life, making way for Leo V (813–20). It was at this point, when he was 14 years old, that Ignatios (then called Niketas – Ignatios was his monastic name), together with his brother, was castrated and also forced into monastic retirement. However, Ignatios' star rose again in 847 when he was asked to become patriarch by the iconophile Empress Theodora, regent for her young son Michael III (842–67). Ignatios fell again in 858 when he opposed Bardas, brother of the Empress Theodora and would-be power behind Michael's throne. Bardas had wanted Ignatios to tonsure Theodora and her daughters. Ignatios had also taken a stand against him as it was rumoured that he had separated from his wife and was having an affair with his (widowed) daughter-in-law. Ignatios was replaced by the famous Photios, who had been pursuing a secular career. Ignatios subsequently faced interrogation, torture and exile. When Photios fell foul of a change of regime in 867 – the founding of the Macedonian dynasty by Basil I (867–86) – Ignatios was restored, and died incumbent in 877, aged 80. He was replaced by the rehabilitated Photios.

Very soon after his death Ignatios was commemorated in mosaic in Hagia Sophia, as part of a series of fourteen church fathers which were put up in the north and south tympanums (Figure 7.1).[41] He was the most recent bishop to be depicted, and found himself in the company of such greats as Saints Basil, Gregory of Nazianzus, John Chrysostom, and Athanasius, though one other ninth-century patriarch, Methodios (843–7), was also included. Ignatios' image is one of three that survive intact.[42] Whilst Ignatios is dressed in identical fashion to the other bishops (tunic, chasuble and omophorion), his physical appearance emphasizes his alternative status as a eunuch. Most obviously he is shown beardless, but his radiant aspect, with youthful face and fair hair, adds to the impression of difference.

The textual image of Ignatios is later than the visual image. Traditionally the Life is dated to the early tenth century and the author is thought to be the known literary and historical figure, Niketas David

Figure 7.1. Mosaic of St Ignatios, Hagia Sophia, Istanbul. By permission of Dumbarton Oaks, Byzantine Photograph and Fieldwork Archives, Washington, DC

the Paphlagonian.[43] Niketas was an opponent of the fourth marriage of the Emperor Leo VI (886–912) during the tetragamy crisis (the dispute over the legality of Leo's marriage to his fourth wife Zoe Karbonopsina).[44] He was significant enough to be arrested on suspicion of deserting to the Bulgars, and was also questioned about a tract he had written against the emperor and the patriarch Euthymios. He was only saved by Euthymios himself, whose monastery of St Agathos he then sheltered in. Niketas' choice of subject matter in writing a life of Ignatios is taken to be informed by his attitudes to events of his own day.[45] He is writing about the past, but it has relevance to the present. Ignatios' exclusion of Bardas from communion due to his affair has striking parallels with the patriarch Nikolaos' treatment of Leo VI. As Dvornik states: 'Nicetas was anxious to put before the eyes of his contemporaries the glowing example of a high priest able to resist the whims of secular rulers in defending the rights of the Church.'[46] The text is certainly notable for its interest in and treatment of Photios, who provides a negative contrast with Ignatios, and represents those patriarchs who humour emperors.[47] Rydén observes that 'the main subject [of the life] is the conflict between these two rather than Ignatios himself'.[48] Vinson asserts that the Life presents us with

> an antithesis between two different types, or rather stereotypes, each representing a separate and competing image of Orthodoxy: the one embodied by Ignatios was characterized by the purity and simplicity of a faith uncompromised by secular concerns while that projected by Photios was marked by a degree of enterprise and sophistication that in the context of the *VI* stands in diametrical opposition to the monastic way of life.[49]

In fact the Life of Ignatios is an example of a group of biographies of patriarchs from Tarasios (784–806) to Euthymios (907–12) which developed in the ninth century. Efthymiadis says that these 'constitute a kind of sub-genre in the domain of Byzantine hagiography', have various features in common, but most importantly 'were designed to portray the ideal patriarch and propound a rather particular concept of sanctity . . . their hidden aim was . . . to augment the power of the Church and enhance the prestige of the patriarch over civil authority'.[50]

But what of Ignatios' condition as a eunuch? It seems that Niketas is in fact little interested in this; it is mentioned explicitly only once. The occasion is when the castration was carried out by the usurping Emperor Leo the Armenian, who had the sons of Michael I castrated even though he was their godfather.[51] Thus the interest of Niketas is in the outrageous action of Leo rather than in its effect on the boys. This is reinforced when Leo was himself assassinated and replaced by Michael II (820–9), for Michael then castrated Leo's sons. Niketas comments: 'And so, in the words of the Holy Scriptures, his mischief returned upon his own head and his violent dealing came down upon his own pate'.[52] The issue of castration is thus completed and terminated.

The literary portrait of Ignatios appears to be that of a rather typical holy man. He endures struggle (*athlesis*, *agona*) to achieve sainthood; he undertakes *askesis*.[53] He abstains from vice, and shows prudence and fortitude (*andria*).[54] He is the champion of Christ.[55] Niketas even notes, apparently with a straight face, that one of the great virtues of Ignatios is his chastity. He writes:

> Temperance too he pursued, and not only in terms of his own body's chastity and purity, which he had cultivated from an early age with such hard work and sweat of his brow that he had arrived at a state of absolute mastery over his passions and of complete mortification of his desires of the flesh.[56]

Notwithstanding Ignatios' relatively late castration these assertions still seem rather bold; the mosaic image of Ignatios certainly emphasizes his altered physical state. It is possible that Niketas has assumed the position that, despite their castration, eunuchs still possessed manly passions to control. However, one could also argue that he is deliberately allowing Ignatios to exhibit masculinity, and thus holiness, through the description of the eunuch's struggle with his fleshly desires, though he knew perfectly well that Ignatios, as a eunuch, did not need to make any effort.

Elsewhere Niketas stresses Ignatios' masculinity and fertility. The saint performs a military role, in a vision after his death: he appeared seated on a white horse to a commander in Sicily and dispensed tactical advice on how to defeat the Arabs.[57] Images of fertility and parenthood pile up, as Vinson has noted.[58] Ignatios brought forth for God the sweetest fruits of virtue; his monastic flock multiplies; the seeds of his mercy and generosity are blessed.[59] Such images are especially strong in the after-death miracles: Ignatios' hair induced mothers' milk; holy oil from his tomb cured a barren noble woman; a difficult birth was assisted.[60] There is also an image of marriage: the church was Ignatios' wife, and Photios took it over in an adulterous union.[61] The impression then is that, for Niketas, Ignatios' condition as a eunuch is not an issue. Unlike in the mosaic, in the literary text Ignatios' eunuch-hood is not emphasized. Niketas even resists developing other strategies it seems: he is well aware of the blurring that exists between angels and eunuchs (for example, the famous dream of Bardas),[62] but Niketas does not pursue this to the advantage of Ignatios.[63] Even a dichotomy between wicked court eunuchs and holy church eunuchs is not embraced, for the *praipositos* Baanes has both negative and positive roles to play.[64]

Whether Niketas is consciously ignoring the condition of Ignatios as a eunuch, or is genuinely not affected by it, is hard to tell. Perhaps he was simply more interested in other issues: the innocence of Ignatios, the crimes of Photios. To address the eunuch-hood of the former might have distracted from his case against the latter. It seems then that the hagiographer is either oblivious to any complexities that might be posed by Ignatios' condition as a eunuch, or is deliberately avoiding them. Either way, Ignatios is presented as a typical holy man.

Other holy eunuchs

The Life of Ignatios is of course but one example of the treatment of a eunuch saint. The question arises, to what extent is Niketas David's approach to Ignatios typical of those who write about sainted castrates? Holy eunuchs of the fourth to sixth centuries have been studied by Pascal Boulhol and Isabelle Cochelin, and the approach they have identified is indeed the same as that taken by Niketas David to describe Ignatios.[65] They comment that the eunuch condition of the subjects is mentioned but then the martyrs are treated simply as ordinary men. They note that, in the case of John and Paul, the holy eunuchs conduct themselves like military martyrs rather than slaves of the palace.[66] Like Ignatios, these earlier holy eunuchs are also praised for their chastity and temperance. Holy eunuchs are depicted as the opposite of the stereotypical bad eunuch. Georges Sidéris has echoed this view in his study of Byzantine eunuchs of the fourth to seventh centuries, and suggests that the increasing military role for eunuchs in Byzantium might have earned them the right to be viewed as masculine.[67]

Thus the image Niketas David creates of Ignatios is foreshadowed by early Byzantine examples. Is the same treatment found in the full-blown Lives of middle and late Byzantine holy eunuchs? In the case of Niketas the patrician, one does get a similar impression, as far as one can tell from the surviving text. Niketas does have to purge himself of the mire of passions.[68] He did suffer for his faith in the time of iconoclasm. The fatherhood of Niketas as head of his community is recognized: the monks declare 'we are the fruits of your vine'.[69] Perhaps in this case though the author is willing to emphasize the angelic quality of Niketas. His death is described as God calling Niketas to heaven to join the choir of the bodiless ones, although he had become an angel already; he is also described as an imitator of the angelic choir.[70] Of course it could be argued that such reflections are equally applicable to non-eunuch saints. Not all hagiographers, however, necessarily mirror the method of 'normalizing' eunuch saints. Nikephoros Gregoras, for instance, chooses to engage head-on with the eunuch-hood of his uncle, John of Heraclea, and turns it to his advantage.[71] He spells out vividly that castration did not result in loss of desire.[72] Further, since eunuchs were feminized and more susceptible to passions, John's sainthood is the more remarkable.[73] Alternatively, if we accept that Symeon the New Theologian was a eunuch, other hagiographers might go further than Niketas and not mention the eunuch-hood of their subject at all.

Conclusion

In this chapter I have attempted to explore how the writers of Lives of eunuch saints deal with the gender ambiguities of their subjects, taking as my main example the Life of Ignatios. In general it seems that the complexities of the eunuch identity of castrated saints are not addressed by their hagiographers, who tend rather to treat their subjects as typical holy men. Whilst one might be tempted to view angelic connections and characteristics evident in some Lives of holy eunuchs as the emphasizing of their alternative gender identity, it is evident that such images and models are equally applicable to non-eunuch saints. Of the Lives considered, Nikephoros Gregoras' treatment of his uncle does stand out for the willingness to engage with gender identity, but the objective in doing so is to demonstrate John of Heraclea's superiority as a holy *man*. Thus it would seem that, even for holy eunuchs, the answer to the question 'Is masculinity a requirement for identification as a saint?' is a resounding 'Yes'. Whether that masculinity was inherent or bestowed by the hagiographer is another matter.

Notes

1. P. Stafford and A. B. Mulder-Bakker, 'Introduction', *Gender and History*, 12, 3 (2000), 531–5 (532).
2. See, for instance, chs 8–11 in S. Tougher (ed.), *Eunuchs in Antiquity and Beyond* (London, 2002).
3. For a survey see R. Guilland, 'Les eunuques dans l'empire byzantine: étude de titulaire et de prosopographie byzantines', *Revue des Études Byzantines*, 1 (1943), 197–238.
4. See, for example, K. M. Ringrose, 'Living in the shadows: eunuchs and gender in Byzantium', in G. Herdt (ed.), *Third Sex, Third Gender: Beyond Sexual Dimorphism in Culture and History* (New York, 1994), pp. 85–109; S. Tougher, 'Images of effeminate men: the case of Byzantine eunuchs', in D. M. Hadley (ed.), *Masculinity in Medieval Europe* (London and New York, 1999), pp. 89–100.
5. M. Kuefler, *The Manly Eunuch: Masculinity, Gender Ambiguity, and Christian Ideology in Late Antiquity* (Chicago and London, 2001), pp. 14 and 36.
6. Ibid., p. 35.
7. For this idea see, for example, M. Mullett, 'Theophylact of Ochrid's *In defence of eunuchs*', in Tougher (ed.), *Eunuchs in Antiquity*, pp. 177–98 (p. 180).
8. See, for example, Kuefler, *Manly Eunuch*, pp. 36 and 249.
9. S. A. Harvey, 'Women in early Byzantine hagiography: reversing the story', in L. L. Coon, K. J. Haldane and E. W. Sommer (eds), *That Gentle Strength: Historical Perspectives on Women in Christianity* (Charlottesville, VA, and London, 1990), pp. 36–59 (p. 41).
10. See, for instance, P. Boulhol and I. Cochelin, 'La rehabilitation de l'eunuque dans l'hagiographie antique (IVᵉ–VIᵉ siècles)', *Studi di Antichita Christiana*, 48 (1992), 49–76. Kuefler, *Manly Eunuch*, esp. p. 258, discusses the paradox in the biblical context.
11. See Kuefler, *Manly Eunuch*, pp. 273–82, on the monk as manly eunuch. On mystical castration see Boulhol and Cochelin, 'La rehabilitation de l'eunuque', p. 72, and n. 142. On mystical castration in the medieval West see J. Murray, 'Mystical castration: some reflections on Peter Abelard, Hugh of Lincoln and sexual control', in J. Murray (ed.), *Conflicted Identities and Multiple Masculinities: Men in the Medieval West* (New York and London, 1999), pp. 73–91.
12. See especially K. M. Ringrose, 'Passing the test of sanctity: denial of

sexuality and involuntary castration', in L. James (ed.), *Desire and Denial in Byzantium* (Aldershot, 1999), pp. 123–37.
13   M. P. Vinson, 'Gender and politics in the post-iconoclastic period: the *Lives* of Antony the Younger, the empress Theodora, and the patriarch Ignatios', *Byzantion*, 68 (1998), 469–515 (510–11). As Jacqueline Murray's essay in the present volume notes, the same argument was made in relation to old men and abstinence as well.
14   I will expand on the other Lives below.
15   Christopher C. Craun's essay in the present volume notes that the same paradigms of male and female holiness informed early Syrian saints' Lives as those discussed in this section.
16   For ascetic struggles defined in masculine terms see N. Delierneux, 'Virilité physique et sainteté féminine dans l'hagiographie orientale du IVe au VIIe siècle', *Byzantion*, 67 (1997), 179–243 (226, n. 390); Kuefler, *Manly Eunuch*, pp. 275–7. Kuefler also notes (p. 239) that this masculine asceticism was to compensate for the lack of traditional masculinity (for example, ascetics did not fight in wars, did not marry, avoided political office and sex), and comments 'In some regard, then, all Christian men identified themselves in a gender-ambiguous fashion.'
17   H. Chadwick, 'Pachomios and the idea of sanctity', in S. Hackel (ed.), *The Byzantine Saint* (London, 1981), pp. 11–24 (p. 11). But see also the list of desired qualities in Delierneux, 'Virilité physique', 226.
18   Kuefler, *Manly Eunuch*, p. 281.
19   C. Mango, 'Saints', in G. Cavallo (ed.), *The Byzantines* (Chicago and London, 1997), pp. 255–80 (p. 261).
20   Vinson, 'Gender and politics', p. 501.
21   Ibid., p. 502.
22   Vinson, 'Gender and politics', p. 510, argues that for 'man' we should understand 'eunuch'.
23   Delierneux, 'Virilité physique', p. 185; Kuefler, *Manly Eunuch*, pp. 206 and 226–38. For a general discussion of Byzantine holy women see A.-M. Talbot, 'Female sanctity in Byzantium', in her *Women and Religious Life in Byzantium* (Aldershot, 2001), p. vi.
24   L. L. Coon, K. J. Haldane and E. W. Sommer, 'Introduction', in Coon *et al.* (eds), *That Gentle Strength*, p. 5.
25   For Babylas see Mango, 'Saints', p. 267. On the so-called transvestite nuns see now Delierneux, 'Virilité physique'; Kuefler, *Manly Eunuch*, pp. 223–4 .
26   Harvey, 'Women in early Byzantine hagiography', p. 47.
27   Ibid., p. 48.
28   Delierneux, 'Virilité physique', pp. 199–202. Kuefler, *Manly Eunuch*, especially pp. 221–6, also discusses the genderless ideal of early Christianity.
29   A. Kazhdan, 'Byzantine hagiography and sex in the fifth to twelfth centuries', *Dumbarton Oaks Papers*, 44 (1990), 131–43 (131). However, Kuefler, *Manly Eunuch*, p. 231, stresses the maleness of angels.
30   R. Swanson, 'Angels incarnate: clergy and masculinity from Gregorian

Reform to Reformation', in Hadley (ed.), *Masculinity in Medieval Europe*, pp. 160–77.

[31] Stafford and Mulder-Bakker, 'Introduction', p. 533.

[32] See, for example, Boulhol and Cochelin, 'La rehabilitation de l'eunuque'. *Passions* relate the deaths of saints, whilst *Bioi* relate their whole life story.

[33] See D. Papachryssanthou, 'Un confesseur du second iconoclasme: la Vie du patrice Nicétas (+ 836)', *Travaux et Mémoires*, 3 (1968), 309–51.

[34] Ibid., p. 313.

[35] H. Delehaye, 'Vita sancti Nicephori episcopi Milesii saeculo X', *Analecta Bollandiana*, 14 (1895), 129–66. See also P. Lemerle, *Le premier humanisme byzantin* (Paris, 1973), pp. 243–6.

[36] P. Magdalino, 'The Byzantine holy man in the twelfth century', in Hackel (ed.), *Byzantine Saint*, pp. 51–66 (p. 52, n. 10).

[37] V. Laurent, 'La Vie de Jean, Métropolite d'Héraclée du Pont par Nicéphore Grégoras', *Archeion Pontou*, 6 (1934), 3–67; 'La personnalité de Jean d'Héraclée (1250–1328) oncle et précepteur de Nicéphore Grégoras', *Hellenika*, 3 (1930), 297–315. See also R. Guilland, *Essai sur Nicéphore Grégoras: L'homme et l'œuvre* (Paris, 1923), especially pp. 4–5, 180–3.

[38] See Ringrose, 'Involuntary castration', p. 133.

[39] On Symeon see A. J. van der Aalst, 'The palace and the monastery in Byzantine spiritual life c.1000', in A. Davids (ed.), *The Empress Theophano: Byzantium and the West at the Turn of the First Millennium* (Cambridge, 1995), pp. 314–36 (pp. 323–5). The Life does say that 'after his death Symeon appeared unto a certain Philotheos as a "white-haired, handsome, venerable eunuch"': p. 327.

[40] For the text see PG, 105, cols 487–574; A. Smithies, 'Nicetas Paphlago's "Life of Ignatios": a critical edition with translation' (unpublished Ph.D. thesis, State University of New York at Buffalo, 1987).

[41] See C. Mango and E. J. W. Hawkins, 'The mosaics of St. Sophia at Istanbul: the church fathers in the north tympanum', *Dumbarton Oaks Papers*, 26 (1972), 3–41 (pp. 9–11, 28–30).

[42] Though there are drawings of others. For comment on the image of Ignatios, ibid., pp. 9–11 and 28–30. They note the rarity of images of Ignatios, and suggest that the image is based on an earlier portrait and shows him when he was about 50 years old, thus c.847 when he became patriarch for the first time.

[43] For Niketas David see, for example, P. Karlin-Hayter, *Vita Eutyhmii Patriarchae Cp. Text, Translation, Introduction and Commentary* (Brussels, 1970), pp. 217–19.

[44] On the tetragamy crisis see, for example, S. Tougher, *The Reign of Leo VI (886–912): People and Politics* (Leiden, 1997), ch. 6.

[45] See, for example, R. J. H. Jenkins, 'A note on Nicetas David Paphlago and the *Vita Ignatii*', *Dumbarton Oaks Papers*, 19 (1965), 241–7.

[46] F. Dvornik, 'Patriarch Ignatius and caesar Bardas', *Byzantinoslavica*, 27 (1966), 7–22 (p. 12).

47 P. J. Alexander, 'Secular biography at Byzantium', *Speculum*, 15 (1940), 194–209, comments that the *Life of Ignatios* 'is unique in hagiographical literature in that it combines the praise of its hero Ignatius with blame of his great opponent, Photius' (pp. 202–3).
48 L. Rydén, 'New forms of hagiography: heroes and saints', *Seventeenth International Byzantine Congress* (New York, 1986), pp. 537–51 (p. 544).
49 Vinson, 'Gender and politics', p. 471.
50 See S. Efthymiadis, *The Life of the Patriarch Tarasios by Ignatios the Deacon (BHG 1698): Introduction, Text, Translation and Commentary* (Aldershot, 1998), pp. 3–4.
51 PG 105, cols 492C–493B. Leo's actions and motives here are comparable to some of the instances of enforced hair-cutting discussed by Robert Mills in the present volume.
52 Smithies, 'Life of Ignatios', p. 81.
53 PG 105, col. 498B; Smithies, 'Life of Ignatios', p. 84.
54 PG 105, col. 501C; Smithies, 'Life of Ignatios', p. 88.
55 PG 105, col. 525A; Smithies, 'Life of Ignatios', p. 109.
56 PG 105, col. 501D; Smithies, 'Life of Ignatios', p. 88.
57 Smithies, 'Life of Ignatios', p. 143.
58 Vinson, 'Gender and politics', p. 491.
59 Smithies, 'Life of Ignatios', pp. 82, 83, 86.
60 Ibid., pp. 142–4.
61 PG 105, col. 512A; Smithies, 'Life of Ignatios', p. 96.
62 In a dream Bardas foresees his own divinely sanctioned death: PG 105, cols 533–6; Smithies, 'Life of Ignatios', pp. 117–19. Discussing the origins of dreams, Niketas says some 'are fashioned by God's angels upon God's command'. Bardas describes how in his dream he went to Hagia Sophia with the emperor, and that at all the windows archangels were looking in. When they came to the pulpit two chamberlains (eunuchs) appeared and one dragged away the emperor to the right, and the other dragged him away to the left. He next saw an old man seated on the patriarchal throne looking like an icon of St Peter, flanked by two *praipositoi* (eunuchs). Ignatios was present also, beseeching Peter, and he identified Bardas as the man who had wronged him. Peter then ordered that Bardas be led away and cut to pieces. For some discussion see J. Featherstone, 'A note on the dream of Bardas caesar in the *Life* of Ignatius and the archangel in the mosaic over the imperial doors of St Sophia', *Byzantinische Zeitschrift*, 74 (1981), 42–3. The dream episode also features in the history of Genesios, 4. 21: A. Kaldellis (tr.), Genesios, On the Reigns of the Emperors (Canberra, 1998), p. 92.
63 We are told however that Ignatios' major monastic foundation was that of the Archangel Michael (PG 105, col. 497A; Smithies, 'Life of Ignatios', pp. 83–4). Also, a speech given to Ignatios identifies angels and saints as comrades 'of that most modest abstinence' (PG 105, col. 553C; Smithies, 'Life of Ignatios', p. 135). Further, angels appear in a list of advocates (PG 105, col. 573D; Smithies, 'Life of Ignatios', p. 153).

64 In 861 Baanes Angoures the *praipositos* is one of those sent to Ignatios to warn him not to cause a problem at the forthcoming synod (PG 105, col. 513B; Smithies, 'Life of Ignatios', p. 102). But Baanes also plays a good role when he goes to Photios and finds his slanderous writings against Ignatios (PG 105, col. 540C; Smithies, 'Life of Ignatios', p. 122). Note also the sticky end of the Lydian *sakellarios* following his disrespectful behaviour at Ignatios' tomb (PG 105, col. 565A; Smithies, 'Life of Ignatios', p. 145).
65 Boulhol and Cochelin, 'La rehabilitation de l'eunuque', p. 66.
66 Ibid., pp. 66–7.
67 G. Sidéris, 'Eunuques et pouvoir à Byzance IVe–VIIe siècle' (unpublished Ph.D. thesis, Sorbonne University, Paris, 2001), especially pp. 415–25.
68 Papachryssanthou, 'La Vie du patrice Nicétas', pp. 340–1.
69 Ibid., pp. 348–9. See Kuefler, *Manly Eunuch*, p. 280, on the alternative family of the monastic community, brothers under the leadership of a father.
70 Papachryssanthou, 'La Vie du patrice Nicétas', pp. 342–3, 348–9 (and also pp. 350–1: he was incorporeal even in the flesh). Links with the archangel are established too: Niketas built a church to the bodiless ones at Katisia, and also a church to the Archangel Michael (ibid., pp. 326–7, 336–7). Also a possessed man claimed that Niketas allied with Michael to do him harm.
71 See N. Gaul, 'Eunuchs in the late Byzantine empire, *c.*1250–1400', in Tougher (ed.), *Eunuchs in Antiquity*, pp. 199–219 (pp. 201–3).
72 Laurent, 'La Vie de Jean', p. 36 and n. 2, the image used is of the declawed lion who still attacks. Laurent points to biblical parallels for the idea of persistent desire: Ecclesiasticus 20: 1 (like a eunuch longing to seduce a girl is the man who tries to do right by violence); 30: 21 (he gazes at the food before him and sighs as a eunuch sighs when he embraces a girl). Laurent says he prefers Basil's image of the dehorned bull that continues to butt when it is enraged.
73 Harvey, 'Women in early Byzantine hagiography', p. 40, notes that 'Theodoret of Cyrrhus commented in his *Historia Religiosa* [29. 1] that holy women are worthy of greater praise than men, because they have had to overcome a weaker nature.' The relevant passage here is quoted by Craun.

8

The Signification of the Tonsure

ROBERT MILLS

According to the *Legenda aurea*, Jacobus de Voragine's compendious manual of saints' lives, the tonsure had its origin in the life of St Peter. When Peter began to preach the Gospel at Antioch, so tradition has it, the pagans shaved the top of his head 'as a sign of contempt for the name of Christians', spawning a fashion for trimmed locks that would be the vogue for clerics in Western Christendom for almost two millennia. Jacobus goes on to elucidate a whole range of significations of the tonsure, supporting his argument that what had originally been imposed on the prince of the apostles as a 'badge of shame' was passed on to clerics as a 'mark of honour'. The shaving of the head, he notes, 'signifies a clean, plain, artless way of life', an 'interior cleanness of mind', and a 'lack of concern for external fashion'; it demonstrates 'that there should be nothing between the cleric and God' and that they 'should have the simplicity of doves'.[1]

Jacobus' remarks centre on a principle of sacrifice that was to become commonplace in Christian discourse from the era of persecution up until the present day – indeed, as this chapter will go on to suggest, there is a degree of congruence between his assertions and the findings of modern-day anthropologists. But to understand the significance of the tonsure in medieval culture, it is important that we also look beyond strictly theological notions of self-denial in order to understand the social implications of that message. Hair is a symbol freighted with cultural meaning. Variously deployed as a marker of social status, racial alterity, physical maturity, age, sexual potency and, most strikingly, gender, hair communicates a society's values. This chapter will seek to unravel some of the gendered ideological messages that the presence and absence of hair conveyed in medieval culture at large, thereby revealing aspects of tonsure symbolism left largely unexplored by commentaries like the *Legenda aurea*. How did the ritual of head shaving and the wearing of tonsures as a sign of clerical difference impact upon a person's understanding of gender and sexuality? How did gender seize upon bodily inscriptions like the tonsure as a way of securing – and naturalizing – constructions of sexual difference? And to what extent did the custom throw such projects into disarray?

I pose these questions, too, as part of an effort to construct a loose analogy between the tonsure and the phallus. The phallus is a category that has been influential in modern gender criticism, not least in the context of feminist responses to psychoanalysis. When invoked by Freud, the term is generally deployed as a synonym of penis, whereas the French psychoanalyst Jacques Lacan takes a less literal view, preferring to explore the phallus as it relates to imaginary and symbolic existence. In his paper 'The signification of the phallus', Lacan suggests that it operates as a social signifier, representing what male subjects (think they) have and what female subjects (are considered, culturally speaking, to) lack. Moreover, the phallus is an object circulated within networks of symbolic exchange: emblematic of the structure of language, it establishes the conditions for signifiability.[2] The privileged position accorded to the phallus in psychoanalytic theory has been subject to a good deal of critique in feminist writings, but the distinction Lacan posits between phallus and penis has also been avidly defended by certain feminists as offering a means of accounting for sexual difference that is irreducible to biological or anatomical models.[3] His account suggests that the meaning of the phallus is culturally and politically motivated, that it has no given content or signified and that it is capable of enveloping other objects and body parts than male genitalia alone. This chapter will not go so far as to suggest that the tonsure was an emphatically 'phallic' signifier in medieval culture, or that it was a symbol bound up entirely in constructions of masculinity. But I would like to recommend that we not reject analogies between modern psychoanalysis and medieval rhetoric out of hand. Lacan, after all, occasionally acknowledges in his work the historical dimensions of phallic symbolism: in another context he is quoted as saying that 'the phallus is not a question of a form or of an image, or of a phantasy, but rather a signifier, the signifier of desire. In Greek antiquity, the phallus is not represented by an organ but as an insignia'.[4] What I take this statement to mean is that the phallus, in ancient Greece, can be interpreted within a sociopolitical frame. Family insignia, which positioned subjects within a social hierarchy according to what they had or to what they lacked, prevented slaves from accessing the Greek family name – they were a method of dispensing power akin to modern discourses emphasizing the presence and absence of the penis.

Tonsures are not, to the mind of writers like Jacobus de Voragine, noticeably gendered as attributes – if anything, they symbolize a denial of selfhood and sexual status connected above all to the vow of chastity. But it could be said that they too operate as 'signifiers of desire': they are a sign, in Jacobus' words, that 'clerics should be immediately united to God and should behold the glory of the Lord with face unveiled'.[5] Moreover, as will hopefully be apparent from the material that follows, tonsures fulfilled functions related to social hierarchy and self-definition: like the phallus, they operated as a crucial signifier in the distribution of power, authority and language in medieval culture. Taking this analogy as its starting point, then, this chapter will suggest that tonsures potentially positioned subjects within a gendered social geography too; that, set against a wider backdrop of capillary symbolism in the medieval period, they also had the capacity to meet needs related to the construction of manhood.

First and foremost, the tonsure was a badge of male social position – it designated, above all else, clerical status. This had not always been the case: it was only after the seventh century that texts began to mention the practice of having the top of the head shaved in the form of a circle – the so-called *corona* tonsure or crown – and it was not until the late eleventh century that tonsures began to be elevated to the status of a church institution.[6] But from this point on, tonsures became an attribute required by law. The Council of Toulouse, in 1119, threatened excommunication to 'the monk, canon or clerk who would maintain his hair and beard like the layman', and in 1215 the Fourth Lateran Council ordained that clerics wear a 'suitable crown and tonsure'.[7] The legal significance of the tonsure is manifested in fourteenth-century German law books describing how Jews and clerics were forbidden to carry weapons; in an example from Heidelberg, the tonsured cleric is depicted sitting astride a horse, sword at his side, beckoning to a pointy-hatted Jew behind him (Figure 8.1).

Figure 8.1. Heidelberg Sachsenspiegel (1300). Heidelberg University Library, MS cod. pal. ger. 164, fo. 12ᵛ

Given the rigour with which church councils enforced the habit of head shaving, the wearing of the tonsure was thus subject to a good deal of anxiety in this period. In 1268 the Council of London denounced as scandalous the fact that the eye could not distinguish clerics from laymen and, for this reason, forbade ecclesiastics from hiding their tonsures under a hat.[8] Much, after all, was riding on the tonsure's visibility in society at large. In the twelfth and thirteenth centuries, the tonsure had been used to establish benefit of the clergy – the right of a criminous clerk to be tried by an ecclesiastical court and thereby escape the death penalty.[9] Evidently, however, this was a test of eligibility that could be faked. Thirteenth-century legal records suggest that gaolers themselves were suspected of bestowing 'tonsures' on willing criminals: the justices of gaol delivery at Newgate prison were so dubious about the authenticity of a certain Robert de Neuby's claim to immunity from secular justice that they proceeded to investigate the possibility that he had obtained it while in custody – all this 'because his tonsure (*sua corona*) is newly shaved'.[10] In the fourteenth and fifteenth centuries a more reliable test was developed, which made external appearance less important: the accused was judged on his ability to read a passage from the Bible in Latin.[11]

But tonsures were also the mark of a specifically gendered form of authority – they represented above all male access to God. This is remarked upon explicitly in the commentary on Peter Lombard's *Sentences* by Bonaventure (d. 1274), who remarks that it is appropriate that clerics be tonsured with the corona (*tonsurari cum corona*) for the sake of distinction and instruction . . . You are an elect race, a royal priesthood (*Vos estis genus electum, regale sacerdotium*); for that reason a royal mark, most rightly, has the capacity to distinguish them.

Bonaventure proceeds, however, to ask the question 'whether the male sex is required for the reception of orders', and is adamant that women cannot become priests because the priesthood, the authority of God, has to be symbolized by a male: first in his list of reasons is the announcement that 'no one has a capacity for orders who does not have the aptitude for a tonsure and crown; and no one has a natural aptitude for this for whom it is fitting always to have the head veiled'.[12] Bonaventure takes his cue here from the prescriptions of St Paul in Corinthians that men who keep their heads covered do themselves a dishonour whereas women do not: 'For a man indeed ought not to cover his head, forasmuch as he is the image and glory of God: but the woman is the glory of the man.'[13] Hence, perhaps, the significance of the scene to the right in the Heidelberg law book, which depicts the punishment meted out to a pregnant woman (see Figure 8.1). The prisoner undergoes whipping and shearing of the hair, suggesting the extent to which hair cutting was, for women, a grave humiliation.

Nonetheless, there are several instances in which women are represented as assuming tonsures or short hair in order to symbolize their ability to bypass the misogynistic prescriptions of writers like Bonaventure. St Euphrosine, a so-called 'transvestite' saint who, according to her *vita*, sought shelter in a male monastery in order to escape marriage and protect her virginity, as well as changing into male clothing, had her hair cut short as part of her disguise.[14] In Bonaventure's own day, Clare of Assisi (d. 1253) was one of a number of young women who chopped off their hair as proof of consecration to God.[15] Hair cutting was, after all, a normal part of the nun's veiling ceremony in this period: a Middle English ritual for the ordination of nuns describes how, after the nun receives the habit and mantle, the prelate 'with a payr of schers beggyn forto kut hir hair befor at þe toppyng . . . And þen sal þe priores kut o-way þe remnaunt.' Unlike the tonsured monk, however, the rite continues by prescribing that the newly shorn head be covered up soon after with a wimple.[16]

The link between tonsures and religious authority was not without its problems in other contexts too. When writers like Hugh of St Victor pronounced that the summit of the clerk's head was shaved naked and rendered visible 'to make it known that this man is chosen to participate in the royal power of Christ', they were refuting centuries of negative tradition surrounding shaved heads.[17] For, in both secular and biblical contexts, extreme haircuts had long been associated not with victory but with humiliation. The ancient Hebrews cherished thick, dark long hair as an attribute conveying vitality and strength.[18] David's son Absalom, proud of his gorgeous tresses, cut or 'polled' them only once a year. Samson, reared as a Nazarite, explained to Delilah that 'if I be shaven, then my strength will go from me and I shall become weak and be like any other man'; Delilah, having discovered the secret of his potency, caused his head to be shaved in his sleep.[19] The book of Leviticus goes so far as to forbid the shaving of heads altogether: 'They shall not make baldness upon their head', the book rules.[20] Often in ancient societies, the removal of hair from the head was a practice associated with acts of social demarcation: the marking out of slaves; rituals of mourning and penance; the humiliation of criminals and conquered peoples; and medical interventions associated with the prevention of vermin.[21] In the light of these attachments, it is not surprising that St Jerome and other early Christians registered dissatisfaction at the thought of priests shaving their heads or indeed any part of their bodies: given that among Greeks and Romans shaved heads were a badge of slavery, it was hardly appropriate that tonsures be adopted by the early church during the age of persecutions.[22]

One particularly striking example of early Christian anxiety surrounding hair removal appears in the writings of the Greek theologian Clement of Alexandria (d. c.215), who has much to say on the subject of hair and hairiness in relation to constructions of gender. God, he announces:

> planned that woman be smooth-skinned, taking pride in her natural tresses, the only hair she has, as the horse in its mane. But man He adorned like the lion, with a beard, and gave him a hairy chest as proof of his manhood and a sign of his strength and primacy . . . His beard, then, is the badge of a man and shows him unmistakeably to be a man . . . By God's decree, hairiness is one of man's conspicuous qualities and, at that, hairiness distributed over his whole body . . . it is sacrilege to trifle with the symbol of manhood.[23]

Of course, Clement is thinking less specifically here of the custom of tonsures than the practise of shaving the beard and other parts of the body – he reserves particular venom for those men who have their pubic regions plucked.[24] Yet his remarks are telling nonetheless, signalling as they do the importance of reading hair removal not just as a marker of clerical status but also as a symbol inflected with gendered significance.

That tonsures were subject to anxiety in the early medieval period is indicated, too, by the writings of Gregory of Tours (d. 594), whose *History of the Franks* is replete with incidents of involuntary head shaving as a method of deposing kings. The Visigothic church in the seventh century announced that 'no one tonsured under the bait of religion or shamefully scalped or having a servile origin shall come to the head of the kingdom', a ruling that sparked a craze for forcibly tonsuring kings in the barbarian kingdoms of pre-Carolingian Europe.[25] Gregory supplies an especially striking example in a passage describing the accession of Clovis to the Frankish throne. Clovis, having imprisoned King Chararic and his son, 'had their hair cut short. He ordered Chararic to be ordained as a priest and he made his son a deacon. Chararic objected to this humiliation and burst into tears.' Chararic's son played things a little cooler, however, announcing boldly that 'These leaves have been cut from wood which is still green and not lacking in sap. They will soon grow again and be longer than ever.' More fool him: Clovis, hearing the son's threat, decided that tonsures were not a permanent enough measure and promptly arranged for the pair's decapitation.[26]

Of course, it was especially humiliating that Merovingian royals undergo radical hair therapy: removal of their manes took away the very mark around which the *reges criniti*, the 'long-haired kings', constructed their public image. In this context, tonsuring royal progeny was an act so humiliating that, in another episode in the *History of the Franks*, Queen Clotild, taking care of two Merovingian princes threatened with forcible tonsure, declared: 'If they are not to ascend the throne, I would rather see them dead than with their hair cut short.'[27] Such episodes do not, of course, deal directly with constructions of manhood – tonsuring occurs within a field of numerous other categories of meaning, not least those bound up in concepts of class and social hierarchy. But, keeping in mind my initial analogy with the symbolic phallus, it is evident that head shaving could be deployed, in certain contexts, as a kind of figurative castration. The act of tonsuring not only symbolized the change from lay to clerical status but also denied the recipient the privileges that were their birthright as male heirs.

The negative implications of head shaving made it appropriate as a means of labelling of fools and other marginal or outlawed figures. This is especially noticeable in literary contexts, where romances such as the Tristan legend sometimes represent the hero passing himself off as a fool in order to infiltrate the court of King Mark and to be reunited with his lover Queen Yseut: one of the ways in which Tristan alters his appearance in order to assume the guise of a madman is to have his head 'shaven and shorn'.[28] Medieval medical writings similarly expressed misgivings about the loss of one's locks, linking an abundance of hair with male sexual potency. According to authors of late medieval medical treatises, hairiness was related to libido in men, the theory being that the same natural heat and moisture that caused the growth of hair in males was also necessary for the production of semen, which in turn was thought to be connected to the ability to sustain an erection: the writings of the French surgeon Guy de Chauliac, translated into Middle English in the fifteenth century, make such a connection, describing how eunuchs do not go bald due to the moisture in their brains; he goes on to conclude that baldness is 'euel and suspecte, for it semeth þat deth haþ applied his baner to þe hede'.[29]

Such perceptions find their way into literary representations, for instance the B-text of Langland's *Piers Plowman* (c.1377–9), where, in the final passus, the dreamer is attacked by the figure of Elde (Old Age) who, making him 'balled bifore and bare on the croune', suffers a distressing change in circumstance. Lamenting his affliction by old age, the dreamer's wife expresses hope that he will be put out of his misery soon, since he has lost the power to pleasure her in bed:

> For the lyme [member] that she loved me fore, and leef [loved] was to
>   feele –
> On nyghtes, namely, whan we naked weere –
> I ne myghte in no manere maken it at hir wille,
> So Elde and heo [she] it hadden forbeten [enfeebled].[30]

If baldness expressed impotence, there were also circumstances when it could conversely be associated with lust. In Chaucer's *Shipman's Tale*, when the rich merchant is away on business, the monk John takes advantage of the situation by paying the merchant's pretty wife a visit. Introduced initially as a person 'manly of dispence' (generous/virile in spending), he strikes a bargain with the wife to sleep with her all night long in return for gold; significantly he arrives at the house 'with

Figure 8.2. Wild man, in *The Luttrell Psalter* (*c*.1335–40). London, British Library, MS Add. 42130, fo. 70ʳ. By permission of the British Library

crowne (tonsure) and berd al fressh and newe yshave'.[31] This connection between clean-shavenness and virility is, it would seem, admissible within the symbolic economy of Chaucerian fabliau precisely because, in these contexts, the narrative relies on a formula of lustful clerics cuckolding men who are, on the surface, materially better off. (In the *Shipman's Tale*, the merchant loans money to the monk.) Elsewhere, however, the reverse is true: wild men or women, depicted with increasing frequency as the medieval period drew to a close, express the opposite extreme by personifying an association between hair and exuberance.[32] An especially hirsute wild man inhabits the borders of a folio in *The Luttrell Psalter* (*c*.1335–40): he crawls on all fours in a posture that links him with madness as well as animalistic sensuality (Figure 8.2).[33] Such scenes are reminiscent of images of hairy anchorite saints, such as St John Chrysostom and Mary of Egypt, which proliferated in the late Middle Ages: again, here, excessive hair is linked with sexuality, and more specifically sexual misconduct.[34] Given these associations, it would be worth countenancing the possibility of a cultural resonance, in tonsure symbolism, between the repression of

Figure 8.3. A bird monster cracks a monastic nut, in *The Luttrell Psalter* (c.1335–40). London, British Library, MS Add. 42130, fo. 179ᵛ. By permission of the British Library

sexual desire required by clerical celibacy and the excess of virility and sexual potency associated with retaining one's hair.

Whether or not one posits a direct relationship between the meanings communicated by hereditary pattern baldness, clerical head shaving and wild men and hair-covered saints, it is clear from these examples that tonsures had the ability to communicate negative as well as positive meanings. While the tonsure was a perfectly acceptable symbol for priests wishing to toe the line of Christian orthodoxy and to renounce their sexual appetites, it was evidently a matter of concern for the lusty, fun-loving priests and monks who were the targets of late medieval anticlerical derision. In another marginal illumination in *The Luttrell Psalter*, a monstrous hybrid – half-cow and half-monk – is depicted crowned with a rotund, egg-like tonsure, which gets attacked in turn by a long-necked, big-beaked bird – a representation of clerical hypocrisy. The monk's solemn, even brooding, demeanour contrasts wildly with the golden linings of his habit; the egg- or nut-cracking motif presumably denotes the collapse of his shell-like exterior (Figure 8.3). In a further

THE SIGNIFICATION OF THE TONSURE

Figure 8.4. A fighting cleric with a tonsure and a naked cleric, in *The Luttrell Psalter* (c.1335–40). London, British Library, MS Add. 42130, fo. 54ʳ. By permission of the British Library

miniature in the manuscript, a cleric, seated beneath his fighting colleague, attempts to cover his nakedness. Both figures sport a somewhat unusual style of tonsure, a minuscule circle in the centre of their heads (Figure 8.4). The implication is that the pair are embarrassed by their vocation: just as the lower cleric is ashamed to reveal his nudity, so he is averse to declaring his clerical status by leaving his head bare.[35]

In a sermon by the fourteenth-century preacher John Bromyard, we are told about just such individuals: clerics who 'are ashamed of the tonsure and therefore cultivate a fashionable head of hair, or have a small tonsure, so as not to be recognized as priests'.[36] Figures of this kind are also epitomized in literature of the period. The character Absolon, one of the two young clerks in the Chaucer's *Miller's Tale*, is described as possessing an especially extravagant hairdo:

> Crul was his heer, and as the gold it shoon,
> And strouted as a fanne large and brode;
> Ful streight and evene lay his joly shode.[37]

Langland, by way of contrast, presents a group of clerics who are properly shorn but whose tonsures are mere empty signifiers, imparting not absent presence (in keeping with the schema outlined in the *Legenda aurea*) but contemptible and unassailable lack. In Passus XI of *Piers Plowman*, the Emperor Trajan rails against priests who have neither 'konynge ne kyn', but only a tonsure – a 'crowne' – with which to earn a living in times of trouble. Complaining that such individuals are more likely to obtain an ecclesiastical benefice through their title, their 'tale of noght' (empty name), than through their knowledge or reputation for virtue, the implication is that hair removal is only ambiguously connected with power – it also has the capacity to connote, precisely, nothing.[38] The fifteenth-century Parisian poet François Villon likewise assumes a connection between hair removal and lack, but hair removal of an even more extreme kind: the narrator of the *Testament*, describing the epitaph he hopes will mark his grave, explains that his tonsure, the outward sign proving clerical status, has itself been violently eliminated through an act of total hair removal:

> Il fut rez, chief, barbe, sourcil
> Comme ung navet c'on ret ou pelle.
>
> [He was shaved, head, beard, brow,
> Like a turnip that's shaved or peeled].[39]

Here the denuding of the scalp is publicly felt: while no one can take his learning from him (competence in Latin was the other minimal attribute of clerics), the *Testament*'s narrator suffers the loss of the only visible trait that signals his social identity.

There is another circumstance, too, in which holy hair loss seems to have provoked anxiety, a circumstance that is at the very centre of Christian tradition. In late medieval art, Christ was almost never depicted bald. This would not necessarily be significant of course, were it not for the fact that late medieval writings describing the passion repeatedly mention the pulling out of Christ's hair and beard. A mid-fourteenth-century passion meditation ascribed to Richard Rolle, for instance, describes how his persecutors hit him on the head till it was as 'bolned as an ouene kake, and tugged vp þe heer bi the rootes'.[40] Nonetheless, despite a substantial textual tradition describing Christ's hair loss, scenes depicting the passion in late medieval panel painting invariably show Christ sporting a beard and hair: a fifteenth-century

Figure 8.5. Artist in Rueland Frueauf the Elder's circle, *Carrying of the Cross* (c.1440–1507). Regensburg, Regensburg City Museum

panel depicting the carrying of the cross, part of a large passion altarpiece painted by an artist in Rueland Frueauf the Elder's circle, shows Christ having his hair tugged by a tormentor, but his curly brown mop nonetheless remains completely intact (Figure 8.5). Artists did not flinch from depicting all the other grisly torments inflicted on Christ's body – the hideousness of the wound in his side, the pains of the flagellation – but they could not bring themselves to represent him without all the hair on his head. If anything, Christ's tormentors were more likely to be represented with bald or balding crowns than Christ himself: in the *Carrying of the Cross* panel, the figure tugging Christ's mane is himself hatless and short-haired. The portrayal of a hairless Christ in visual media evidently had the capacity to unsettle medieval viewers and patrons to the extent that artists were rarely motivated to depict him with anything less than a full head of hair.[41]

It is of no small significance that Christ's shearing was sometimes alluded to in theological discussions of the clerical tonsure, which interpreted it as a symbol representing the honour and glory of Christ's passion.[42] But given the anxieties that hair removal apparently aroused, beyond the intellectual justifications of theologians, why did the tonsure assume such authoritative status as an institution from the twelfth century on? How could it shift from being a sign communicating abasement, impotence and even emasculation to an attribute signifying clerical privilege and power? These are questions that concern studies of masculinity in any period, of course, since they ask that we consider the extent to which submission – say in the form of figurative castration and feminization – produces the effect of domination. Readings that envisage a degree of complicity between authoritarian and submissive forms of masculinity allow us to see beyond the apparent opposition between 'phallic' and 'feminized' men in order to reveal spaces where they cooperate and coincide: submission does not necessarily equate with devirilization.[43] But was a similar dynamic at work in the ritual of the tonsure? Did members of the clergy wear shaved heads to signify their dissent from the gendered supremacy to which they had been accustomed or did they, on the contrary, see it as an ultra-virile thing to do?

Anthropologists provide one answer to this question: they have long recognized tonsures as markers of status elevation. After all, the ritual of tonsure, as with other acts of shaving and hair cutting, frequently takes on the significance of a rite of passage – the 'first tonsure' was accorded the significance of an initiatory ordeal in Catholic ordination ceremonies until 1972.[44] Individuals who accepted the procedure effectively entered into a state of liminality, marked by the humiliating renunciation of their natural locks – and it is this condition of remaining permanently on the threshold that, according to writers like Victor Turner, effectively endows the recipients with sacred power.[45]

The anthropological insight has implications for an understanding of masculinity too: as with the 'blissful castration' of the twelfth-century philosopher Abelard, which allowed him, in his own words, to 'advance in many ways',[46] it is evident that in certain areas of medieval culture experiences of unmanning could be socially beneficial. But it is also important to note that the dignity of submission was, for the most part, closely related to its *wilful* acceptance by the subject: whereas the Merovingian kings were forced against their will to undergo the ordeal of head shaving, clerics accepted the tonsure voluntarily and thus did not suffer the same degree of humiliation. As such, tonsures partook of an ethics of self-sacrifice – which perhaps explains what endowed them with the ability to convey authority and social power. Indeed, this is a sleight of hand that was performed routinely in Christian discourse. Just as, for medieval martyrs, voluntary submission to pain was often represented as a source of power and transcendence,[47] in the lives of medieval clerics, tonsures were unhooked from their negative associations in order to signify as markers of absence but also, paradoxically, presence. Designating both the desire of the Other (in Christian discourse, God) and a repository of repressed desire (celibacy), tonsures embodied the sacrificial trope that less equals more.

We have, in a sense, come full circle, returning to the explanation in the *Legenda aurea* with which I opened: I do not pretend to have discovered a definitive answer to the question posed at the outset about the tonsure's impact in society at large. Nor has it been possible, given the disparate nature of the material, to make precise historical claims regarding the tonsure's signification at any one point in time, or to conclude that the tonsure operated as a signifier possessing the same sort of gendered privileges as the phallus in psychoanalytic discourse – that would be to overstate the case. The cutting of hair was able to carry a whole bundle of significations within the medieval mind, some of them gendered, some of them not. In certain contexts, it functioned negatively, communicating humiliation of a sort inappropriate even to representations of Christ; in other contexts, it functioned positively, as a symbol of ascetic triumph. Indeed, in anthropological terms, one structure of meaning may have provided the conditions for the other. The tonsure was an ambivalent symbol in the Middle Ages, and its signification cannot be determined in advance of its possible quotidian uses. The analysis presented in this chapter has adopted a brush that is deliberately broad, but hopefully the picture I have painted will help draw attention to some of the gendered contexts for those uses. Tonsures were embedded in a network of meanings of which masculinity was just a part, and the versions of masculinity with which it was entangled circulated variously between authoritarian and submissive forms. But if, as this volume demonstrates, the intersections between holiness and masculinity are a topic worthy of study, then an investigation of one of the most visible manifestations of those intersections would be the proper place to start.

Notes

1. Jacobus de Voragine, *Legenda aurea*, ed. Theodor Graesse (Dresden and Leipzig, 1846), pp. 182–3; Jacobus de Voragine, *The Golden Legend: Readings on the Saints*, 2 vols, tr. William Granger Ryan (Princeton, 1993), vol. 1, pp. 165–6.
2. Jacques Lacan, 'The signification of the phallus', in *Écrits: A Selection*, tr. Alan Sheridan (London, 1977), pp. 281–91 (p. 290).
3. Elizabeth Grosz, *Jacques Lacan: A Feminist Introduction* (London, 1990), pp. 116–26, presents a useful summary of the status of the Lacanian phallus in feminist theory, along with a cogent critique.
4. Jacques Lacan, *Speech and Language in Psychoanalysis*, tr. Anthony Wilden (Baltimore, MD, 1981), p. 187.
5. Jacobus, *Legenda aurea*, p. 182; Jacobus, *Golden Legend*, vol. 1, p. 166.
6. General accounts of the development of the Christian tonsure include Louis Trichet, *La Tonsure: Vie et mort d'une pratique ecclésiastique* (Paris, 1990), especially pp. 69–160; T. J. Riley, 'Tonsure', in *New Catholic Encyclopedia*, 15 vols (New York, 1967), vol. 14, pp. 199–200; P. Gobillot, 'Sur la tonsure chrétienne et ses prétendues origines païennes', *Revue d'histoire ecclésiastique*, 21 (1925), 399–454.
7. Council of Toulouse, *Sacrosancta concilia ad regiam editionem exacta quæ nunc quarta parte prodit auctior*, ed. Philippe Labbe and Gabriel Cossart, 17 vols (Paris, 1671–2), vol. 10, col. 858; 'Canons of the Fourth Lateran Council, 1215', in *English Historical Documents*, ed. David C. Douglas, 12 vols (London, 1955–77), vol. 3, *1189–1327* (1975), pp. 643–76 (canon 16 at p. 653).
8. *Sacrosancta concilia*, ed. Labbe and Cossart, vol. 11, col. 872.
9. Leona C. Gabel, *Benefit of Clergy in England in the Later Middle Ages*, Smith College Studies in History, 14 (New York, 1969), p. 63.
10. Ibid., p. 64.
11. Ibid., pp. 64–73.
12. *Commentaria: in quatuor libros sententiarum Magistri Petri Lombardi*: distinction 24, article 1, question 1, and distinction 25, article 2, question 1, in St Bonaventure, *Opera omnia*, 11 vols (Quaracchi, 1882–1902), vol. 4 (1889).
13. Corinthians 11: 4–7.
14. Ælfric, 'St Eufrosia (or Euphrosyne)', in *Ælfric's Lives of the Saints*, 2 vols, ed. Walter W. Skeat, EETS OS 76, 82, 94 and 114 (Oxford, 1966), vol. 2, pp. 334–55 (p. 342); Raymond T. Hill (ed.), 'La Vie de Sainte Euphrosine', *Romanic Review*, 10 (1919), 191–232 (p. 205).
15. Other female religious figures who cut off their hair in the late Middle Ages include Catherine of Siena (d. 1380) and Columba of Rieti (d. 1501): see Caroline Walker Bynum, *Holy Feast and Holy Fast: The Religious Significance of Food to Medieval Women* (Berkeley, CA, 1987), p. 146.
16. *Vespasian Ritual for the Ordination of Nuns*, in *Three Middle English*

Versions of the Rule of St Benet and Two Contemporary Rituals for the Ordination of Nuns, ed. Ernst E. Kock, EETS OS 120 (London, 1902), pp. 145–50 (p. 146).

17   Hugh of St Victor, De Sacramentis, PL 176, col. 421.
18   Ruth Mellinkoff, Outcasts: Signs of Otherness in Northern European Art of the Late Middle Ages, 2 vols (Berkeley, CA, 1993), vol. 1, pp. 181–2.
19   2 Samuel 14: 26; Judges 16: 17.
20   Leviticus 21: 5.
21   Mellinkoff, Outcasts, vol. 1, p. 182; Gobillot, 'Sur la tonsure chrétienne', p. 404.
22   William H. W. Fanning, 'Tonsure', in The Catholic Encyclopedia, 17 vols (New York, 1907–18), vol. 14 (1912), p. 779.
23   Clement of Alexandria, Christ the Educator, tr. Simon P. Wood (Washington, DC, 1954), pp. 214–15.
24   Ibid., p. 215.
25   Edward James, 'Bede and the tonsure question', Peritia: Journal of the Medieval Academy of Ireland, 3 (1984): 85–98 (p. 89), quoting VI Toledo (638), constitution 17, in Concilios visigóticos e hispano-romanos, ed. José Vives, Tomás Marín Martínez and Gonzalo Martínez Díez, España Christiana, Textos I (Madrid, 1963), pp. 244–5.
26   Gregory of Tours, The History of the Franks, tr. Lewis Thorpe (London, 1974), p. 156 (book 2, ch. 41). For further discussion, see James, 'Bede and the tonsure question', pp. 91–2.
27   Gregory of Tours, History of the Franks, pp. 180–1 (book 3, ch. 18).
28   Beroul, The Romance of Tristan and the Tale of Tristan's Madness, tr. Alan S. Fredrick (London, 1970), p. 153. On the association between fools and shaved heads or tonsures, see Angelika Gross and Jacqueline T. Schaefer, 'Sémiotiques de la tonsure de l'"insipiens" à Tristan et aux fous de Dieu', in Le clerc au moyen âge (Aix-en-Provence, 1995), pp. 245–75.
29   The Cyrurgie of Guy de Chauliac, ed. Margaret S. Ogden, EETS OS 265 (Oxford, 1971), pp. 422, 426; Joan Cadden, Meanings of Sex Difference in the Middle Ages (Cambridge, 1993), pp. 181–2.
30   William Langland, The Vision of Piers Plowman: A Critical Edition of the B-Text Based on Trinity College Cambridge MS B.15.17, ed. A. V. C. Schmidt (London, 1995), pp. 353–4 (Passus XX, ll. 195–8).
31   Geoffrey Chaucer, The Riverside Chaucer, 3rd edn, ed. Larry D. Benson (Oxford, 1987), pp. 203, 207 (ll. 43, 309).
32   Richard Bernheimer, Wild Men in the Middle Ages: A Study in Art, Sentiment, and Demonology (Cambridge, MA, 1952), pp. 121–75.
33   Michael Camille, Mirror in Parchment: The Luttrell Psalter and the Making of Medieval England (London, 1998), p. 291.
34   Cadden, Meanings of Sex Difference, p. 182.
35   Jacqueline Murray's essay in the present volume discusses some of the paradoxes inherent in clerical attempts to negotiate and represent their own masculinity as strong yet celibate.

[36] G. R. Owst, *Literature and Pulpit in Medieval England: A Neglected Chapter in the History of English Letters and of the English People* (Cambridge, 1933), p. 262.

[37] Chaucer, *Riverside Chaucer*, pp. 69–70 (ll. 3314–16).

[38] Langland, *Piers Plowman*, p. 181 (Passus XI, ll. 296–300).

[39] *Testament*, in François Villon, *Complete Poems*, ed. and tr. Barbara Sargent-Baur (Toronto, 1994), p. 184 (ll. 1896–7).

[40] *Meditation A*, in *Richard Rolle: Prose and Verse, Edited from MS Longleat 29 and Related Manuscripts*, ed. S. J. Ogilvie-Thomson, EETS OS 293 (Oxford, 1988), pp. 64–8 (p. 65).

[41] Mellinkoff, *Outcasts*, vol. 1, pp. 181–94, especially p. 184; James H. Marrow, *Passion Iconography in Northern European Art of the Late Middle Ages and Early Renaissance* (Kurtrijk, 1979), pp. 68–76.

[42] Mellinkoff, *Outcasts*, p. 184; Marrow, *Passion Iconography*, pp. 70 and 277, n. 275.

[43] Christopher Newfield, 'The politics of male suffering: masochism and hegemony in the American renaissance', *differences*, 1, 3 (1989), 55–87; Amelia Jones, 'Dis/playing the phallus: male artists perform their masculinities', *Art History*, 17 (1994), 546–84.

[44] On the decline and disappearance of the Christian tonsure, see Trichet, *La Tonsure*, pp. 165–77.

[45] Victor Turner, *The Ritual Process: Structure and Anti-Structure* (New York, 1969), especially pp. 166–203; Arnold van Gennep, *The Rites of Passage*, tr. Monika B. Vizedom and Gabrielle L. Caffee (London, 1960), p. 106; Howard Eilberg-Schwartz, 'Introduction: the spectacle of the female head', in Howard Eilberg-Schwartz and Wendy Doniger (eds), *Off with her Head! The Denial of Women's Identity in Myth, Religion and Culture* (Berkeley, CA, 1995), pp. 1–13; Edmund Leach, 'Magical hair', *Man: Journal of the Royal Anthropological Institute*, 88 (1958), 147–68; James, 'Bede and tonsure question', p. 95.

[46] Peter Abelard, *Historia calamitatum*, PL 178, cols 206D and 207A; Yves Ferroul, 'Abelard's blissful castration', in Jeffrey Jerome Cohen and Bonnie Wheeler (eds), *Becoming Male in the Middle Ages* (New York, 1997), pp. 129–49 (p. 142).

[47] Robert Mills, 'A man is being beaten', *New Medieval Literatures*, 5 (2002), 115–53.

9

Christian Sanctuary and Repository of France's Political Culture: The Construction of Holiness and Masculinity at the Royal Abbey of Saint-Denis, 987–1328

DAWN MARIE HAYES

The later medieval church of Saint-Denis was at one and the same time a holy sanctuary and an important centre of French political culture.[1] Tradition held that the abbey church had been consecrated by Christ himself and this encouraged people to venerate as relics the ruins of the early medieval churches on which it laid. The special status of the church derived from the relics it housed: the bones of St Denis, protector of the realm and patron of the king.[2] In this sacred space spiritual authority and monarchical might fused, elevating each other to create a unique repository for both powers. As a church that served as custodian to some of the best-known symbols of France's political and military power, Saint-Denis offers us a unique opportunity to observe a particular set of relationships between holiness and masculinity in the Middle Ages. These were shaped by the agendas of the Capetians and the monks of Saint-Denis. We can see the interplay between holiness and masculinity both within the abbey itself and informing wider representations of the Capetian kings.

I would like to begin by considering the abbey itself and the ways in which its monks perceived it in specifically gendered terms. During the years 987–1328, which bracket direct Capetian rule in France, the institutions of monarchy and monasticism joined forces as each shared its distinctive powers and prestige with the other. United in a lord–vassal relationship solidified in the late eleventh century, the Capetian kings and the monks of Saint-Denis carefully cultivated a masculine culture at the abbey that was founded on the belief that each protected the other and that together they defended the interests of the kingdom. Adding nuance to this alliance between the Capetians and the royal abbey was the medieval perception of churches as female bodies that offered sustenance to their communities, similar to the way mothers nurture their young. Suger, the famous twelfth-century abbot of Saint-Denis who played such an important role in its design and appearance, clearly related to his abbey church as a son does to a mother. In his *Libellus Alter de Consecratione Ecclesiae Sancti Dionysii* (On Consecration) Suger discusses the monastery's resolve for the expansion of the church, the mother of his fraternal community.[3] In his *Liber de Rebus in Administratione Sua Gestis* (On Administration) he refers to the church as having fostered his brothers and sons from 'mother's milk to old age'.[4]

The fact that the great abbot had been handed over to the abbey as an oblate at the age of 10 gives us pause to consider the possible emotional ramifications as the pre-pubescent boy transferred his identity from his family to the community of monks. John Benton notes that although the names of his father, a brother and a sister-in-law have been recorded, we do not know Suger's mother's name and he did not mention her in his writings.[5] Whether she was alive or not when he entered the monastery remains uncertain, but it is very clear that his filial feelings were fully directed at 'mother church'. At other times the monks conceived of a different relationship with the church-as-female: Suger states that, according to custom, the community granted to a number of chapels a dowry to offset the costs of their lights.[6] Just as brides had dowries, so too did many churches and chapels, including those at Saint-Denis; before Christ could be married to his bride the monks had to settle proper dowries for her upkeep. Suger and his monks, therefore, perceived the church at Saint-Denis as a feminine body and, moreover, as occupying specific familial and social roles in relation to themselves. In becoming monks they had relinquished these relationships with women as mothers and wives, as well as the masculine identities that accompanied the roles of son and husband. But here we see the monks replicating both the relationships and the roles in their representations of the church. Their status as guardians of the church was therefore predicated, in part, on the standards of lay masculinity, whereby men were expected to honour and protect their female relations. Indeed, by taking the abbey as a spiritual bride, the monks could become spiritual fathers and raise spiritual children within the monastery.[7]

The extremely masculine nature of monastic culture at the abbey was probably, at least in part, a result of the abbey's close links to the monarchy, for it was constructed both by the monks and by the Capetian kings. The monks wanted to identify their abbey more closely with the emerging monarchy while the kings busily worked to infuse their reigns with a sacred character.[8] The documentary connection between the two was established early, perhaps during the sixth century, when the royal court began to deposit at the abbey copies of royal documents that would become the seeds for the writing of many of the early histories of France, including the famed *Grandes Chroniques* (Great Chronicles) also known as the *Chroniques de Saint-Denis*.[9] At times the association between king and abbot became extremely close, so close that they could assume each other's responsibilities. During Louis VII's absence Suger became regent of France and, as John Benton notes, for all practical purposes was 'chief of state' for two years as the king participated in the Second Crusade from 1147 to 1149.[10] It was after this experience that Suger's role as abbot, or spiritual father, assumed an even greater dimension when he received the secular-sounding masculine epithet, 'father of the fatherland'.[11] Although primarily a man of peace, the pious abbot did not refrain from participating in battle and had accompanied Louis VI on a number of expeditions.[12] And for two decades he was a major player in the diplomatic relations between Louis VI and Henry I of England.[13]

Another example of an abbot from Saint-Denis serving as regent of France is Matthew of Vendôme, who served for Louis IX during the crusade of 1270. Although the reigns fall outside the scope of this article, it should be noted that power could also transfer in the other direction, such as when a number of late Carolingian kings became lay abbots of Saint-Denis, a practice begun by Charles the Bald. Most of his successors continued this tradition, which was not ended until Hugh Capet relinquished it as part of the monastery's reform in the tenth century.[14] If the roles of king and abbot could be, on occasion, interchangeable, this would account for the importance of hegemonic masculinity to the public identity of the abbot: a variety of active, lay masculinity that he would not usually be expected to perform. Indeed, this contention is illustrated by the fact that, although Suger appears to have been fairly comfortable with his role as peacemaker and protector of France, alongside the king, he was apparently uneasy about his military past. Writing at about the age of 60, Suger uses his 'On Administration' and *Ordinatio A.D. MCLX uel MCLXI* (Ordinance of 1140 or 1141) to express regret about taking up arms.[15] Suger is reassured that this role was divinely sanctioned by comparing himself to the biblical King David. Suger rejoiced that, unlike David, God did not refuse him the privilege of building a house of worship.[16] Instead, God's forgiveness of him was made manifest by the fact that Suger was permitted to refashion Saint-Denis, one of the most beautiful churches of the period. David was not as lucky; the task of building the Temple was left to David's son, Solomon, whom God calls 'a man of peace'. It should be kept in mind that Suger's regret here was expressed in retrospect; at the time it seemed that he was quite prepared to take on all the qualities required of a surrogate king.

Thus, in partnership with the king of France, the church of Saint-Denis, and in particular its abbot, provided spiritual and physical protection for the French realm and its people. Its role as defender of France was reflected in the very architecture of the building. In *The Royal Abbey of Saint-Denis* Sumner McKnight Crosby argues that the church's exterior façade was divided into two themes that made statements about the forces it harnessed: powers that were both holy and masculine. Crosby notes that the west façade included symbols of secular, royal authority that were distinct from those of the authority of the church, which were concentrated at the eastern end, the part which was dominated by the clergy.[17] For example, the west façade of the church contained crenellations that, Crosby suggests, 'remind us that the patron saint was protector of the monarchy and that the church guarded the regalia and oriflamme'[18] (Figure 9.1).

Crosby's interpretation is in keeping with the intentions of Suger, who stated that the crenellations were made 'both for the beauty of the church and, should circumstances require it, for *practical purposes*' (my emphasis).[19] The crenellations fitted with the rest of the complex, including the Porte de Suger, the monastery's principal gate, which, according to F. N. Martinet's engraving, included fortified towers capped by even more crenellations[20] (Figure 9.2).

The church's architecture, therefore, reflected the community's concern to be both a holy sanctuary and a defensive structure that

Figure 9.1. Sumner McKnight Crosby's reconstruction of Saint-Denis's west façade as imagined by Suger. Drawing by Gregory Robertson. From S. M. Crosby, *The Royal Abbey of Saint-Denis from its Beginnings to the Death of Suger, 475–1151*, ed. and completed by Pamela Z. Blum (London and New Haven, 1987), p. 172, fig. 72. By permission of the press

Figure 9.2. F. N. Martinet's engraving of the main entrance to the abbey as it may have looked during Suger's abbacy. From Crosby, *Royal Abbey*, p. 125, fig. 44. By permission of the press

protected against threatening forces. Abbey and kingdom were further linked by the statue-columns of Saint-Denis' west façade, which displayed prophets, priests and kings from the Old Testament – 'forbears and models of the French *regnum* and *sacerdotium*'.[21] Crosby even suggests that the west façade's three arches might have been modelled on the well-known triumphal arches of Constantine or the one that existed at Orange, which Suger probably had seen with his own eyes.[22] The relationship between holiness and masculinity is even emphasized in the rare image of Christ in the tympanum of the central portal of the west façade, which simultaneously portrays him as the

Figure 9.3. Christ on the tympanum of the west façade's central portal. From Crosby, *Royal Abbey*, p. 185, fig. 79. By permission of the press

enthroned Son of God and the crucified Son of Man (Figure 9.3). To use Crosby's phrase, '[h]e is at once seated on his throne and suspended on the cross', revealing his divine and human natures.[23]

Behind Saint-Denis's impressive façade and within its sanctuary walls were contained extraordinarily valuable symbols of political authority. The abbey was the custodian of the regalia, the symbols of authority used at royal coronations, which usually included some variation of crown, orb, vestments, fibulae, armband and dagger.[24] King Eudes had removed the regalia for his coronation in 888 and his successors were slow in returning them. After receiving the orb in 987 and crown during the reign of Philip I (r. 1052–1108), Louis VI signed an official document that restored the regalia to the abbey in 1120.[25] In 1261 the Capetian saint, Louis IX, agreed that the regalia would be permanently stored in the abbey's treasury and taken to Reims on the occasion of a royal coronation. As Anne Robertson notes, thirteenth- and fourteenth-century ordinaries from Reims make it clear that the abbot was always present to guard the treasures.[26] This agreement was important since it gave Saint-Denis a prominent role in the creation of French kings, emphasizing the part the abbey played in their consecration while increasing the competition between the community and the archbishop of Reims. The cathedral used alternative traditions to try and establish its primacy over Saint-Denis, but was not successful in this respect.[27] The collection of regalia continued to expand until it was scattered and some objects melted down during the Revolution.[28] As only a man could rule France the regalia can be identified as specifically masculine emblems of power.

Another symbol of masculinity stored at Saint-Denis was the oriflamme, the red battle flag that the marshal of France's armies received during the mass that preceded the king's departure for war.[29] Suger relates that in 1124 Louis took the banner from the high altar of the abbey as a sign of recognition that St Denis was the 'special patron, and after God, the most powerful protector of the kingdom'.[30] This act reinforced the notion emphasized during the reign of Philip I that the king was the vassal of the monastery while lending a sacred character to the impending conflict.[31] Guided by the banner Louis managed to rally enough opposition to prevent the Germans and English from joining forces and the intended invasion of France ended in failure. Suger notes that this was a remarkable event since the king put aside his dignity and engaged in the task of a simple knight.[32] Later in the same century Philip took 'the oriflamme or vexillum' from Saint-Denis's altar as he embarked on the Third Crusade. The standard followed the holy cross carried by the papal legate during Louis IX's attack on Damietta.[33] And Philip IV attributed his success against Flanders in 1304 to St Denis, under whose banner he fought.[34] Indeed, custody of the oriflamme was a privilege that set Saint-Denis apart from other churches and monasteries in a highly competitive spiritual climate; as France's armies charged into the manly sport of war, they were guided – literally and figuratively – by a battle standard that had been charged by the relics of numerous saints and sheltered in this most holy of Christian sanctuaries.[35]

So far the focus of this study has been the political and military culture of Saint-Denis and how it contributed to the abbey's rich and complicated relationship with holiness and masculinity. Yet Capetian-centred evidence also highlights this relationship. For example, as noted above, to be a Capetian monarch was to be a male.[36] Vern Bullough has observed that, in the Middle Ages, a man's maleness was felt to be demonstrated by the sex of his child.[37] Furthermore, Jacqueline Murray has noted that

> The manner in which duty and responsibility could influence and define gender was perhaps nowhere as central as in the role and image of the

king. At this highest level of society, the expectations and imperatives to manliness, masculine prowess and bravery, patriarchal authority, sapiential wisdom and good governance all intersected. The king had much invested in his appropriation and performance of masculine identities.[38]

What, therefore, might have been suggested about a king's masculinity if he had been incapable of producing a son? Fortunately, one of the Capetian dynasty's most notable achievements was consistently to produce male heirs throughout its 341-year history. The Capetians' lucky streak continued until 1328, when Charles IV died without a male heir and the title of king passed to the Valois line, ultimately leading to the Hundred Years War. As the concept of male succession developed throughout the Capetian centuries, so too did the idea of the holy king.[39] Andrew Lewis locates the first uses of holiness as a royal attribute in late twelfth-century documents written to celebrate the birth of Philip Augustus 'Dieudonné', who, as this epithet demonstrates, was thought to have been given to Louis VII by God, because Louis had been married three times and had to wait many years for the birth of a son.[40] To Giles of Paris Philip was the sacred portion taken from his father's loins. Later William the Breton referred to the gestating Louis VIII, Philip's son, as the holy burden in his mother's womb.[41]

The Capetian kings' reputation for holiness was built on two principles: the kings were the vassals of God and St Denis and, due to their promise to serve both lords, they were able to access divine power for the good of the kingdom. That the Capetians had special relationships with God and the patron saint of France was revealed in personal behaviours that demonstrated the legitimacy of the dynasty: Louis VI died a monk; the relics of Philip Augustus were said to have miraculous powers and the dead king was believed to have appeared to people accompanied by St Denis; and Louis VII, Louis VIII, St Louis and Philip III were all praised for their chastity.[42] Of all the powers that the Capetians were said to possess, perhaps the one that demonstrated their holiness most dramatically was the miraculous royal touch that they used to cure scrofula[43] (Figure 9.4).

Another powerful statement of the holiness of the Capetian kings came with the adoption of the fleur-de-lis into the dynasty's symbology. A sign of christological and Marian significance, Brigitte Bedos Rezak observes that the fleur-de-lis begins to appear on Louis VII's seals during the last quarter of the twelfth century.[44] At Saint-Denis the tree in the Tree of Jesse window (c.1144) was replaced by a

Figure 9.4. Louis IX cures scrofula, *Grandes chroniques de France*, British Library, Royal 16 G VI, fo. 424ᵛ. By permission of the British Library

large fleur-de-lis in an effort to 'establish a visual bond between the Capetian kings, as represented by their heraldic symbol, and the kings of the Old Testament . . . and to affirm, by means of the culminating figure of Christ, the divine character of the Capetian monarchy'.[45] Use of this symbol, which some people considered to represent the Trinity, also suggested a link between the kings and the Godhead itself.[46] By the fifteenth century many people in France believed that their kings were born with the mark of the fleur-de-lis on their bodies, though during the Capetian centuries the royal birthmark had been thought to be a cross.[47] Whatever its shape, it is clear that by the thirteenth century popular legend held that the kings of France were born with a sacred symbol on their bodies that announced their legitimacy to rule, symbols that were painted and in relief (along with the arms of Castille) inside the abbey church.[48] Thus individual behaviours, healing miracles and sacred symbology were used to foster and popularize a sacred character for the Capetian monarchs.

The union between the holy Capetians and the abbey of Saint-Denis was most visible in the burials of the kings in the monastic church.

There, inside its walls, the two façades of Christian sacred space – building and body – became one.[49] During the late twelfth and thirteenth centuries, attitudes towards the remains of the kings had changed as people began to lavish upon them the same kind of attention given to the relics of saints.[50] This did not escape the attention of the monks of Saint-Denis. Hoping that it would become a royal cemetery for many years, by the thirteenth century the monks expanded the transept in all four directions to accommodate the growing number of corpses.[51] The Capetian king who oversaw the tomb programme, Louis IX, was eager to establish Saint-Denis as a royal necropolis; it also was his wish to reserve burial at the abbey to the males who continued the dynastic line, a strategy that would have further emphasized the bond between the male kings and the holy monastery. In fact, his actions may have been somewhat defensive for Wright argues that 'the tomb program was conceived in a period when men were conscious of the frailty of the king's newly-won territorial and political power and equally conscious of the political power of the mystique of kingship'.[52] The tradition of burying France's kings in the abbey may have begun as early as the sixth century, but it was during Capetian reign that the practice became regular. Only two kings of the dynasty, Philip I and Louis VII, were buried elsewhere. The others were all laid to rest at Saint-Denis.

Three tombs probably attracted the greatest amount of contemporary attention: those of Philip Augustus, Louis VIII and St Louis IX.[53] There is evidence that all of these monuments were covered in silver and gold. Suspended over the tombs were golden boxes, perhaps suggesting that the surrounding area, nestled between two altars, functioned as a shrine and the boxes contained relics, remains of the holy kings.[54] Brown argues that the kings, like saints,

> were becoming first quasi- and then fully public persons and their bodies thus, in a sense, the possessions of their own faithful, the subjects whom they ruled. The elevation of the spiritual status of the kings of France, which was fully developed by the mid-fourteenth century, in part accounts for the changed attitude to the king's earthly body. Further, respect for royal remains signaled the increased reverence for the king and crown which emerged in the later Middle Ages, and also the greater impressiveness of the king's power over the kingdom, reflected both in his legislative authority and the ceremonial of the court.[55]

St Louis, through his roles as father, monarch, crusader, pious Christian and, in death, miracle-worker, may have better embodied the ideal combination of holiness and masculinity than any monarch of the Middle Ages. His connection to St Denis was firm; even when the king was away from the abbey and in residence in Paris he likely worshipped in a chapel dedicated to the saint that was conveniently located next to his bedroom.[56] That the king had struck an ideal balance between holiness and masculinity in life was testified to by the miracles that occurred at his tomb in death, which contributed to the sacred profile of an already holy place.[57] The balance was maintained in the first chapel dedicated at the abbey to the royal saint, completed around 1304, whose eight glass panels portrayed Louis as brave crusader, pious prisoner, instructive father, disciplined penitent, dedicated leader, charitable almsgiver, dying king and venerated saint. With the exception of the imprisonment, all events were included in the office for Louis's feast day, composed after 1301.[58] The altar consisted of three strata: the top or retable contained scenes of miracles performed by Louis and vows made to him; the bottom depicted scenes from the king's earthly life. A crucifix that graced the centre layer joined both strata.[59]

To conclude, by the early fourteenth century the two cornerstones of Capetian kingship – male blood-right and holy character – had been closely associated in the Capetian royal court.[60] Holiness and masculinity had been joined in the community of Saint-Denis as well as in the person of the Capetian monarch. Although the two ingredients may have been combined in different proportions, the recipes for the success of each were very similar. And as the Middle Ages wore on they blended – literally and figuratively – at the royal abbey, where the holiness and masculinity of the kings fused with the holiness and masculinity of the abbey itself. The power that emanated from both combined to create an immaterial substance of power from which monarchy and monastery would sculpt their increasingly complex identities and wage their campaigns of self-promotion. Yet although their relationship was in many ways rooted in self-interest, it was also mutually beneficial, with each contributing to the welfare of the other. The monks of Saint-Denis and the Capetian kings received and mediated God's protective power. The monks were the custodians of the protection offered by the relics of St Denis as well as the 'royal relics' such as the Crown of Thorns and the Holy Nail, which they used for the benefit of the kings of France.[61] The Capetian kings, on the other hand, defended the interests of the abbey. Yet the exchange of protective power did not stop there; France also benefited from these relationships as the kings protected its physical interests while the abbey tended to its spiritual well-being. Such was the balance achieved between holiness and masculinity in Capetian France.

Notes

This essay is dedicated to my mother, Anne Tabony. I would like to thank Mr Trevor Smith of the Borough of Manhattan Community College's A. Philip Randolph Memorial Library and the staff at the New York Public Library's Humanities and Social Sciences Library for their assistance in locating a number of the sources on which this study draws.

1. Like Sumner McKnight Crosby's convention I will distinguish the saint from the abbey. I refer to the former as *St Denis* and to the latter as *Saint-Denis* (hyphenated). See Crosby, *The Royal Abbey of Saint-Denis from its Beginnings to the Death of Suger, 475–1151*, ed. and completed by Pamela Z. Blum (London and New Haven, 1987), p. 453 and 'Introduction to Part I'. Other important studies of the medieval history of the abbey include: Caroline Astrid Bruzelius, *The Thirteenth-Century Church at St.-Denis* (London and New Haven, 1985); Paula Gerson (ed.), *Abbot Suger and Saint-Denis: A Symposium* (New York, 1986); Anne Lombard-Jourdan, *Montjoie et Saint-Denis: le centre de la Gaule aux origines de Paris et de Saint-Denis* (Paris, 1989); and Françoise Autrand, Claude Gauvard and Jean-Marie Moeglin (eds), *Saint-Denis et la royauté* (Paris, 1999).
2. Crosby, *Royal Abbey*, pp. 122–3; see also Anne Lombard-Jourdan, 'La légende de la consécration par le Christ de la basilique mérovingienne de Saint-Denis et de la guérison des lépreux', *Bulletin Monumental*, 143 (1985), 237–69.
3. Erwin Panofsky (ed. and tr.), *Abbot Suger: On the Abbey Church of St.-Denis and its Art Treasures*, 2nd edn, Latin text and English tr. on facing pages (Princeton, 1979), pp. 98–9.
4. Ibid., pp. 40–1: 'sicut a corpore ecclesiae beatissimorum martyrum Dionysii, Rustici et Eleutherii, quae nos quam dulcissime a mamilla usque in senectam fovit.'
5. John Benton, 'Introduction: Suger's life and personality', in *Abbot Suger and Saint-Denis*, pp. 3–15.
6. Panofsky, *Abbot Suger*, pp. 98–9: 'Nos autem tantae benedictionis pro fructu impensi laboris Dei dono participes effici toto affectu desiderantes, quasi pro dote, sicut solet fieri, ad expensas emendorum luminariorum, plateam quandam cimeterio collimitantem juxta ecclesiam sancti Michaelis, quam quarter viginti libris a Willelmo Cornillonensi emeramus.' 'Dos' could mean 'wedding gift' as well as 'church endowment'.

7   For more on spiritual fatherhood, see Megan McLaughlin, 'Secular and spiritual fatherhood in the eleventh century', in Jacqueline Murray (ed.), *Conflicted Identities and Multiple Masculinities: Men in the Medieval West* (London and New York, 1999), pp. 25–44, where she explores 'how, deprived of biological fatherhood, medieval clerics, nevertheless constructed roles for themselves as spiritual fathers, capable of begetting and raising "children of the faith"', pp. xiii–iv.
8   See, for example, Andrew W. Lewis, *Royal Succession in Capetian France: Studies on Familial Order and the State* (London and Cambridge, MA, 1981) and Gabrielle M. Spiegel, 'The cult of Saint Denis and Capetian kingship', *Journal of Medieval History*, 1 (1975), 43–69.
9   Crosby, *Royal Abbey*, p. 9; Jules Viard (ed.), *Les grandes chroniques de France*, 10 vols (Paris, 1920–53).
10 Benton, 'Introduction: Suger's life and personality', p. 6.
11 Ibid. William of Saint-Denis, Suger's biographer, refers to him as: 'tam a populo quam principe pater appellatus est patriae', *Vita Sugerii*, p. 398. As already noted, the image of spiritual fatherhood was a conventional one for an abbot, but this title appears to have more firmly lay connotations, especially given the context.
12 For a discussion of how Suger's writings – particularly his *Deeds of Louis the Fat* – help modern historians better understand twelfth-century warfare see Michel Bur, 'Suger et l'art militaire de son temps', *Académie des Inscriptions et Belles-Lettres: Comptes-Rendus des Séances*, 3 (1994), 689–704.
13 Benton, 'Introduction: Suger's life and personality', p. 6.
14 See Bruzelius, *Thirteenth-Century Church*, p. 9.
15 Panofsky, *Abbot Suger*, pp. 44–5; see also the *Ordinatio*, pp. 122–3.
16 1 Chronicles 22: 8: 'But the word of the Lord came to [David], saying: "You have shed much blood and have waged great wars; you shall not build a house to my name, because you have shed so much blood in my sight on the earth."'
17 Crosby, *Royal Abbey*, p. 281.
18 Ibid., p. 282.
19 Panofsky, *Abbot Suger*, pp. 46–7. Note that the Latin word Suger uses for crenellations, 'propugnacula', has a much more bellicose tone than its English translation.
20 Crosby, *Royal Abbey*, p. 124 and figs 44 and 125. See also p. 482, n. 24, which notes that the engraving was first published in Edme Beguillet and J.-Ch. Poncelin de la Roche, *Description historique de Paris et de ses plus beaux monuments gravés en taille douce par F. N. Martinet* (Paris, 1780), vol. 2, p. 122.
21 Georgia Sommers Wright, 'A royal tomb program in the reign of St. Louis', *The Art Bulletin*, 56 (1974), 224–43.
22 Crosby, *Royal Abbey*, p. 282. See also Paula Gerson, 'The west façade of St. Denis: an iconographical study' (unpublished Ph.D. thesis, Columbia University, 1970).

23 Crosby, *Royal Abbey*, p. 184.
24 On the regalia see Gabrielle M. Spiegel, *The Chronicle Tradition of Saint-Denis* (Brookline, MA, 1978), pp. 31–3; Percy E. Schramm, *Der König von Frankreich*, 2 vols (Weimar, 1960), pp. 132 and 204–15; and Sumner McKnight Crosby, *L'abbaye royale de Saint-Denis* (Paris, 1953), pp. 8–9.
25 Crosby, *Royal Abbey*, p. 11.
26 Anne Walters Robertson, *The Service-Books of the Royal Abbey of Saint-Denis* (Oxford and New York, 1991), p. 50, n. 215: 'que omnia abbas beati dyonisii in Francia de monasterio suo debet Reims adportare, et stans ad altare custodire'. Reims, Bibliothèque de la Cathédrale, 330 (fourteenth century). Robertson notes that slightly modified versions of this passage also may be found in Reims, Bibliothèque de la Cathédrale, 328 (thirteenth century) and in Reims, Bibliothèque de la Cathédrale, 329 (fourteenth century).
27 Crosby, *Royal Abbey*, p. 10.
28 Ibid., p. 11. See Michel Félibien, *Histoire de l'abbaye royale de Saint-Denys en France* (Paris, 1706), pp. 536, 538, 540, 542, 544 and plates I–V.
29 For further information on the oriflamme, see Laura Hibbard Loomis, 'The oriflamme of France and the war-cry "Monjoie" in the twelfth century', in Dorothy Miner (ed.), *Studies in Art and Literature for Belle de Costa Greene* (Princeton, 1954), pp. 67–82; and Philippe Contamine, 'L'oriflamme de Saint-Denis aux XIVe et XVe siècles: étude de symbolique religieuse et royale', *Annales de l'Est*, 25 (1973), 179–244. For a discussion of the mass that directly preceded the reception of the standard, see Robertson, *Service-Books*, pp. 97–8.
30 Crosby, *Royal Abbey*, p. 11. Also p. 460, n. 74.
31 Bruzelius, *Thirteenth-Century Church*, pp. 9–10.
32 Ronald James Braud, 'Suger and the making of the French nation' (unpublished Ph.D. thesis, University of Southwestern Louisiana, 1977), p. 330.
33 Spiegel, 'Cult of Saint Denis', 43–69.
34 Ibid.
35 Contamine, 'L'oriflamme de Saint-Denis', 179–244. See especially p. 207.
36 On Capetian royal succession see Lewis, *Royal Succession*, passim.
37 V. L. Bullough, 'On being male in the Middle Ages', in C. A. Lees (ed.), *Medieval Masculinities: Regarding Men in the Middle Ages* (Minneapolis, MN, 1994), pp. 31–45.
38 Murray, 'Introduction', *Conflicted Identities*, pp. ix–xx (pp. xviii–xix).
39 Lewis, *Royal Succession*, pp. 122–33.
40 Ibid., p. 122.
41 Ibid.
42 Ibid., pp. 129 and 278–9, nn. 114–21. See also John W. Baldwin, *The Government of Philip Augustus: Foundations of French Royal Power in the Middle Ages* (Oxford and Berkeley, CA, 1986), pp. 391–92.
43 Marc Bloch, *The Royal Touch: Monarchy and Miracles in France and England*, tr. J. E. Anderson (New York, 1961). Medieval writers had claimed thaumaturgic power for all but three of the kings, though it was

44 Rezak, 'Suger and the symbolism of royal power: the seal of Louis VII', in Gerson, *Abbot Suger and Saint Denis*, pp. 95–103.
45 Ibid., p. 100.
46 Lewis, *Royal Succession*, p. 148.
47 Bloch, *Royal Touch*, pp. 141–5. See also Ferdinand Lot, 'La croix des royaux de France', *Romania*, 20 (1891), 278–81 and Antoine Thomas, 'Le "signe royal" et le secret de Jeanne d'Arc', *Revue Historique*, 103 (1910), 278–82.
48 Bruzelius, *Thirteenth-Century Church*, p. 12.
49 For more on the royal tombs, see Wright, 'Royal tomb program'; Alain Erlande-Brandenburg, *Le roi est mort: étude sur les funérailles, les sépultures, et les tombeaux des rois de France jusqu'à la fin du XIIIème siècle* (Paris and Geneva, 1975).
50 Elizabeth A. R. Brown, 'Burying and unburying the kings of France', in Richard C. Trexler (ed.), *Persons in Groups: Social Behavior as Identity Formation in Medieval and Renaissance Europe* (Binghamton, NY, 1985), pp. 241–66.
51 Bruzelius, *Thirteenth-Century Church*, p. 36; Spiegel, 'Cult of Saint Denis', *passim*.
52 Wright, 'Royal tomb program', 243; Brown, 'Burying and unburying', *passim*.
53 Wright, 'Royal tomb program', 241–66.
54 Lewis, *Royal Succession*, pp. 132–3.
55 Brown, 'Burying and unburying', p. 241.
56 Bruzelius, *Thiteenth-Century Church*, p. 12.
57 It should be noted, though, that Louis's piety also included characteristics that were traditionally seen as feminine. Renate Blumenfeld-Kosinski argues that by manifesting the virtues of hands-on charity and peacemaking Louis IX performed roles usually allotted to women saints and, therefore, transgressed gender boundaries. Yet Louis's concern for these virtues may have been influenced by a practical concern: political rebellion. If this indeed was the case, then the traditionally feminine manifestations of Louis's piety can be seen as ultimately underpinning his masculine roles of maintaining political power over his realm. Renate Blumenfeld-Kosinski, 'Saintly scenarios in Christine de Pizan's *Livre des trois vertus*', *Medieval Studies*, 62 (2000), 255–92.
58 Elizabeth A. R. Brown, 'The chapels and cult of Saint Louis at Saint Denis', *Medievalia*, 10 (1984), 279–331.
59 Ibid.
60 Lewis, *Royal Succession*, p. 125.
61 Perhaps another sign of the bond between abbey and monarchy, Colette Beaune observes that the monks of Saint-Denis credited cures obtained at the abbey to the Crown of Thorns and the Holy Nail rather than the relics of St Denis. The 'royal relics' had been deposited there in the ninth century by Charles the Bald. Colette Beaune, *Naissance de la nation France* (Paris, 1985), p. 94.

10

Self-Mastery and Submission: Holiness and Masculinity in the Lives of Anglo-Saxon Martyr-Kings

EDWARD CHRISTIE

The original cover of Kaja Silverman's influential book, *Male Subjectivity at the Margins*, is a slightly cropped image of a medieval painting. Andrea Mantegna's portrayal of St Sebastian (1480) depicts the muscular, statuesque saint bound to a ruined Roman column. The saint's mostly naked body is marred only by understated trickles of blood, and stands in a conventional posture (observable in similar fifteenth-century portaits of his passion by Piero de la Francesca, Antonello de Messina and Alessandro Botticelli). With one leg straight and the other slightly bent, his hip is thrust gently sideways, and with his arms tied behind his back, both his pelvis and chest are pushed slightly outwards. Despite being pierced by many arrows, his body shows no contortions of pain, but lines of suffering are etched on his face (by contrast with the smooth, youthful face of Mantegna's 1459 study of the same subject) and his upturned eyes seem to seek God's compassion and, indeed, release from his suffering. The same image is placed at the head of Silverman's fifth chapter, 'Masochism and male subjectivity', a chapter that compares the masochism theorized by Freud with the spectacle of Christian suffering, in which the body is 'centrally on display' and for which Christ's crucifixion is the 'master tableau'.[1] The portrayal of Sebastian's suffering, however, is never referred to in Silverman's argument. Nonetheless, the juxtaposition of this image with the argument suggests the symbolic importance of Christian suffering to the dynamics of medieval male subjectivity. Martyrdom and masochism, of course, cannot be equated, but the willingness with which martyrs often meet their death, their passivity in the face of aggressors, suggests the action of a death drive: a desire described by Freud in very biological terms as a bodily instinct to return to a state of quiescence such as that before birth.[2] Ælfric's lives of Anglo-Saxon martyr-kings reinforce, as do other Old English texts, a heroic ideology that finds its drive towards unity and peace manifested in the body of the sacrificed king. Their martyrdom may be seen as a kind of masochism and thus, as Silverman observes, 'has radically emasculating implications, and is in its purest forms intrinsically incompatible with the pretensions of masculinity'.[3] But is this true of the martyr-kings of whom Ælfric writes?

In the martyrdom of Saints Edmund and Oswald, the former of which the homilist Ælfric of Eynsham explicitly connects with the model of St Sebastian, masculinity is also connected to the models of heroic kingship depicted in poems like *Beowulf*. In their cases, however, we also see the potential for the emulation of Christ to undo their heroic identity. Ælfric's version of their respective passions is at pains to bypass these negative effects. If, as Silverman writes, the compulsion to re-enact past suffering (particularly the trauma of war) is driven by a desire for mastery, then the life and death of the martyred king represents submission as a new and better kind of mastery.[4] Taken together, the similarly structured passions of Anglo-Saxon kings, repeating the suffering of Sebastian, may be read as the cultural compulsion of a war-beset Christian nation. The deaths of these martyrs, narrated as they are, attempt to deny the masochistic, emasculating potential of Christian suffering and elevate it to a new position of power; to maintain, in other words, the symbolic equation of penis and phallus which sustains the ideological reality of our society, and, it has been argued, Anglo-Saxon society.[5] It is only through this denial that Ælfric may hope to reconcile heroic values with Christian ideology.

Ælfric's *Natale Sancti Oswaldi Regis et Martyris* (Life of Saint Oswald, King and Martyr) and *Passio Sancte Eadmundi Regis et Martyris* (Passion of St Edmund, King and Martyr) are the twenty-sixth and thirty-second items in his *Lives of Saints*. Represented by Walter Skeat, its editor for the Early English Text Society, as a third series in Ælfric's collections of Catholic homiles, this work was penned around 998, only a few years after Ælfric had completed his earlier volumes of homiles.[6] Bede records that the Northumbrian King

Oswald (d. 642) 'held under his sway all the peoples and kingdoms of Britain'.[7] Prior to Oswald's reign, Northumbria had been terrorized by the alliance of the British King Cadwalla and the Mercian Penda. The former, though a Christian, was according to Bede nonetheless a 'barbarian at heart' who raged with 'bestial cruelty'.[8] He was responsible for the deaths of several Northumbrian kings before Oswald, and was unstopped until Oswald met him at a place called 'Heavenfield' and, raising the sign of the cross, marched his inferior force to victory. Nine years later, however, Penda conquered Oswald at Maserfield, where Oswald's head and arm were cut off. This arm did not decay, the story goes, in accord with the blessing of Bishop Aidan, who had earlier grasped Oswald's hand in delight at Oswald's pious care for the poor and pronounced a blessing. Ælfric's version of Oswald's *vita* adheres to a typical formula. It recounts biographical details and the exemplary behaviour of the king, follows with an (albeit brief) account of his martyrdom, and ends by reporting the miracles attributed to him *post mortem*. The moment of death is not drawn out in Oswald's *vita* as it is in the passion of Sebastian or Edmund. Nonetheless, his decapitation and his death for the protection of his people demonstrate the same sacrificial dynamic. He dies, Ælfric reports, in the defence of his people, and when his death is inevitable, his final thoughts are for the well-being of his people: 'Þa geseah he genealecan his lifes geendunge and gebœd for his folc þe þær feallende sweolt' (then he saw approach his life's ending, and prayed for his people who died falling).[9]

Edmund was king of East Anglia from 855 until *c*.870, when he was killed by Viking invaders. Regarding Edmund's death, the *Anglo-Saxon Chronicle* records only that an invading army of Danes rode into East Anglia, where 'King Edmund fought against them, and the Danish took the victory, and killed the king, and conquered all that land'.[10] More elaborate traditions grew regarding the details of Edmund's death, and are reflected in the hagiographical account by Abbo of Fleury some hundred years later. The progress of events, as epitomized by Ælfric, is as follows. Having ravaged East Anglia, Danish invaders sent boasting messages to Edmund, demanding that Edmund surrender his people's wealth in order to save his own life and live as an under-king. Despite the advice of a convenient bishop, Edmund determines that he will neither capitulate nor flee. He returns the messenger to tell Hingwar that he will not submit unless Hingwar first converts to Christianity. At this Hingwar and his army arrive in

Edmund's hall to mock, beat and finally kill him by shooting him with arrows and cutting off his head.[11]

He was a good king, Ælfric writes, because he 'gewissode his folc / symle to riht-wisnysse, and þam reþum styrde' (guided he people ever to righteousness and controlled the violent).[12] Like the life of Oswald, that of Edmund emphasizes the role of the king as protector, controller of threats from outside. Sebastian, again, appears as the model of the protector. As Ælfric relates in his verson of the life of St Sebastian, when Christians flee Rome for fear of persecution by the Emperor Diocletian, among those who stay are the pope and Sebastian, whom the pope 'gesette him eallum to mund-boran' (constituted protector of them all).[13] The scene of martyrdom that passes so quickly as to be almost absent in Ælfric's life of Oswald, is at the core of the passion of Edmund. Edmund refuses to submit to a king whose military superiority is unquestionable. He refuses to save his own life by becoming Hingwar's 'under-kyning' (under-king) because Hingwar offers clemency only on the condition that Edmund 'dœlan þine digelan gold-hordas and þinra yldrena gestreon ardlice wið hine' (divide [his] hidden gold hoards and [his] ancestors' wealth quickly with him).[14] Edmund is seized by Hingwar's men and pierced with javelins 'oð þæt he eall wæs besæt mid heora scotungum swilce igles byrsta swa swa Sebastianus wæs' (until he was all beset with their shots as with porcupine bristles, just as Sebastian was).[15] When finally he is beheaded, the local people come out of hiding to find that the Vikings have hidden Edmund's head somewhere far from his body, but it is recovered by two miraculous events. First, a wolf, a creature renowned for its violent and voracious hunger but tamed by God, protects Edmund's head from other animals. Second, Edmund's head remains sentient, and calls out to his people so that they may locate it. Ælfric recounts later miracles associated with Edmund, mostly involving the suffering of those who seek to see the relics of saints. The hortatory purpose of his version of Edmund's passion appears not only to encourage the veneration of holy places, but also to curtail an unseemly popular fetish: to actually see or touch the saint's body.

Both of these lives represent the king as a source of unity against external threats of division, and this role is symbolized by the disintegration and mystical reintegration of the king's body. If decapitation is a symbolically emasculating gesture, Ælfric's Passion of St Edmund asks, what happens when the head keeps talking? The answer to this question, it will be seen, complicates the image of the warrior-aristocrat once typically taken to represent Anglo-Saxon masculinity. Scholarship regarding masculinity in Old English literature has, understandably, attempted to read poems such as *Beowulf* so that they might not be considered simply, as Gillian Overing has put it, 'tale[s] of men dying'.[16] Part of my purpose is nonetheless to explore the psychoanalytic reading of Anglo-Saxon heroism that Overing bypasses, since the passions of martyr-kings are by definition tales of men dying (even while they invoke the heroic ideals modelled in *Beowulf*). The martyr-king in fact sacrifices the very capacity to subject others to his will that is a prime factor in heroic masculinity and, instead, subjects himself entirely to the will of God. The capacity of these saints' lives to stimulate identification in an Anglo-Saxon warrior-aristocrat thus rests on convincing propaganda – the representation of this surrender as neither emasculating nor unheroic.

Gillian Overing characterizes the 'masculine economy' of *Beowulf* thus:

> Not unexpectedly, Beowulf is an overwhelmingly masculine poem; it could be seen as a chronicle of male desire, a tale of men dying. In the masculine economy of the poem, desire expresses itself as a desire for the other, as a continual process of subjugation and appropriation of the other. The code of vengeance and the heroic choice demand above all a resolution of opposing elements, a decision must always be made.[17]

Overing goes on to suggest that Beowulf himself is the 'ultimate binarist' since 'the hero says "I will do this or I will die" '.[18] Her point is that the poem escapes the psychological reading that reduces it to a 'chronicle of male desire' which inevitably ends in death. Overing's argument, however, confuses what Beowulf himself explicitly claims about his behaviour and what the poem shows us about the character of such a hero. The hero himself might say 'I will do X or die', but what finally happens is that Beowulf does X *and* dies. Thus, while Beowulf professes a heroic binary, the poem does not force a decision between success and death. The 'masculine economy' of Beowulf is more than a simple binary even in the case of its exemplary hero.[19] Where Overing has suggested that the 'masculine economy' of Beowulf is one driven by the desire of the masculine hero, the distinction between Beowulf's binary claim and the resolution of that binary in both conquest and death suggests that this economy is a mechanism by which the death drive is manufactured in the hero. The hero's society, in a sense, *wants* him to think in binaries, and supports a code of behaviour that leads him to self-destruct. The binary 'I will do this or die' tacitly privileges death rather than the successful exploit because it is thus that the warrior is sacrificed and thus that his society protects itself from his power turning back upon them.

The society of 'exploit' is explained in the work of nineteenth-century American economic theorist Thorstein Veblen in his *Theory of the Leisure Class*. Veblen begins his critique of early American capitalism with a survey of the anthropological roots of the 'leisure class' in 'barbaric' (as he calls them) societies where activities are divided between 'exploit' (aligned with the masculine and aristocratic) and 'industry' (aligned with the feminine and labour class).[20] The prior of these two roles was privileged, consisting of the aggressive capture of goods for, or actions taken for the good of, the community, and the symbolization of this success in gold that is exemplified, for example, in *Beowulf*. The barbarian value of 'exploit' was depicted in the seventh century by the Frankish chronicler Fredegar, who described a barbarian king adjured by his mother:

> If you wish to perform an exploit and make a name for yourself, destroy all that other people have built up and kill the entire people whom you have conquered; for you cannot put up a building better than those constructed by your predecessors and there is no finer exploit with which you can make your name.[21]

This expression of the ideal of exploit is dominated by eagerness for fame, an eagerness that is potentially a fatal flaw in Beowulf himself. The will to destruction depicted by Fredegar is almost cartoonish, and perhaps invites us more to judge the bloodthirsty queen than her son the warrior. Nonetheless, the important revelation it makes is that the king does not exist in a vacuum: his urge to relentless violence is derived from social pressure. This relentless urge, as we will see, appears also to motivate the pagan kings who persecute Oswald and Edmund, so that 'exploit' becomes identified with paganism. Without any depth, these enemies are simply tokens of violence itself. Since, as Ælfric writes, a defining quality of the good king is to 'control the violent', the heroism of Oswald or Edmund appears in direct opposition to this ideal.

The tension in societies of exploit, as Freud points out in *Totem and Taboo*, is that the magical potency of the warrior, king or priest is a source of great anxiety to his own people.²² The very violence that protects them may also be turned inwards. Freud invokes Frazer, who writes that '[a] king must not only be guarded, he must be guarded against'.²³ This anxiety is registered throughout *Beowulf*, where examples of bad kingship are consistently thrust beneath the hero's nose. The poem's logic appears on many occasions to be precisely to guard against the inward turn of the hero's strength, to distinguish between the 'gōd cyning' (good king), the king who is a protector but not an aggressor, and the hero whose success makes him 'bolgen-mōd' (enraged) and 'blōd-rēow' (bloodthirsty).²⁴ Freud also invokes the anthropological studies of Frazer to demonstrate a scapegoating pattern, whereby he who is invested with such taboo power is also the one sacrificed for the good of the community. In some cases the danger to his own society from a king or priest of great power is such that the conventions governing his behaviour restrict him to sitting on the throne, lest his slightest motion topple the kingdom.

It is with this sacrificial function in mind that we should consider the lives of English martyr-kings like Edmund and Oswald. Like the taboo of the king who may not move, the characteristic which represents the martyr-king's triumph is constraint: not the imposition of his will upon others, but the surrender of his will and the deliberate disavowal of his martial power. It is through this self-mastery that he is seen to frustrate attempts by a pagan persecutor who is represented as his antithesis: excessive, proud and confident in his own fulfilment of the ideals of heroic exploit – the capacity to exert his will over others through violence or the threat of violence.²⁵ The means of avoiding violence offered by the pagan king is precisely the *division* of the kingdom about which Ælfric expresses concern. In Ælfric's *Life of Oswald*, for example, Oswald's first opponents are 'þone modigan Cedwellan, mid his micclan werode, þe wende þæt him ne mihte nan werode wiðstandan' (the arrogant Cadwalla and his great band, who thought that no army might withstand them).²⁶ Cadwalla's pride, his confidence in his overwhelming martial strength, is aligned with paganism. Oswald falls in battle at the hands of Penda, 'oð þæt he ofslagen wearð for his folces ware' (so that he was slain for his people's protection).²⁷ The sacrificial nature of Edmund's death is made even clearer, as he says to his bishop that 'leofre wære þæt ic on feohte feolle wið þam þe min folc most heora eardes brucan' ([he] would rather fall in battle so that my people continue to possess their land), and proclaims that he will never turn aside from God 'swelte ic, lybbe ic' (whether I live or die).[28] This assertion, indifferent to death, provides an interesting counterexample to the binary between life and death that Overing identifies as the key to the masculine economy of *Beowulf*. As Edmund expresses it, the choice that the Christian hero must make is no choice, since his will is absorbed in obedience to God.

On account of this submission the martyr becomes protector of his people not through the aggressive exploit of war, but through the passive acceptance of deferred authority. It is important to note, however, that this acceptance is portrayed as willing abstinence from the use of an unquestioned potency. Edmund implies confidence in his own power, much as Cadwalla had done, saying to Hingwar's messenger:

> Witodlice þu wære wyrðe sleges nu, ac ic nelle afylan on þinum fulum blode mine clænan handa, forðanþe ic Criste folgie, þe us swa gebysnode, and ic bliðlice wille beon ofslagen þurh eow gif it swa god forsceawað.
>
> Verily you would now be worthy of death, but I will not foul my clean hands with your impure blood, because I follow Christ, who gave us example, and I happily will be slain by you if that is what God decrees.[29]

Edmund is represented as master of the situation, despite his intention to submit to Hingwar and his obedience to Christ. A more abstract model of this obedience is exemplified in the *Dream of the Rood*. Like Edmund, the rood is 'all wounded with shafts' and recounts its own restraint in refusing to fight: 'þær ic þa ne dorste ofer dryhtnes word / bugan oððe berstah, þa ic bifian geseah / eorðan sceatas. Ealle ic mihte / feondasgfyllan, hwœðre ic faste stod' (There I dared not bend or break against God's will, though I saw the earth's edges tremble. I might have felled them all, yet I stood fast).[30] The rood also insists on its superior might. Its surrender is not to Christ's enemies but to the will of God.

The model of heroic behaviour in these Lives is thus, of course, driven by the desire to imitate Christ. This desire in turn is ultimately a desire for death. While the rood actually participates in one and the same sacrifice, Edmund dies 'wolde geœfenlecan Cristes gebysnungum' (desiring to imitate the example of Christ).[31] The result of literary moments like these is the depiction of obedience as a heroic virtue. Valorizing submission appears to threaten the model of heroic behaviour premissed on exploit, but this threat is resolved by the transference of that submission into submission to God rather than the enemy, and as a result obedience becomes the ultimate heroic triumph. The symbolic struggle this causes, and the need to resolve it through repetition of the troubling scene, are developed in the spectacle of the king's martyrdom, but also in the miraculous recuperation of his body after death. These later recuperations signal an ongoing desire to negate the submission of the king, to represent his emasculation as not really emasculating after all.

Central to the construction of masculinity in the lives of Edmund and Oswald is, of course, the moment of martyrdom itself. The deaths of these two kings are 'spectacles' of suffering ending in decapitation. In an article on sexual violence in the Old English *Judith*, Karma Lochrie describes the specular nature of Holofernes's gendered violence, and argues that head-taking is a specifically sexual act of violence: a symbolic castration which disrupts the 'masculine economy' of Anglo-Saxon war.[32] Judith turns the tables on Holofernes, who intends to rape her, and decapitates him. Lochrie draws on Luce Irigaray and Toril Moi to explain the masculine gaze, which functions to define the masculine subject by 'objectifying others and arrogating to itself the prerogative of looking. Subjectivity, authority, and power are constituted through the gaze while the feminine is objectified and made a spectacle – or mirror – of masculinity.' Lochrie quotes Toril Moi to further define the gaze as a means of domination which 'enacts the voyeur's desire for sadistic power, in which the object of the gaze is cast as passive, masochistic, feminine victim'.[33] In the passion of Edmund, Hingwar's 'desire for sadistic power' is explicit, as he attempts to force Edmund's submission. Edmund's body is rendered literally passive by being bound. To force his submission to Hingwar's rule, Edmund is repeatedly wounded, penetrated by arrows. The scene of Edmund's death can be read as feminizing, relying on the spectacle of his humiliation as an objectifying process that defines him as the 'mirror' of Hingwar's masculine power. Hingwar's frustration at Edmund's resistance indicates that his desire is not to kill Edmund, but to force his submission. The *vita*, however, represents Edmund's death as a sacrifice and thus attempts to override the feminizing implications of the oppressor's gaze.

The wounding of the martyr is obviously given its significance by identification with the suffering of Christ. Lochrie has shown elsewhere that 'the feminization of Christ is usually considered to be one of the most distinctive features of late medieval piety'.[34] The wounds of

Christ are often represented as vaginal in later medieval paintings, and in mystical writing of the thirteenth century he gives birth through them.[35] The confusingly gendered Christ, Caroline Walker Bynum suggests, posed problems for twelfth-century Cistercians since, 'if the God with whom they wished to unite was spoken of in a male language, it is hard to use the metaphor of sexual union unless they saw themselves as female'.[36] The desire of the martyr is not for the same union with God, but is to emulate Christ. Nonetheless, the submission this entails is similarly feminizing. If Christ's crucifixion is indeed the 'master tableau' of medieval Christian suffering, then the spectacle of crucifixion has already implicitly feminized such suffering by objectifying and passifying him. The feminizing implications of later, monastic desire for union with Christ are prefigured in the desire of the Christian, Anglo-Saxon warrior, whose emulation of Christ rests in remaining passive where the masculine role of 'exploit' had defined the pagan warrior.

As the *vita* tells us, Edmund has renounced the signs of his heroic-masculine identity – he throws away his weapon and will not fight, 'desiring to imitate the example of Christ', just as the rood mystically bleeds with Christ's wounds. The martyr's passivity is thus not simply forced on his body. It is self-imposed upon his will. Though he will not fight, neither will he submit, and endures torture, making 'þa hœþenan þa for his geleafan wurdon wodlice yrre' (the heathen's madly angry because of his faith).[37] Thus, 'ða geseah Hingwar, se arlease flotman, þœt se aþela cyning nolde Criste wiðsacan . . . het hine beheafdian and þa hœþenan swa dydon' (when Hingwar, the wicked seaman, saw that the noble king would not deny Christ . . . he commanded men to behead him, and the heathens did).[38] The beheading of the king is represented as the angry resort of a pagan who, despite his obvious physical mastery of the saint, is nonetheless impotent against the self-imposed passivity of the martyr who already 'awearp hi wœpna wolde geœfe-lœcan cristes gebysnungum' (threw away his weapons, wishing to imitate Christ's example).[39]

The association of masculinity with weapons (literal and figurative) is evident in one Old English term for 'man', 'wœpnedmann'. A variety of compounds signifying the male sex testify to the understanding of 'weapon' as metaphorical penis: 'wœpnedcild' (male child), 'wœpned-healf' (male line), and so forth. It is also worth noting that, in the notorious Exeter Riddle 44 ('Key'), the man in question intends to greet a familiar hole 'mid his hangellan heafde' (with his hanging *head*).⁴⁰ The phallic-symbolic identification of a man's 'head' is thus reinforced lexically – appearing to leave little doubt that beheading could have been perceived as a symbolic castration by Ælfric himself. This theme of impotence, of discarded or unusable weapons, continues later when grave-robbers are frozen in the martyr's tomb, 'œlcne swa he stod strutigend mid tole' (each as he stood toiling with his implement).⁴¹ Thus, the bodily subjugation of the martyr comes to represent not his own emasculation but the impotence of his persecutors. Edmund's masculinity is wondrously protected by God. This is most startlingly revealed in that his decapitation does not disable his head, which keeps on talking.

Edmund's head is later discovered miraculously rejoined to his body, when '[þ]a wæs micel wundor þæt he wæs eall swa gehal swylce he cucu wære' (there was great miracle, in that he was all whole as if he were alive, with clean body, and his neck was healed which before had been cut through).⁴² If this subjugation of the martyr and his decapitation are indeed symbolically threatening to his masculinity because they construct him as the passive object of his persecutor's tormenting gaze, then these events after his death seem to assure the saint of symbolic remasculation guaranteed by the will of God, and represented by the miraculous *post mortem* unity of his body. Similarly, Oswald's head and arm, though not reattached to his body, do not wither, but remain 'clean' and intact long after his death. Ælfric makes a point of showing this healing to be a reversal of the pagans' torture. Of Edmund he writes that 'þa wunda, þe þa wælhreowan hæþenan mid gelomum scotuungum on his lice macodon, wæron gehælede þurh þa heofonlican God' (the wounds, which the bloodthirsty heathen had made in his body by their repeated shots, had been healed by the heavenly God).⁴³

It is clear that, from the beginning of his suffering through the fragmentation and miraculous reconstruction or preservation of his limbs, the saint's body is the locus of the construction of his holiness *and* his masculinity. A sign of inward purity, it can be overwritten by the wounds of his heroic-masculine (pagan) persecutor, but this persecutor has power only over the corporeal. It is telling that the pagan kings in the lives of Edmund and Oswald are not described physically, but identified only by their demeanour: pride, arrogance and violence. Hingwar is at his most embodied in the simile that compares him to a wolf. That Edmund's head is later protected by a wolf, a beast of battle domesticated by God's will, is a further token that his self-mastery triumphs over the violence of physical 'exploit'. While control of wild animals is a common miracle in saints' lives, the wolf has a particular significance in that it symbolizes ravenous violence, and pagan kings are often described by figurative association with wolves. Nebuchadnezzar, in the OE *Daniel*, is the archetypal, arrogant and enraged pagan king, and is described as 'wulfheort cyning' (wolf-hearted king). Hingwar had, likewise, stalked across East Anglia: 'swa swa wulf on lande bestalcode and þa leode sloh' (like a wolf stalked over the land and killed the people).[44] Thus, while the 'wolf-hearted' pagan asserts his will through violence, the martyred Christian king (indeed, his 'head' with all its gendered connotations) controls the violence of the wolf, even after he has been decapitated.

The example of Edmund assures the Anglo-Saxon warrior that his Christian behaviour will not impinge upon his masculinity according to the heroic-masculine rule.[45] By self-controlled, self-imposed passivity he has demonstrated a subjugation more potent than the simple physical potency of subjugating others. By surrendering his will to God he subjugates his own desire for the 'exploit' that signals the *pagan* hero. He nonetheless remains defined by the heroic-masculine economy because the fame that motivates the warrior remains the reward of the martyr in the ongoing veneration of his body long after his death. His eternal glory supersedes earthly fame, and his control over his enemies will be the greater. In this way the martyr's death is depicted as the ultimate heroic exploit. The desire for death that drives the 'masculine economy' of *Beowulf* is not replaced in the life of the martyred king like Edmund, but is instead channelled or sublimated. The sacrifice of the martyr shifts his heroism from an 'exploit' of taking to an exploit of giving, and from the subjugation of the body to the subjugation of the non-corporeal. This self-mastery is represented as a choice, not a lack of power, but a decision to endure suffering and death rather than renounce his loyalty to the Christian faith, and to one God. The heroism of these kings is thus consistent with the representation of Beowulf's heroism, analysed by Overing as centring on a choice that polarizes successful exploit and death. The martyrdom of these kings, while still emphasizing the choice, suggests a different binary: one between brutal rage and violence controlled. Rather than success or death, these narratives equate success *with* death.

Steven Kruger argues that medieval sexual identities are always embedded in and intersected by other cultural designations of differentiation and opposition, such as gender, ethnicity, race and religion.[46]

What I hope to have demonstrated is that the category of gender, in the particular case of Anglo-Saxon martyr-kings, is similarly implicated in the opposed categories of pagan heroism and Christian sacrifice. 'Exploit' is represented not as a definition of heroism, but of a specifically *pagan* heroism. The spectacle of the martyr-king's suffering is the meeting of an heroic masculinity premissed on the subjugation of others and a masculine-holiness premissed on the mastery of self. The triumph of the latter is represented as the ultimate form of mastery, so that superior and lasting fame are achieved by the Christian king only, paradoxically, through their denial. In both the narrative content of these lives, and in the anxieties expressed by Ælfric about writing them, troubling complexities of authority, compromises between Christian and pagan kings, are rejected in favour of unity: one king, not two; submission only to God. Desiring to imitate Christ, the good king dies to preserve not only his faith, but so as not to divide the wealth of his people. The dismemberment of the martyr's body, which signifies the threatening divisions of war and paganism, as well as the symbolic castration of the hero, is miraculously undone. The king's submission is thus brought within the realm of the exploit and his heroic-masculine identity protected.

Notes

1 Kaja Silverman, *Male Subjectivity at the Margins* (New York and London, 1992), p. 197.
2 Sigmund Freud, *Beyond the Pleasure Principle* (New York and London, 1961), pp. 45–6.
3 Silverman, *Male Subjectivity*, p. 198.
4 Ibid., p. 58.
5 Ibid., pp. 15–16, p. 62; Clare A. Lees, 'Men and Beowulf', in Clare A. Lees (ed.), *Medieval Masculinities: Regarding Men in the Middle Ages* (Minneapolis and London, 1994), pp. 129–48; Gillian Overing, *Language, Sign, and Gender in 'Beowulf'* (Carbondale, IL, 1990). See also the articles cited in n. 32 below.
6 *Ælfric's Lives of Saints*, ed. W. W. Skeat, 4 vols (London, 1881); James Hurt, *Ælfric* (New York, 1972), p. 60. All references to saints' lives are to Skeat's edition. Unless otherwise noted, translations are mine. Where I have retained Skeat's translations they are modernized.
7 Bede, *The Ecclesiastical History of the English People*, tr. Bertram Colgrave (Oxford, 1994), p. 118.
8 Ibid., p. 105.
9 *Ælfric's Lives of Saints*, vol. 2, p. 134.

[10] *Anglo-Saxon Chronicles*, ed. and tr. Michael Swanton (London, 2000), p. 70.
[11] For further discussion of the hagiographic elaboration of the life of St Edmund see Katherine J. Lewis's essay in the present volume.
[12] *Ælfric's Lives of Saints*, vol. 3, p. 315.
[13] Ibid., p. 139.
[14] Ibid., p. 318.
[15] Ibid., p. 322.
[16] Gillian Overing, *Language, Sign, and Gender in 'Beowulf'* (Carbondale, IL, 1990), p. 70.
[17] Ibid., p. 70.
[18] Ibid.
[19] Robert Morey, for example, has shown in his article 'Beowulf's androgynous heroism' that Beowulf also appears to '[fulfil] his society's idealized feminine role: that of peace-weaver', *Journal of English and Germanic Philology*, 95, 4 (1996), 486–96.
[20] Thorsten Veblen, *The Theory of the Leisure Class* (New York, 1994), p. 8.
[21] Quoted in Jacques Le Goff, *Medieval Civilization 400–1500*, tr. Julia Barrow (New York, 1988), p. 17.
[22] Sigmund Freud, *Totem and Taboo* (New York and London, 1950), pp. 52–61.
[23] Ibid., p. 52.
[24] See *Beowulf*, ll. 1713 and 1719. Frederick Klaeber, *Beowulf and the Fight and Finnsburg* (Lexington, MA, 1950), p. 64.
[25] The same contrast between Edmund and his pagan persecutors is also drawn in later medieval versions of the life, as noted in Lewis's essay.
[26] *Ælfric's Lives of Saints*, vol. 2, p. 126.
[27] Ibid., p. 134.
[28] *Ælfric's Lives of Saints*, vol. 3, pp. 318, 320.
[29] Ibid., p. 320.
[30] Elaine Treharne (ed.), *Old and Middle English: An Anthology* (Oxford, 2000), p. 110, ll. 35–8. My tr.
[31] *Ælfric's Lives of Saints*, vol. 3, p. 320.
[32] Karma Lochrie, 'Gender, sexual violence, and the politics of war in the Old English *Judith*', in Britton J. Harwood and Gillian R. Overing (eds), *Class and Gender in Early English Literature* (Bloomington, IN, 1994), pp. 1–20. See also Jeffrey Jerome Cohen, 'Decapitation and coming of age: constructing masculinity and the monstrous', in *The Arthurian Yearbook*, vol. 3, ed. Keith Busby (New York, 1993), pp. 171–90.
[33] Lochrie, 'Gender, sexual violence, and politics of war', p. 9
[34] Karma Lochrie, 'Mystical acts, queer tendencies', in Karma Lochrie, Peggy McCracken and James Schulz (eds), *Constructing Medieval Sexuality* (Minneapolis, 1997), pp. 180–200 (p. 187).
[35] Ibid.
[36] Quoted ibid.
[37] *Ælfric's Lives of Saints*, vol. 3, p. 322.

[38] Ibid., p. 322.
[39] Ibid., p. 320.
[40] Treharne, *Anthology*, p.72.
[41] *Ælfric's Lives of Saints*, vol. 3, p. 328.
[42] Ibid., p. 330.
[43] Ibid.
[44] Ibid., p. 318.
[45] Aldhelm's saints' lives make the same assurance, as discussed by Emma Pettit in the present volume.
[46] Steven F. Kruger, 'Conversion and medieval sexual, religious, and racial categories', in Lochrie *et al.* (eds), *Constructing Medieval Sexuality*, pp. 158–79.

11

Edmund of East Anglia, Henry VI and Ideals of Kingly Masculinity

KATHERINE J. LEWIS

The manner in which duty and responsibility could influence and define gender was perhaps nowhere as central as in the role and image of the king. At this highest level of society, the expectations and imperatives to manliness, masculine prowess and bravery, patriarchal authority, sapiential wisdom and good governance all intersected. The king had much invested in his appropriation and performance of masculine identities.[1]

Despite Jacqueline Murray's assertion of the vital relationship that existed in the Middle Ages between successful kingship and gender performance, recent studies of medieval masculinities have paid scant attention to the masculinity expected of and performed by kings.[2] This essay seeks to shed light on these issues by exploring some of the attempts that were made to mould the kingly masculinity of a young Henry VI, and the ways in which St Edmund of East Anglia was held up as a model for him.[3] I shall consider the relationship between the hagiographic representation of St Edmund and the ideal king who emerges from a different genre: the 'Mirrors for Princes' tradition. These didactic texts outline the character, behaviour and function of the ideal king and were very popular in later medieval England.[4] The most popular of all, the *Secreta secretorum* (Secret of Secrets) for example, survives in at least eleven Middle English translations and many more individual manuscripts known to have been owned by members of the royal family and nobility.⁵ John Watts has demonstrated the ways in which these mirrors constructed a conceptual framework within which the norms of kingship were expressed and against which the actions of individual kings were interpreted in fifteenth-century England.⁶ Focusing on John Lydgate's Middle English life of St Edmund this analysis will explore the ways in which the representation of a king-saint can be seen to intersect with the normative qualities of ideal kingship, and of kingly masculinity outlined by the *Secreta secretorum*. We will see that St Edmund, as king of East Anglia, is explicitly presented to the young Henry VI as the epitome of an ideal king, with respect to behaviour, function and gender performance. Edmund provides a model of the ways in which holiness and masculinity can be successfully blended in the figure of a king.

What makes Lydgate's life of St Edmund particularly appropriate for such a study is the fact that it was written for Henry VI, to commemorate the visit of the 12-year-old king to the abbey of Bury St Edmunds in 1433. It was commissioned from Lydgate by the abbot, William Curteys.⁷ Lydgate was a monk there, thus having access to a wealth of hagiographic materials relating to Edmund. According to the *Anglo-Saxon Chronicle*, Edmund was killed by the Danes in 870, but other than some coins issued during his reign, this is all we know about the 'real' Edmund, before a cult grew up around his remains.⁸ The first life of St Edmund was written by Abbo in the 980s and this formed the basis for the later medieval tradition, which became quite elaborate, with the addition of extra episodes relating the story of Edmund's birth and upbringing, as well as the accretion of miracles through the centuries.⁹ From the Anglo-Saxon period onwards there seems to have been a particular connection between the cult of St Edmund and royalty; for example, the West Saxon kings of the tenth century used it to justify their take-over of East Anglia, and after the Conquest many kings of England showed conspicuous devotion to St Edmund and to his shrine at Bury.¹⁰ Earlier versions of Edmund's life had described Edmund as an exemplar of ideal Christian kingship; Abbo's life is predicated on this image for example.¹¹ But in Lydgate's version it forms the governing principle behind his description of Edmund, which must surely be related to the identity of its intended recipient. At the beginning of the life of Edmund Lydgate announces 'Tencresse his [Henry's] virtues, Edmund shal been his guyde', and explicitly states that Edmund will be 'an exaumplaire and a merour' to the reader (Prologue: 45, 1. 419–20).¹² The prayer at the end of the life entreats

Edmund to protect both Henry and his kingdom and also asks that Edmund should 'Encresse our kyng in knyhtly hih prowesse' (3. 1513). Edmund's exemplary status within the life derives in part from his sanctity, of course. Lydgate describes his undaunted faith and willingness to suffer torture and martyrdom, so in common with other saints he provides a universally applicable Christian example. But, importantly, in presenting him as a model for Henry, Edmund's behaviour is seen to be exemplary, not solely in these general terms, and not primarily because he is a saint, but rather because he is an excellent king.[13]

The *Secreta secretorum* will be used as a comparison for Lydgate's description of Edmund as an ideal king, partly because it was such a popular work, but also because we know of one version that was written for Henry, and partially composed by Lydgate himself.[14] Apart from this we know of at least one other didactic work that was written expressly for Henry, *Tractatus de regimine principum ad regem Henricum Sextum* (*A Tract on the Regiment of Princes to Henry VI*), written in 1436–7.[15] We also know a fair amount about the context in which such works would have been read by the young king. In 1428 Richard Beauchamp, earl of Warwick, 'the best-nurtured man in England', was appointed to serve as Henry's guardian, to guide him in 'good manners, letters, languages, nurture and courtesy', as well as religion and morality.[16] Moreover, Warwick was instructed, as Watts notes, 'to use examples culled from history books to teach the young king to "love, worship and drede God"'.[17] It was presumably felt particularly important to provide Henry with models of good kingship to imitate because he had never had the opportunity to observe a real king in action before becoming one himself when only a few months old, and it is very likely that Warwick would have used the *Secreta secretorum* or something similar as part of Henry's education.

Of course, it is impossible to know for sure if Henry ever actually read any of the 'Mirrors for Princes' material directed at him. Although if we assume that he did, Watts suggests that he may have got the 'wrong idea of what kingship involved' from these texts.[18] This would, perhaps, partly explain his failings as a king. Certainly, one long-standing historiographical stereotype about Henry suggests that he did not pay much attention to ideas about ideal kingship, because he was too pious and otherworldly.[19] It could be argued, therefore, that setting up St Edmund as a model of exemplary kingship for the young Henry VI to imitate was not such a good idea. Indeed, it is often assumed that the reason Henry himself subsequently came to be seen as a saint is because he was so holy. This implies that the definition of a king-saint as a man who is too 'good' to be an effective king, and who therefore seeks to withdraw from the world, was the only one which had currency in the Middle Ages.[20] In fact the lives of many later medieval king-saints establish that a great part of their status as a saint actually rests *on* their outstanding performance of kingship, not on the fact that they would rather have been a monk. Gabor Klaniczay has recently argued that the eleventh-century legends of king-saint Stephen of Hungary played a crucial role in the creation of a new model of the Christian king and in presenting it as a blueprint which other kings should seek to follow.[21] Similarly M. C. Gasposchkin has recently explored the ways in which Boniface VIII emphasized Louis IX of France's exemplary kingship as an intrinsic element of his sanctity when he was canonized in 1297.[22] 'Mirrors for Princes' assign the king a role which enjoined patronage and protection of the people upon him and these are exactly the roles that a saint was also expected to perform. So perhaps a king-saint like Edmund becomes a sort of super saint: already trained and accustomed to helping his people, he now has supernatural powers which allow him do this even more effectively. This is also aided by the contemporary notion that any king was already invested with an amount of sacred glamour by virtue of his office.

Certainly Lydgate makes it very clear that Edmund is a saint because he is a king, not in spite of it. For Edmund sanctity lies in carrying out his kingly duties in an exemplary way, not in shirking them, so the model of the king-saint as a king who would really rather not be a king is not applicable here, as the following analysis will illustrate. Edmund is, naturally, very pious; every morning he goes to his chapel to hear divine service (1. 1068–72). But proper religious observance and devotion are not seen to be incompatible with his exercise of kingly duties. Nor is he seen to be at odds with his knights in this respect, as they all accompany him (1. 1069). Indeed, Edmund's court as a whole is so exemplary that it is subsequently described as 'liht and lanterne / To alle uertuous how thei shal hem gouerne' (2. 139–40). This is entirely in keeping with the *Secreta secretorum*, which devotes a chapter entitled 'Of a kyngis goodness and holynes' to the importance of religion in the conduct of a king and in the successful running of his household and realm.[23] Crucially the reader is shown that Edmund achieves the correct balance between his spiritual and secular responsibilities, Lydgate explaining: 'Thus toward heuene he was contemplatiff, / Toward the world a good knyht of his liff' (1. 1073–4). In fact Lydgate reinforces this point by having used a very similar formula to describe Edmund's father, King Alkmund, earlier in the text: 'Thus in two wise his noblesse did shyne: / Toward the world, in knyhtly hih prowesse, / And toward god, in parfit holynesse' (1. 267–9). As Karen Winstead notes, 'Lydgate consistently praises characters who are able to reconcile spiritual and temporal pursuits.'[24]

Edmund's status as an ideal king is described in great detail in the life and there is only space to discuss a few instances here. For example, Edmund's conduct is shown to be governed by the four cardinal virtues of prudence, justice, temperance and fortitude.

> Yong of yeeris, old of discrecioun,
> Flouryng in age, fructuous of sadnesse [with the fruits of stability],
> His sensualite ay soget [subject] to resoun,
> And of his counsail discrecioun was maistresse;
> Foure cardynal sustre [sisters], Force and Rihtwisnesse,
> Weied alle his werkis, by Prudence in balance,
> Al passiouns voide in his Attemperance. (1. 396–402)[25]

This element of Edmund's representation is clearly underpinned by the precepts of the *Secreta secretorum* and illustrates perfectly this passage:

> Sothly, nobill lorde, many Pepill shall ye well gouerne, whyle that reyson gouernyth yow. And yf ye . . . youre-Selfe gouerne aftyr this boke, and aftyr the iiije cardynale virtues that here lyke as y fynde writte in dyuers bokis declarid shal be, than shall ye doutles youre-Silfe gouerne by reysone, to godis wyrschupp and youris, and profite to al yours [your people].[26]

Self-governance is identified as the key to successfully governing others and this is why Lydgate stresses that Edmund's sensuality is subject to reason, as will be discussed in more detail below. Returning to the extract from the life of Edmund quoted above, the reference to his youth is also significant. This is something that Lydgate repeats several times, at one point claiming that Edmund was 15 at his coronation (1. 857). This makes Edmund a very approachable model for Henry: they are both teenaged kings.

One section of the life is entitled 'the Roial gouernance of seynt Edmond aftir he was crownyd kyng of Estyngland', and is entirely given over to a description of Edmund's rule. It could be removed from its hagiographic context and function as a mirror for princes in its own right, for it holds up King Edmund as the embodiment of desirable kingly conduct which Henry VI should seek to imitate. We are shown the ways in which Edmund translates the symbolic significance of his coronation regalia into action with his practice of good government:

> That blissid Edmond by goddis ordynance
> Hadde of Estyngland hooli the gouernance:
> Tholi gost beyng euer his guyde,
> First for his rewm thus he gan prouyde.
> Lawes he sette of trouthe and equite.
> Them establysshid upon ryhtwisenesse;
> First so disposyng his royal mageste
> Twen sceptre and swerd tattempre his noblesse,
> That ther were founde in nouther noun excesse,
> But with the sceptre conserue his peeple in pees,
> Punysshe with the swerd folk that were reklees.
> For, as a sceptre is smothe, long and round,
> The hier part of gold and stonys ynde [Indian jewels]:
> So semblably this noble kyng Edmond
> Was meek of maneres and vertuous, as I fynde,
> Vp to godward hadde most his mynde.
> Mercy preferryng, examyned euery deede,
> Delaied rygour, listnat of haste proceede.
> In his on hand the sceptre of pees he heeld,
> Cherisshynge his peeple in reste and quyeete;
> And wher that he espied or beheld
> Ryot or trouble of folk that were vnmeete [badly behaved],
> Of manly prudence in his royal seete
> Anoon he took his swerd of rihtwisnesse,
> Of fals rauyne [rapine] alle surfetis to redresse. (2. 861–85)

Lydgate here follows the convention of using the sword and sceptre as symbols of King Edmund's two main functions: defence of his kingdom and its people and the provision of justice.[27]

Edmund's excellence as a ruler is made manifest with respect to a variety of arenas and activities. To give a few examples: he is concerned for what Lydgate refers to as the 'Rem publicam' (matters of state) (2. 891), ensuring that the church, the law and trade in particular are bastions of honesty directed by appropriately virtuous men (2. 892–934). His realm is represented by Lydgate as an 'ymage' (2. 940), which is the conventional one of the body politic, with Edmund at the head ensuring that all of the other limbs, from nobility to labourers, fulfil their proper duties as part of an organic whole (2. 941–76).[28] Edmund is a protector of the church and takes a harsh attitude to heterodoxy: 'Lollardis that tyme fond in him no confort' (2. 1014) (perhaps intentionally redolent of Henry V's treatment of heretics). We have seen that Edmund is devout, and he is also extremely generous to the sick and needy (2. 1084–8). He is also a knight of great prowess, and ensures that all his nobles are properly trained using 'Vigecius' (2. 906). Lydate is here referring to another extremely popular instructional work which was often owned by medieval royalty and nobility, Vegetius' *De re militari* (On Military Matters), so the life provides further illustration of the precepts of didactic literature by showing Edmund making use of such a book himself.[29] Edmund also encourages his nobles to imitate him by choosing appropriate games and pastimes, such as hunting, as well as accompanying him to church (2. 904–6, 1047–54). Edmund possesses a king's ideal personal and physical qualities too; well-formed and temperate, never given to overindulgence of any kind (2. 984–1007). The entire description in this section functions as a practical illustration of the theories of good kingship promulgated by the *Secreta secretorum*, a point that is underlined in the text when we are told that Edmund has the love of his people who cry 'Longe mote he leue, longe mote the kyng endure!' (2. 983).

The text further develops the depiction of Edmund's exemplary kingship by presenting him as a martial hero, opening the text with a description of the saint's war banner, and later describing him fighting against the Danes. This is a departure from other versions of the legend in which Edmund is never seen to take up arms against his enemies.[30] Lydgate, however, describes Edmund's exploits in the field thus:

> For with his knyhtis that kyng Edmond ladde
> Of paynym blood ful gret plente he shadde.
> Edmond that day was Cristis champioun,
> Preeuyng him-silf a ful manly knyht;
> Among sarseynes he pleied the lioun:
> For they lik sheepe fledde out of his syht.
> Maugre [In spite of] the Danys he put Hyngwar to flyht:

> For wher his swerd that day dide glyde,
> Ther was no paynym afforn him durste abyde.
> The soil of slauhtre I-steynyd was with blood,
> The sharp swerd of Edmond turnyd red:
> For ther was noon that his strook withstood
> Nor durste [dared] abide afforn him for his hed. (3. 376–89)

Earlier Lydgate prays that Edmund will help Henry VI to 'rassemble by tryumphal victory / To his fadir, most notable of memory' (Prologue: 163–4), so it is fitting that he presents Edmund as the consummate warrior, every bit as accomplished as Henry V on the battlefield.

Lydgate's description of Edmund as a 'manly knight' brings us on to consideration of the ways in which the life is informed not just by ideas about the ideal king, but by ideas about ideal kingly masculinity. The elements already discussed plainly establish that Edmund's gender identity adheres strictly to normative definitions of royal manhood, and Lydgate emphasizes this by using the adjective 'manly' to describe him on several occasions.[31] Edmund's correct performance of masculinity is also highlighted through comparison with the villains of the piece, the Danish princes Vbba and Hygwar.[32] They are cruel, brutal, greedy, lustful, unjust and intemperate, and, as such, are the perfect example of bad kings, clearly set up as foils for Edmund (3. 8–18).[33] They are also self-important and ignorant, for they swagger about proclaiming:

> Ys ther any leuyng now these daies,
> Kyng or prynce, so myhti of puissance [power]
> In any rewm, knowen at alle assaies, [trials]
> On londe and water that hath gouernance,
> Which rassemblith or is like in assurance
> To vs in manhood, yf it be declaryd,
> Which to our noblesse of riht may be comparyd? (3. 22–8)

They are absolutely furious when their father, King Lothbrok, tells them that they could never match Edmund's nobility and 'manhod', qualities that have made him well-known to the world (3. 43–70). His sons enviously vow to revenge themselves on Edmund's 'noblesse' for showing up the sham of their own claims to kingly excellence (3. 71–84). This is just one of the ways in which the text stresses that proper masculinity is the key to proper kingship. It is not enough to be more powerful than other men (as Vbba and Hyngwar wrongly believe, boasting that they can bend anyone to their will), unless that strength is tempered by appropriate virtues.[34]

It is this issue of tempering and temperance to which I shall turn for the last part of this essay. As a starting point here, it has to be said that there is one glaring aspect of Edmund's conduct that is, of course, not at all in keeping with the demands of ideal kingship: his virginity, because it prevents him from fathering an heir. However, Lydgate does not play down Edmund's virginity; in fact it is a central element of his sanctity.[35] Lydgate underlines this by repeating the formula 'martyr, maid and king' to describe him throughout the life (for example, Prologue: 49–56; 3. 413, 827). It could be argued that this is an area in which the depiction of the king-saint diverges from the ideal king, particularly with respect to contemporary notions of lay masculinity.[36] Indeed, Henry VI is often seen to provide the prime example of a king who aroused suspicion in some of his contemporaries precisely because he did not exhibit appropriate levels of kingly heterosexuality: only one child after eight years of marriage and a strong suspicion that he had not been keen to consummate it at all.[37] Under the circumstances we might therefore question why Edmund's virginity is stressed by Lydgate. It seems rather a counter-kingly quality, and, given that contemporary discourses of virginity tend to associate it with women far more than with men, might it not run the risk of rendering Edmund rather an effeminate figure?[38]

The explanation for Lydgate's emphasis here lies in the importance of sexual temperance to a king's identity, and explicitly to his gender identity. This is something that the *Secreta secretorum* makes very clear, because while virginity (a complete absence of sexual intercourse) may not be vocationally appropriate to a king, chastity is deemed to be crucial. The *Secreta secretorum* warns that its opposite quality, lechery, is not simply an evil in itself, but is the first step downwards on a slippery slope of sin:

> leve bestly desires and flesshely, for they ben corruptible. fflesshely desires bowith the hert of mane to delitis, which are corrupcioun to the sowle, and it is bestialle without discreeccioun. And he that ioyneth him to bodily corrupcioun, he corruptith the vndirstondyng of man. And wite welle þat suche desires engendrith flesshely loue: And flesshely loue engendrith avarice: Auarice engendrith desiris of ricchesses: Desiris of ricchesse

makith a man without shame: Man without shame is prowd and without feith: Man without feith drawith to thefte: Thefte bryngith a man to endles shame, and so cometh a man to kaytifnes [captivity] and to fynalle distruccioun of his body.[39]

Moreover, chastity (understood here as licit sexual relations with his queen) is extremely desirable in a king because immoderate indulgence in intercourse will have a disastrous effect on his manhood:

> sett nought thyn hert in lecherie of women, for þat is the lyf of swine. Ioy and worshipe shalt thou noon haue, while thou governyst the aftir that lijf and aftir the lijf of vnresonable bestis. Dere sone, lecherie is destruccioun of body abreggyng [shortening] of lijf and corrupcioun of virtues; Enemy to conscience, *and makith a man oft femynyne*. In whiche is oft tyme found cowardnes, and þat is the grettist point of repreef that may be vnto Chyvalrie.[40]

A king might believe that sex with women would serve to make him more masculine, but the advice literature is at pains to point out that the reverse is true; too much sex will leave him effeminate, and unknightly. This is a point that is developed in a section of one version of the *Secreta secretorum* dealing with temperance:

> A grete Clerke Vegece vs tellyth in his boke of Chyualrie, that hit appartenyth not to a good knight to lowe ayse [ease] ne delytes of body. Alsmoch is abstinence auenaunt [becoming] to a knight and mesure, as to a monke . . . loue of women and brandynge fylthed [burning filth] of lechurie nesshyth [softens] a manes herte and hym makyth lyke a womon, So that he lesyth his Streynth, and hardynesse, and manhode, and chyualrie. More accordyth to a lechurere a Styfe-stafe [distaff] than a Swerde, and an hechil [comb to card wool] than an chelde [shield] or a boklere [buckler].[41]

It is therefore perhaps no coincidence that Lydgate tells us that Edmund uses Vegetius himself to train his own knights.

I would argue that, using the standards of the *Secreta secretorum*, Lydgate seeks to enforce an understanding of Edmund's virginity as anything but an anomalous or problematic quality in a king. Nor is it seen to be the sign of imperfect manhood; quite the reverse, for male continence was not an easy option. It took strength of will to overcome the unruly body, as Jacqueline Murray's recent work on the sexuality of medieval men demonstrates.[42] As in the earlier quotation, the king must be controlled by reason, whatever his flesh tries to tempt him to, and Lydgate tells us at the very beginning of the life that Edmund 'vnto reson . . . gaff the souereynte' (Prologue: 10). Edmund's virtue allows him to control himself (both with respect to fleshly and other bodily appetites, such as eating and drinking) and it is this which should be imitated by Henry. It is, of course, exemplary moral conduct for anyone, but it is especially important for a king, because this self-control is what qualifies him to rule over others: 'By this Vertu Temporancia a man gouernyth hym-self, and with the Vertu of Iustice other men. But rather and more Providabille [profitable] ys to a man to gouern hynself than other mene.'[43] If a king cannot control himself, he has no business trying to control other people – a point also stressed in another work written for Henry VI, *The Book of Illustrious Henries* by John Capgrave; here quoting Godfrey of Viterbo's assessment of the Emperor Henry VI, which is explicitly given as advice for King Henry VI to imitate in his own conduct as king:

> And, whatso'er thou doest, 'Know thyself.'
> 'Twere better thou shouldst learn to rule thyself
> Than conquer many nations and their kings, –
> King of thyself – thou art a king indeed! . . .
> Govern thyself or cease to govern me![44]

As already noted, this is a point that Lydgate illustrates in the life of Edmund by comparing the king to Vbba and Hyngwar. The fact that they cannot control themselves and indulge in an orgy of slaughter, rape and pillage is shown to compromise their knighthood, just as the *Secreta secretorum* warns it would, for all their strength is to no avail against the virtuous army of knights which the virgin King Edmund leads against them, nor against the similarly virginal King Fremund (Edmund's cousin) who takes revenge on the Danes after Edmund's martyrdom, killing them in battle (3. 523–49). So, while Henry was certainly not expected to remain a virgin himself, Edmund's virginity was a figuratively invaluable example for him nonetheless. Indeed, Lydgate tells us that God allows Edmund to protect both Henry and England because of his virginity. In the prologue he describes a special banner belonging to St Edmund which protected him in battle, and which still protects England and we are told:

God grantyd it hym for a prerogatyff,
Be-cause al heete off lust and flesslyheede
Were queynt [quenched] in hym during al his leyff. (Prologue: 38–40)

This theme of Edmund's protection of England is taken up in the prayer at the end of the life too, as noted above, and, again, Edmund's virginity is central, Lydgate addressing him here as 'gemme of virgynyte' (3. 1466). Thus, Edmund's virginal body stands as a symbol of the inviolate kingdom of England.[45] This is a point which becomes particularly significant when we remember that England's other great king-saint, St Edward the Confessor, was also a virgin, a very different situation from countries where king-saints such as Louis IX or Stephen of Hungary had fathered children. This would suggest that there was something extremely significant about the performance of virginity to the ideology of kingship in later medieval England, especially given the existence of a poem addressing the newly crowned Edward IV as an undefiled, virgin knight, in terms that recall Lydgate's description of Edmund.[46] The fact that Edward IV's body was not actually virginal did not stop him being able to assume the symbolism of virginity as part of his kingly identity.

As a final point, just as with the mirrors that were written for him, it is impossible to say for sure whether Henry VI ever actually read the life of St Edmund which Lydgate wrote for him. However, the nature of the life and its presentation of Edmund suggest that it was not just intended as a devotional text, but that it would have provided a very useful educative tool as well. It is therefore entirely likely that it was used alongside the histories and other texts with which the earl of Warwick was expected to instruct the young Henry VI in the ideal conduct and ideal masculinity which were required of a king of England. Of course, whether or not Henry tried to follow this advice once he became old enough to rule the country himself is an entirely different matter altogether.

Notes

I would like to thank Joanna Huntington, Alice Cowen, Karen Winstead, Sarah Salih and Christopher Fletcher for their advice and assistance with this essay.

[1] Jacqueline Murray, 'Introduction', in Jacqueline Murray (ed.), *Conflicted*

Identities and Multiple Masculinities: Men in the Medieval West (New York and London, 1999), pp. ix–xx.

2   For example, Clare Lees noted that '"hegemonic" males' such as kings had been explicitly left out of *Medieval Masculinities* lest they 'obscure the rich and varied evidence for men's history': 'Introduction', in Claire Lees (ed.), *Medieval Masculinities: Regarding Men in the Middle Ages* (Minneapolis and London, 1994), pp. xv–xxv (p. xv). Similarly, the study of queens lagged behind the scholarly rise of interest in medieval women, as noted by John Carmi Parsons, 'Family, sex, and power: the rhythms of medieval queenship', in John Carmi Parsons (ed.), *Medieval Queenship* (Stroud, 1994), pp. 1–11 (pp. 1–2). The lack of scholarship on gender in relation to kings and kingship is also noted by W. M. Ormrod in the present volume.

3   Male saints and issues of masculinity also remain relatively unexplored as compared with female saints and issues of femininity in recent studies of medieval saints' lives and cults.

4   For accounts of the development and dissemination of these works see Nicholas Orme, *From Childhood to Chivalry: The Education of the English Kings and Aristocracy 1066–1530* (London and New York, 1984), pp. 86–98; Richard Firth Green, *Poets and Princepleasers: Literature and the English Court in the Late Middle Ages* (Toronto, 1980), pp. 135–67; Jean-Philippe Genet, *Four English Political Tracts of the Later Middle Ages*, Camden Society, 4th series, 18 (London, 1977). For an outline of contemporary ideas about ideal kingship see G. L. Harriss, 'Introduction: the exemplar of kingship', in G. L. Harriss (ed.), *Henry V: The Practice of Kingship* (Oxford, 1985), pp. 1–29. See also Watts cited in n. 6 below.

5   Orme, *From Childhood to Chivalry*, p. 96; Firth Green, *Poets and Princepleasers*, pp. 140–1. For editions of the *Secreta secretorum* see n. 23. Fiona Dunlop's essay in the present volume discusses the *Secreta secretorum* within a late medieval noble context.

6   John Watts, *Henry VI and the Politics of Kingship* (Cambridge, 1996), esp. pp. 16–38 for analysis of the norms of kingship established by mirrors for princes. However, this excellent study does not consider the role of king-saints within this discourse. (See p. 15 n. 6 for Watts's summary of the 'poems, verse histories and similar [instructional] texts' which he considered alongside mirrors for princes.)

7   For an account of Henry's visit see Walter F. Schirmer, *John Lydgate: A Study in the Culture of the Fifteenth Century*, tr. Ann E. Keep (London, 1961), pp. 145–6; Derek Pearsall, *John Lydgate* (London, 1971), pp. 25–7. Pearsall notes that Curteys himself had written a Latin life of St Edmund (p. 25). Surviving manuscripts of the life contain a series of illustrations, including one of Henry VI praying by St Edmund's tomb. There is not space to consider these here, but see Kathleen L. Scott, 'Lydgate's lives of saints Edmund and Fremund: a newly-located manuscript in Arundel Castle', *Viator*, 13 (1992), 335–66, for some reproductions.

8   For the development of the early cult of Edmund see Susan J. Ridyard, *The*

Royal Saints of Anglo-Saxon England (Cambridge, 1988), pp. 61–73, 211–33; Dorothy Whitelock, 'Fact and fiction in the legend of St Edmund', *Proceedings of the Suffolk Institute of Archaeology*, 21 (1969), 217–33.

9 For an edition of Abbo's life see Michael Winterbottom (ed.), *Three Lives of English Saints* (Toronto, 1972), pp. 67–87; for discussion of the circumstances of its composition see Ridyard, *Royal Saints*, pp. 70–3.

10 Ridyard, *Royal Saints*, p. 226; Diana Webb, *Pilgrimage in Medieval England* (London and New York, 2000), pp. 117–20.

11 *Three Lives of English Saints*, pp. 70–1, for Abbo's praise of Edmund's kingship. Ridyard notes that Geoffrey of Wells, author of the twelfth-century text describing Edmund's infancy (*De Infancia Sancti Edmundi*) also showed 'a marked interest in the delineation of Christian kingship': Ridyard, *Royal Saints*, p. 73.

12 All quotations from the life of St Edmund (hereafter referred to by book and line numbers in the text) are taken from C. Horstmann's edition, *Altenglische Legenden: Neue Folge* (Heilbronn, 1881), pp. 376–440.

13 Karen A. Winstead has also noted that Lydgate presents Edmund as an excellent ruler, arguing that this is part of a strategy which seeks to valorize lay life and experience, 'Lydgate's lives of saints Edmund and Alban: martyrdom and prudent pollicie', *Medievalia*, 17 (1991), 221–41.

14 Pearsall, *John Lydgate*, p. 297. The text has been edited as *Lydgate and Burgh's Secrees of the old Philosophers*, ed. Robert Steele, EETS ES 66 (London, 1894).

15 For an edition see Genet, *Four English Political Tracts*, pp. 53–168. Hoccleve's Middle English *Regiment of Princes* was another extremely popular mirror, and was originally dedicated to Prince Henry, later Henry V: *Thomas Hoccleve: The Regiment of Princes*, ed. Charles R. Blyth (Kalamazoo, MI, 1999).

16 R. A. Griffiths, *The Reign of King Henry VI* (orig. publ. 1980; this edition Stroud, 1998), p. 52.

17 Watts, *Henry VI*, p. 54.

18 Ibid., p. 110.

19 This premiss underpins Roger Lovatt's work on John Blacman's memoir of Henry, for example; 'John Blacman: Biographer of Henry VI', in R. H. C. Davis and J. M. Wallace-Hadrill (eds), *The Writing of History in the Middle Ages: Essays Presented to R. W. Southern* (Oxford, 1981), pp. 415–44, and 'A collector of apocryphal anecdotes: John Blacman revisited', in A. J. Pollard (ed.), *Property and Politics: Essays in Later Medieval English History* (Gloucester, 1984), pp. 172–97.

20 Bede provides several examples of this phenomenon in his *Ecclesiastical History of the English People*, as discussed by C. Stancliffe, 'Kings who opted out', in P. Wormald with D. Bullough and R. Collins (eds), *Ideal and Reality in Frankish and Anglo-Saxon Society: Studies Presented to J. M. Wallace-Hadrill* (Oxford, 1983), pp. 154–76.

21 Gábor Klaniczay, *Holy Rulers and Blessed Princesses: Dynastic Cults in*

Medieval Central Europe, tr. Éva Pálmai (Cambridge, 2002), pp. 114–54 (p. 147).

22 M. C. Gasposchkin, 'Boniface VIII, Philip the Fair and the sanctity of Louis IX', Journal of Medieval History, 29 (2003), 1–26 (3).

23 Three Prose Versions of the Secreta Secretorum, ed. Robert Steele, EETS ES 74 (London, 1898), p. 11. For editions of other Middle English versions see Mahmoud A. Manzaloui, Secretum Secretorum: Nine English Versions, EETS OS 276 (Oxford, 1977).

24 Winstead, 'Lydgate's lives', p. 226.

25 Edmund's self-governance according to the four cardinal virtues is reiterated at 1. 664–73.

26 Three Prose Versions of the Secreta Secretorum, p. 146. See Watts, Henry VI, pp. 23–5; pp. 58–9, for discussion of the role of the four cardinal virtues within mirrors for princes.

27 Watts, Henry VI, pp. 21–2, for the delineation of these twin duties.

28 Ibid., pp. 22–3, for representations of the body politic.

29 For De re militari see Firth Green, Poets and Princepleasers, p. 144. It was also tr. into Middle English in the fifteenth century, for an edition see Knyghthode and Bataile, ed. R. Dyboski and Z. M. Arend, EETS OS 201 (London, 1936).

30 For example, Abbo states that Edmund is a keen soldier, but does not show him in battle; Winterbottom, Three Lives of English Saints, p. 73, p. 76.

31 Christopher Fletcher's current work on Richard II will provide a fuller discussion of the implications of 'manly' in relation to medieval kingship.

32 These two had been established as Edmund's persecutors by Abbo, Three Lives of English Saints, p. 71.

33 Similarly Winstead has noted that the confrontation between Edmund, Vbba and Hyngwar is presented 'as a confrontation between just and unjust princes', 'Lydgate's lives ', 228.

34 See Edward Christie's essay in the present volume for the same point made in relation to Ælfric's translation of Abbo's life. The emphasis on contrasts between different versions of manhood is heightened by the virtual absence of any female characters in the events of Edmund's earthly life. Masculinity is here set against another form of masculinity, rather than against femininity.

35 The fact of Edmund's virginity was apparently established at an early stage in the development of his cult. Ridyard argues that, in the first instance, Edmund was presented as a virgin because it suited the interests of the kings of Wessex (who ruled East Anglia from the early tenth century onwards) to claim that, as Edmund could not have fathered any heirs, they themselves were his natural successors, Royal Saints, p. 226.

36 Vern L. Bullough, 'On being male in the Middle Ages', in Lees, Medieval Masculinities, pp. 31–46, for discussion of the importance of sexual activity and procreation to definitions of lay manhood.

37 As noted in Karen A. Winstead, 'Capgrave's Saint Katherine and the perils of gynecocracy', Viator, 26 (1999), 361–76 (368).

38 Kathleen Coyne Kelly has argued that, within medieval texts, 'male virginity is underdetermined, and can be made intelligible only by reference to an elaborate feminized and feminizing system. In effect, these texts broach the subject, only to change the subject, as it were, from masculine to feminine.' *Performing Virginity and Testing Chastity in the Middle Ages* (London, 2000), p. 93. She also argues that 'the male virgin never takes centre stage in the saint's life' (p. 104) but this is certainly not true of the life of St Edmund.

39 *Three Prose Versions of the Secreta Secretorum*, pp. 10–11.

40 Ibid., p. 14; my emphasis.

41 Ibid., pp. 189–90.

42 Jacqueline Murray, ' "The law of sin that is in my members": the problem of male embodiment', in Samantha J. E. Riches and Sarah Salih (eds), *Gender and Holiness: Men, Women and Saints in Late Medieval Europe* (London and New York, 2002), pp. 9–22.

43 *Three Prose Versions of the Secreta Secretorum*, p. 191

44 John Capgrave, *The Book of Illustrious Henries*, tr. F. C. Hingeston (London, 1858), p. 45. For further discussion of the importance of self-control to a king see Harriss, 'Henry V', p. 5; Gaspoleschkin, 'Boniface VIII, Philip the Fair and the Sanctity of Louis IX', p. 16.

45 I am indebted to Sarah Salih for this observation.

46 For an edition of the poem see Richard Leighton Greene (ed.), *The Early English Carols* (Oxford, 1977), pp. 259–60; see also Katherine J. Lewis, 'Becoming a virgin king: Richard II and Edward the Confessor', in Riches and Salih, *Gender and Holiness*, pp. 86–100 (p. 88).

12

Monarchy, Martyrdom and Masculinity: England in the Later Middle Ages

W. M. ORMROD

The history of English monarchy in the later Middle Ages is customarily represented as a series of institutional, constitutional and dynastic crises: the crises of governance brought on by the supposed decline in the crown's fiscal and judicial authority, the political crises generated by factionalism in court and country, and the succession crises precipitated by the forcible removal of rulers who were deemed unfitted to exercise sovereignty. Historians have done a great deal in the last fifty years or so to debunk the myths surrounding the deposition of Richard II, the Lancastrian 'experiment in government' and the Wars of the Roses, and in the process have added much to our understanding of how kingship worked both in the normative and the performative senses.[1] But little attention has been given to the possibility that a *gendered* reading of monarchy might contribute to a deeper appreciation of the dynamics of politics.[2]

This neglect might be explained in two ways. First, there is the assumption that later medieval English monarchy was self-evidently a male preserve, deeply imbued with masculine values and fulfilled in all but exceptional circumstances by men.[3] Secondly, there is the fact that most of the relevant recent work by political historians has been preoccupied with the so-called 'new constitutional history' which, while explicitly engaging with ideas as well as structures, nevertheless tends to steer away from the sort of cultural-historical approaches that we normally associate with the study of gender.[4] In this discussion, I hope to demonstrate that masculinity was in fact a deeply contested issue in the public debate on monarchy in England during the fourteenth and fifteenth centuries, that this manifested itself in the debates that surrounded the depositions of Edward II, Richard II and Henry VI, and that the theme of martyrdom and its associations with sanctity were used by the successors of those kings in order to reclaim the masculinity of deposed rulers and thus to legitimize their own regimes.

In order to assess the degree to which monarchy may be said to have been a gendered concept in England during the later Middle Ages, we need to draw a distinction between, on the one hand, 'monarchy' itself (that is, the *system* of governance by a single individual, usually claiming authority by dynastic right) and, on the other hand, 'kingship' (a phenomenon that we may define in terms of the *exercise* of monarchy by the individual who happened to hold the title of ruler at any one time). It can be argued that, while the *exercise* of monarchy in England had always tended to be the preserve of males, the principles that underpinned the *system* of monarchy continued to represent the institution as genuinely transcending gender.[5] This had two implications. First, and more theoretically, it reinforced the symbolic inclusiveness of the ruler's constitutional and moral authority by representing the body politic of which the monarch was head as an organism with both masculine and feminine attributes and thus symbolically representative of the whole realm.[6] Secondly, and more pragmatically, it required that such a ruler demonstrate not only the 'masculine' qualities of monarchy – leadership, prowess, integrity, equity – but also its 'feminized' virtues of peacemaking, love, mercy and reconciliation. As we know from recent work on the intercessory role of royal women, these feminized aspects of the late medieval royal job specification were most effectively exercised by queens consort, whose actions as mediators for the exercise of royal mercy transformed them from mere trophy wives into real players in the performance of monarchy.[7] The resulting informal division of responsibilities between king and queen tells us much about the manner in which the exercise of monarchy continued to reflect and reinforce the ruler's responsibility to serve a symbolically genderless political community.

If we take this distribution of functions between king and queen as both normative and normal in the functioning of late medieval English monarchy, then we need also to consider the implications of a situation in which there was no queen available to take on the feminized elements of monarchy, or in which either king or queen chose to transgress the declared boundaries and assume some of the functions usually associated with the other partner. Such situations arose on three occasions during the later Middle Ages. The first was in the early fourteenth century, when the inability of Edward II to respond to the masculine model of royal authority created by his father, combined with the public scandal of his political (and possible sexual) subjection to court favourites, precipitated a reaction by his wife, Isabella of France, who led the coup that brought about the deposition of her husband and her own installation as *de facto* regent of England. The second instance was during the reign of Richard II, when for significant periods England lacked a real or active queen, and when the king himself was occupied in demonstrations of uncompromising political mastery that appeared to marginalize, if not confound, the feminine attributes of monarchy. The third case occurred in the mid-fifteenth century, when Henry VI's failure to live up to his father's vision of macho-monarchy, coupled with the onset of his own mental incapacity and deposition, encouraged his wife, Margaret of Anjou, to take up arms in defence of their son's right to the succession – a strategy whose failure quickly brought about the deposition of the king himself. Clearly, gender disorder played a significant – if still under-rated – role in some of the great political crises of later medieval England. The aim of this essay is to treat this wider topic from a specific angle, by looking at how subsequent rulers sought to restore the dignity and legitimacy of deposed kings (and thus, of course, to reinforce their own right to rule) specifically by playing on the theme of martyrdom. I will argue that the presentation of these kings as martyrs had a specifically gendered dimension, and that the effect of creating or promoting a cult of a deposed ruler was not merely to provide a generalized vindication of his monarchy but also to reassert his masculinity and thus to defame the gender transgressions committed by him and/or his wife. In other words, I shall contend, martyrdom offered the rulers of late medieval England a convenient means of fictionalizing the past that denied the gynocratic implications of active queenship and offered a sanitized view of the reigns of controversial kings.

Much has been written in recent years on the phenomenon of 'political saints' in late medieval England. The work of John Mc-Kenna, John Thielmann, Simon Walker and others has revealed how, from the thirteenth century, popular cults associated with figures who had suffered violent deaths in civil strife could become the locus for subsequent expressions of political discontent and opposition: thus the well-known and at least potentially anti-royalist cults of Simon de Montfort, Thomas of Lancaster and Archbishop Scrope.[8] The crown, which sometimes needed and tried to suppress such movements, somewhat ironically responded with a similar strategy by patronizing its own series of royal (and therefore *royalist*) proto-saints in the persons of the martyred Edward II and Henry VI. (The fact that Richard II is not on this list is significant, and a point to which I shall return.) To some extent, the efforts to secure formal canonizations of late medieval English kings can be seen as a response to the elevation of Louis IX of France, within a generation of his death, to the status of sanctity.[9] More immediately, however, royal petitions to the papacy for the canonizations of Edward II and Henry VI were the product, as is well-known, of regimes that felt a special political need to vindicate those kings: in the first instance, Richard II aimed during the 1380s and 1390s to invalidate the notion that Edward II's deposition created a precedent for the enforced abdications of other kings (including Richard himself); and in the second case, Henry VII was eager to associate his new dynasty with the emergent cult of Henry VI and thus to derive credibility for the notion that the Tudors were indeed the legitimate successors of the Lancastrian kings.[10] Partly because the secondary literature has become so preoccupied with the notion of the '*political* saint', however, the scholars who operate in this field do not appear to have given much consideration to the rather wider cultural implications of the cults in question. Furthermore, by focusing on the periods during which royal patronage of those cults produced formal representations to the papacy for canonization, the previous work has perhaps missed some of the wider political implications, at least in the case of the posthumous rehabilitation of Edward II. By starting with that case, and examining it in reasonable detail within the context of gender politics, I hope to suggest some new ways of thinking about the connection between martyrdom and masculinity which I can then apply more briefly and generally to the cases of Richard II and Henry VI.

Following his abdication and deposition in January 1327, Edward II was held in secure custody until his suspiciously timely death in September of the same year.[11] He was buried at Gloucester Abbey (now the cathedral), where a popular cult seems to have developed relatively quickly, possibly at the active encouragement of a chapter of monks who were otherwise somewhat short of relics, pilgrims and income.[12] The immediate effect of the coup of 1327 was to transfer effective power not into the hands of the 14-year-old king but into those of his mother, Queen Isabella, and her lover, Roger Mortimer. Isabella's own upbringing as a princess of France, a daughter of no less a figure than Philip IV 'the Fair', seems to have encouraged her to believe that she had a right to exercise the functions of a regent, even though the specific constitutional position was that her son was of an age to rule.[13] As a result, Isabella had not only transgressed her role as consort to Edward II by overthrowing his regime, but had also artificially extended her authority as queen into the reign of the son that she had brought prematurely to the throne. When Edward III in turn overthrew his own mother and had her lover Mortimer put to death late in 1330, it was therefore especially important and relevant that his regime should seek to re-establish the gender norms implicit in the theory and practice of monarchy.[14]

This was achieved in a number of ways. First, Mortimer was publicly accused at his trial of putting enmity between Edward II and his queen and thus of disrupting what was now constructed, after the event, as a 'normal' marital relationship.[15] Secondly, Edward III clearly imposed on his mother the attributes and limitations of widowhood – not by locking her away, as used to be popularly thought, but by allowing her to develop a regime of pious contemplation such as might suggest her atonement for past offences to political and gender conventions and which culminated in a rather theatrical funeral that involved her burial in full bridal gear and accompanied by the heart of her long-dead husband.[16] Thirdly, Edward III reasserted the feminized aspects of monarchy in an appropriately subsidiary role by constructing his own queen, Philippa of Hainault, as the archetypal wife and mother and, having re-established the appropriate balance between their roles, began to reinforce the status of the queen by allowing her, uniquely, to share in the thaumaturgical powers claimed by Plantagenet kings.[17] Fourthly, Edward III managed public debate on the legacy of Edward II – or at least allowed it to develop – in a way that made it clear that the deposition and murder of the former king was an act of political treachery precipitated chiefly by the queen's own refusal to accept the gender role rightly ascribed to her. This 'royalist' position is especially evident in the chronicle accounts composed in the decades after 1327 – most famously, that of Geoffrey le Baker – and which projected Edward II as a martyr and saint cruelly deprived of his kingship and his life by the henchmen of Isabella 'the Jezebel'.[18]

The final, and in the present context most significant, way in which Edward III may be said to have reinstated gender norms in the public image of the royal family was through his patronage of the cult that grew up around the resting place of Edward II at Gloucester Abbey. Because there is no direct evidence that Edward III petitioned the papacy for his father's canonization, it is easy to assume that he deliberately downplayed the local cult that sprang up, perhaps spontaneously, perhaps under the self-interested patronage of the monks of Gloucester, during the period after Edward II's interment in 1327. Nevertheless, the gifts that he bestowed on the abbey were certainly taken as official markers of royal patronage, and the visits to Gloucester that we know him to have undertaken in person (and arranged for his sons) suggest that the cult was given some prominence at court.[19] The absence of canonization petitions to the curia before Richard II's time is not, then, to be taken as necessarily marking the reluctance of Edward III's regime to be associated with the cult of Edward of Caernarfon. Far from it: the image of Edward II as a martyr for the cause of hereditary and lifelong monarchy was a very necessary part of the official or royalist stance on what had happened in the coup of 1327, just as much so under Edward III as under Richard II. What needs particularly to be stressed in the present context, however, is the way that the deposed king's alleged martyrdom can be read as part of a concerted and coherent strategy on the part of Edward III to reassert his father's masculinity and thus reestablish the gender norms of monarchy temporarily disrupted by Queen Isabella's role as principal perpetrator of the deposition. This is essentially the line of argument elaborated in Geoffrey le Baker, who portrayed Edward II as a Christ-like figure tested and purified by the terrible death that awaited and finally took him.[20] Not everyone, of course, agreed: the red hot poker thrust into the deposed king's anus became, in subversive renderings of the story, a metaphor for his reputation as a sodomite and thus, in itself, a direct and enduring challenge to normative masculinity.[21] But it was precisely the existence and persistence of this hostile view of Edward II's kingship that necessitated what has here been characterized as a royalist assertion of gender norms in monarchy achieved through the elevation of Edward II to the status of martyr, the demonizing of Queen Isabella as a disruptive virago and the representation of the complementary kingship and queenship of Edward III and Queen Philippa.

When we move to Richard II's treatment of the cult of Edward II during the 1380s and 1390s, by contrast, we find very different political motives at work and very different cultural implications to be drawn.

Richard II was the first and only king to make formal representations to the papacy for the canonization of Edward II.[22] In recent years there has been a growing awareness that both Richard and his enemies showed a keen interest in the historical past and that the similarities that modern historians have long drawn between the politics of the 1390s and those of the 1320s were also appreciated by those who participated in the political events that culminated in Richard's deposition.[23] Although documentary evidence falters for the last years of the reign, it is therefore reasonably credible to suggest that, when the papacy showed no interest in pursuing the cause of St Edward of Caernarfon, Richard continued to persist with a private and personal cult of his ancestor. That cult could have provided him, while king, with an elusive sense of divine protection and consequent political impunity (witness the connection that both Edward II and Richard II asserted with the tradition of the holy oil of St Thomas Becket).[24] It could also have provided him, after deposition and imprisonment at Pontefract, with a ready-made role model for his own impending martyrdom.[25] There is good reason, in short, to suppose that while Edward III's patronage of the memory of Edward II was perfectly prepared to play on the theme of *political* martyrdom, it was really only the heightened political circumstances of Richard II's reign that caused a king himself overly preoccupied with the theology of monarchy to elevate that martyrdom to the level of *holiness*.

If that is the case, what were the gender implications, if any, of Richard's public and private treatment of the cult of his great-grandfather? It was suggested above that Edward III's rehabilitation of Edward II was, at least in part, a vindication of the right of both kings to rule without the unwarranted interference of Queen Isabella. In Richard's case, however, the problem lay not in an overmighty consort but in the lack, for much of his reign, of an authoritative embodiment of the feminine attributes of queenship. I have argued elsewhere that, although the king's mother, Joan of Kent, princess of Wales, performed some of the functions normally associated with the king's consort during the early years of the reign, she lacked both the public credibility and (very importantly for someone like her son) the formal investiture of coronation and anointing to fulfil adequately the void that had been left since the death of her mother-in-law, Queen Philippa, in 1369.[26] Once Richard was married, in 1382, to Anne of Bohemia, all this supposedly changed: Anne was treated by contemporaries, and has been much analysed by historians, as the very incarnation of the queenly attributes of mercy and reconciliation.[27] Certainly, her death in 1394 was and is held to have had a destabilizing effect on Richard.[28] A gendered reading can be articulated in terms of his apparent inability or refusal to accommodate the queen's function as political peacemaker into his own performance of solitary kingship.

I should like to take these fairly well established ideas a little further by suggesting that Richard's posthumous treatment of Queen Anne was itself a concerted attempt actually to suppress the notion that the queen had distinct attributes and responsibilities, and thus to create within his own increasingly internalized image of monarchy an argument that all power operated through the king alone. In this isolationist view of monarchy, the support of a consort (or of other lesser royals) was deemed no more substantive or significant than the loyalty that was due from the king's subjects at large.[29] Evidence suggesting this idea of the suppression or assimilation of the queen's separate political role may be found in two forms: the double tomb that Richard commissioned for himself and his first wife; and his choice of a child to act as his second consort. To take the second matter first, it is to say the least striking that Richard II should have chosen, or been content with the offer of, an infant French princess as the replacement for Queen Anne: the prospect of five to ten years before the consummation of the marriage and the assumption of an active political role by the new Queen Isabelle may have allowed Richard the sense of distance and independence that he needed in order to recraft the gender identity of his monarchy.[30] As for the Westminster tomb: late medieval aristocratic double tombs are often read as statements of the *parity* of the marriage partners, and there is good reason to see some royal examples in this light.[31] But the tomb of Richard II and Anne of Bohemia, commissioned by Richard after Anne's death, and the first such royal double tomb, can also be interpreted in another manner: namely, as a statement by the king that the attributes of queenship had been *subsumed* into his royal authority following the death of his first wife. Not for Anne the very public representation of queenship that had been accorded to Eleanor of Castile through the Eleanor Crosses and the three tombs at Lincoln, London and Westminster.[32] Rather, the double tomb commissioned by Richard II may epitomize the more general sense in which Anne created no identity and left no memory save those which the king chose to allow her: the uncharacteristically close proximity in which the king and queen spent so much of their time (and which is one reason why no separate accounts survive for

Anne's household) is suggestive not merely of Richard's fondness for his wife but also for his desire to control her, and his destruction of the couple's favourite palace of Sheen is indicative not merely of his grief at her death but also of his desire carefully to focus organized memorialization of the queen at his own liturgical headquarters of Westminster Abbey.[33] In this sense, then, the feminine attributes of monarchy may be said to have expired with the death of Queen Anne and been claimed back assertively by a king who had his own effigy and legend carved on 'her' tomb. The fact that the politics of Richard's last years – those of his so-called 'tyranny' – were so lacking in the exercise of queenly moderation and pacification was simply another way of putting across the king's increasing obsession with his policy of demanding the uncompromising obedience of his subjects.

If it can thus be argued that there are important gender issues to the royal politics of the 1380s and 1390s, we might also ask whether this can in any sense be connected back to Richard II's interest in the cult of Edward II. The gender implications of Richard's close association with Edward the Confessor have been fruitfully explored by Katherine Lewis, who has argued that the association signified not simply a general and necessary veneration for the last of the canonized kings of England but a particular preoccupation with the theme of chastity: Richard's devotion to the Confessor suggests that, perhaps during his marriage to Anne and almost certainly after it, the king undertook a vow of chastity that turned him, in effect, into a reconstructed virgin, undefiled either by sins of the flesh or, metaphorically and more potently, by the political mistakes and the constitutional challenges of the early years of his reign.[34] This theme of virginity chimes with my earlier suggestion about Richard II's assimilation and sublimation of the feminine qualities of monarchy into his performance of monarchy after 1394. What I would like to suggest now is that the cult of Edward II, in the manner in which I earlier characterized it, could also have fitted with Richard's view of the capacity and right of the king to exercise all the functions of monarchy, whether they were masculine or feminine, kingly or queenly. If I am correct in suggesting that part of Edward III's strategy in memorializing his father was to re-establish the gender norms of monarchy briefly disrupted by the political intervention of Queen Isabella, then the idea that the king had the right and capacity to regulate queenly functions – and even, in the absence of an active consort, to *incorporate* those functions – may surely have struck a chord with Richard II after the death of Anne of Bohemia and his marriage to the infant Isabelle of France. The degree to which such ideas might have worked through in the longer term is, however, part of counterfactual history: in 1399 Richard lost his throne not through betrayal by a queen but through the treachery of a male cousin, and the deposed king's final engagement with the memory of Edward II was doubtless within the emotionally charged and self-destructive context of political martyrdom.

The cases of Edward II and Richard II provide models and possible precedents in relation to the third of my case studies, that of the cult of Henry VI. We can move fairly quickly over this ground, not because it is uncontested but because at least some of the conceptual framework in which I wish to set it has already been established in earlier parts of this paper. Henry VI died a deposed and imprisoned king, and a broken and deranged man, in the Tower of London in 1471. Despite the careful attempts of his usurper, Edward IV, to hide the body away at the royal abbey of Chertsey, a popular cult soon sprang up; and after the overthrow of the Yorkists and the succession of the Tudors, who claimed their right to the throne through the Lancastrian line, the monarchy gave official support to the cult and began a long, though ultimately unsuccessful campaign for the canonization of Henry VI.[35] Modern historians have, not surprisingly, been quick to categorize Henry as a *political* saint, implying that the unofficial cult would never have received royal patronage had it not been for the Tudors' desire and need to buttress their otherwise tenuous claim to the rightful succession.[36] Scholarly attention has therefore tended to concentrate on a fairly cynical deconstruction of the cult, and of its apologist, John Blacman, in an effort to demonstrate the mismatch between Henry's posthumous reputation as a saintly ruler and the incontrovertibly disastrous political record of his reign.[37] This, however, as Katherine Lewis has again pointed out, is rather to miss the point: our aim ought to be to understand the cultural messages provided by the legends of the pious Henry VI, not simply to test and discredit their actual historical veracity.[38] In the present context, it may be possible to push the discussion of this material a little further by exploring in particular the manner in which it sought not merely to rehabilitate Henry's political record but to reclaim his masculinity in order to serve a particular dynastic imperative.

There is no doubt that Henry VI had all the credentials of a political martyr: he lost his throne, and finally his life, to a usurping cousin in the person of Edward IV. The degree to which any mileage might be made of that fact was, however, a different question: the situation at Henry's death in 1471 was, after all, quite different from that which had attended Edward II's demise, for it involved not merely a change of king but a major disruption to the normal line of succession and the advent of a new dynasty to the throne.[39] Whereas I have argued that the popular cult of Edward II was cultivated – even managed – by the crown from an early stage to add credence to both Edward III and Richard II's visions of kingship, the dynastic changes arising from the Wars of the Roses meant that the cult of Henry VI was treated as suspicious, subversive and in need of suppression, at least so long as Edward IV was alive. There was something of a change of heart under Richard III, who was instrumental in having Henry's remains exhumed from Chertsey and reburied at Windsor. This could be regarded as a distinct phase in the development of the cult, not in itself connected to the process of canonization. It gave formal royal support to the cult – and thus, by the way, confirmed that the ex-king was indeed dead – but it did not mean that the current monarch was signed up to support his predecessor's claims to sainthood. There are important similarities here with Henry V's decision to exhume Richard II's remains from Kings Langley and rebury them in the tomb that the latter had prepared for himself and his wife at Westminster: in both cases, there are no hints of any direct royal sympathy for the holiness of the deceased king, and the intended messages were about the continuity and strength of royal power.[40] The *second* and distinct stage in the process of posthumous rehabilitation – that reached, in the case of Edward II's cult, when Richard II chose to press for formal canonization – occurred for Henry VI only after Richard III's deposition and the arrival of a neo-Lancastrian ruler in the person of Henry VII.[41] The political parallels between these royal campaigns of canonization are obvious: by seeking validation of the miracles performed in death by a previous ruler of his own dynasty, a king could both invalidate the legitimacy of that earlier monarch's deposition and provide proof that his was indeed the line of succession justified in the eyes of God. It is this dynastic imperative that probably also explains why no one ever thought to pursue the canonization of Richard II: as things worked out, no king in fifteenth-century England needed to argue that his claim to the throne rested on a dynastic association with Richard of Bordeaux.

While there is therefore an undoubted abundance of political interpretations of the canonization process of Henry VI, it may also be that a cultural-historical – and specifically a *gendered* – reading of the material adds depth and strength to the argument that seeking saintliness represented an effective form of royalist propaganda in late medieval England. It is my contention that Henry VI's canonization process sought to rehabilitate him as *man* as well as king, and thus to normalize the distribution of gender roles within his own and (equally as important) his Tudor successors' regime. The strategy was something akin to that which I have posited for Edward III in using the memory of Edward II as a means of distancing himself from the overbearing influence of Queen Isabella. In the case of Henry VI, however, the line of thinking can be carried further, and argued more substantively, because of the survival of documentary evidence relating directly to the cult and the royal patronage that it latterly received. These materials – particularly the writings of John Blacman – indicate that the case for Henry's canonization was built not only (as was the case with Richard II's campaign for Edward II's sainthood) on the reports of miracles worked by the king after his death, but also on the holiness of his earlier life in this world. One outcome of this new, sanitized view of the regime of Henry VI was to blacken the name and memory of Margaret of Anjou. While Margaret's intentions in taking charge of her husband's regime during the 1450s had always been projected in terms of her desire to defend the rights of succession of their son, Prince Edward, her attempts to assume a kind of regency during Henry's bouts of mental incapacity, and her donning of armour at the outbreak of civil war, presented disturbing signs of the disruption of normative gender roles within the performance of monarchy. One effect of the new emphasis on Henry VI's holiness during the 1480s was therefore to denigrate and marginalize Margaret, to distance her from the spiritual values on which Henry's monarchy was now seen to have rested, and to perceive her flouting of gender roles as itself contributing to the destruction of his regime.[42] Thus, by default at least, the exercise of monarchy was reasserted as a specifically masculine enterprise and Henry's kingship was vindicated.

To press this point just one step further, we might wish to speculate on the degree to which the habit of demonizing queens for gender transgression as a means of excusing the personal and political deficiencies of their kings was, in the case of Margaret of Anjou at least, especially driven by the dynastic exigencies of the moment. We surely cannot ignore the fact that the king who first petitioned for Henry VI's canonization, Henry VII, had taken to wife Elizabeth of York, a direct claimant to a rival line of succession. For all the elaborate strategies that Henry VII deployed to demonstrate that his kingship did not depend on his wife, he was very much aware of the potency of her position, especially when it suited him to configure it in Tudor royal iconography.[43] What Elizabeth lacked, however, and what her husband gained through his patronage of the cult of Henry VI, was a recent saint in the family. The gearing up of the cult of Henry VI to a new level of activity with formal, royally sanctioned petitions for canonization therefore demonstrated to the realm, and to the Christian world, that the Lancastrians – and thus the Tudors – were a legitimate dynasty. In the light of the foregoing arguments, it might also be said that it also represented them as the guardians of a monarchical tradition in which gender roles were appropriately divided and ordered to guarantee the dominance of the masculine. The great irony of the situation, of course, is that the whole reassertion of the masculinity of monarchy here attributed to Henry VII had to be turned on its head within two generations, when the Reformation put a stop to the prospect of *any* more royal saints and the accession of Mary I and Elizabeth I required a fundamental reconfiguration of the gendered performance of English monarchy.[44]

From the foregoing discussion, two conclusions may now be offered. First of all, in terms of the gendering of monarchy: I hope I have set out coherently an argument that, specifically because there *was* an acknowledged element of gender identity within the range of functions and qualities associated with the performance of monarchy, the actual distribution and effective delivery of those elements in the job specification could become contested between kings and queens and, in the process, challenge some of the wider gender norms of contemporary society. Kings and queens were not ordinary husbands and wives, but they did provide a set of role models for conjugal relationships: consequently, the transgression of boundaries by queens, as in the cases of Isabella of France and Margaret of Anjou, represented an image of the 'woman on top' that was both politically and culturally disruptive. I have suggested that the cults of Edward II and Henry VI were managed by their successors at least in part to reassert the masculine elements of monarchy and to restore the sense of political and social stability that came with the appropriate division of responsibilities between the king and his consort. I hope thereby to have added another dimension to the theme and debate on so-called 'political saints' by suggesting that cultural politics, as well as matters of state, had a bearing on the posthumous fortunes of the martyred kings of late medieval England.

The second of my concluding remarks comes back to the theme of this book and attempts to assess what messages may be drawn from my discussion in terms of the connection between holiness and masculinity. Underpinning much of what I have said here is a sense that, while a whole range of activities and representations of royalty during the later Middle Ages upheld the principle that monarchy was ungendered and required the appropriate application of masculine *and* feminine characteristics to create effective and merciful government, the processes of popular and formal canonization only ever applied themselves to kings and tended to create and perpetuate a version of royal holiness which, for political reasons, was consciously gendered as masculine. It is interesting in this respect to see how, although late medieval culture repeatedly looked to the Virgin Mary and other female saints to provide very precise role models for queens of England, the elaborate regimes of religious devotion which became more and more a part of the female royal lifestyle towards the end of the Middle Ages never generated any candidates for sanctity from among them. If piety was the duty of queens, holiness was evidently the prerogative of kings – or rather, more specifically, of martyred kings. It is for others to consider the degree to which this state of affairs – women as recipients of a preordained devotional regime, men as continuing contenders for the heavenly hierarchy – represents a wider trend in the gendering of late medieval devotion and sanctification. Kings – and queens – are of course very special and likely exceptional cases. But that is also what makes them so interesting. I hope to have suggested here that, even in the supposedly well-trodden path of high politics, there is much for the historian of culture to explore about the nature both of holiness and of masculinity in late medieval England.

Notes

I am grateful to Katherine Lewis for assistance with this project, and to current and former members of the Centre for Medieval Studies, University of York (especially Joel Burden and Joanna Laynesmith), for their fruitful contributions to my thinking on this topic.

[1] The outstanding contribution is John Watts, *Henry VI and the Politics of Kingship* (Cambridge, 1996).

[2] An important exception is the new work currently in development by Christopher Fletcher on the masculinity of Richard II.
[3] For discussion of 'the single principle that males were preferred to females' and exceptions to the same, see Armin Wolf, 'Reigning queens in medieval Europe: when, where and why', in John Carmi Parsons (ed.), *Medieval Queenship* (Stroud, 1994), pp. 169–88.
[4] For this 'new constitutional history', see Edward Powell, *Kingship, Law, and Society: Criminal Justice in the Reign of Henry V* (Oxford, 1989), pp. 1–20.
[5] The most important point to be made in this respect is the distinction between the ability of a woman to exercise the office of king and her ability to transmit a claim to the throne to her son. Denial of the former did not necessarily denote denial of the latter, though the matter came under some discussion both in England and in France during the fifteenth century. Michael J. Bennett, 'Edward III's entail and the succession to the crown, 1376–1471', *English Historical Review*, 113 (1998), 580–609; Craig Taylor, 'Edward III and the Plantagenet claim to the French throne', in J. S. Bothwell (ed.), *The Age of Edward III* (Woodbridge, 2001), pp. 155–69; Craig Taylor, 'The Salic Law and the Valois succession to the French crown', *French History*, 15 (2001), 358–77.
[6] Ernst H. Kantorowicz, *The King's Two Bodies: A Study in Medieval Political Theology* (Princeton, 1957), pp. 394–5.
[7] Paul Strohm, *Hochon's Arrow: The Social Imagination of Fourteenth-Century Texts* (Princeton, 1992), pp. 95–119; John Carmi Parsons, 'The queen's intercession in thirteenth-century England', in J. Carpenter and Sally-Beth McLean (eds), *Power of the Weak: Studies in Medieval Women* (Urbana-Champaign, IL, 1995), pp. 147–77; John Carmi Parsons, 'The pregnant queen as counsellor and the medieval construction of motherhood', in John Carmi Parsons and Bonnie Wheeler (eds), *Medieval Mothering* (New York, 1996), pp. 39–61; John Carmi Parsons, 'The intercessionary role of Queens Margaret and Isabella of France', in Michael Prestwich, R. H. Britnell and Robin Frame (eds), *Thirteenth Century England*, vol. 6 (Woodbridge, 1997), pp. 144–56; Carolyn P. Collette, 'Joan of Kent and noble women's roles in Chaucer's world', *Chaucer Review*, 33 (1999), 350–62; W. M. Ormrod, 'In bed with Joan of Kent: the king's mother and the Peasants' Revolt', in Jocelyn Wogan Browne, Rosalynn Voaden, Arlyn Diamond, Ann Hutchison, Carol Meale and Lesley Johnson (eds), *Medieval Women: Texts and Contexts in Late Medieval Britain: Essays for Felicity Riddy* (Turnhout, 2000), pp. 277–92 (pp. 287–91).
[8] J. W. McKenna, 'Popular canonisation as political propaganda: the cult of Archbishop Scrope', *Speculum*, 45 (1970), 608–23; J. W. McKenna, 'Piety and propaganda: the cult of King Henry VI', in Beryl Rowland (ed.), *Chaucer and Middle English Studies in Honour of Rossell Hope Robbins* (London, 1974), pp. 72–88; Christopher Page, 'The rhymed office for St Thomas of Lancaster: poetry, politics and liturgy in fourteenth-century England', *Leeds Studies in English*, NS 14 (1983), 134–51; Thomas W.

French, 'The tomb of Archbishop Scrope in York Minster', *Yorkshire Archaeological Journal*, 61 (1989), 95–102; John M. Theilmann, 'Political canonization and political symbolism in medieval England', *Journal of British Studies*, 29 (1990), 241–66; John Edwards, 'The cult of "St" Thomas of Lancaster and its iconography', *Yorkshire Archaeological Journal*, 64 (1992), 103–22, and 67 (1995), 187–91; Simon Walker, 'Political saints in later medieval England', in R. H. Britnell and A. J. Pollard (eds), *The McFarlane Legacy: Studies in Late Medieval Politics and Society* (Stroud, 1995), pp. 77–106.

[9] Elizabeth M. Hallam, 'Philip the Fair and the cult of Saint Louis', *Studies in Church History*, 18 (1982), 201–14.

[10] Nigel Saul, *Richard II* (London, 1997), p. 323; Chris Given-Wilson, 'Richard II, Edward II, and the Lancastrian inheritance', *English Historical Review*, 109 (1994), 553–71; Bertram Wolffe, *Henry VI* (London, 1981), pp. 351–8.

[11] The present discussion accepts the orthodox account, though there has been a recent revival of interest in the tradition that Edward II escaped his fate and fled to the continent.

[12] W. M. Ormrod, 'The personal religion of Edward III', *Speculum*, 64 (1989), 849–77 (870–1).

[13] Frank L. Wiswall III, 'Politics, procedure and the "non-minority" of Edward III: some comparisons', in James L. Gillespie (ed.), *The Age of Richard II* (Stroud, 1997), pp. 7–25.

[14] For some legal and gender implications of Isabella's actions, see Charles T. Wood, *Joan of Arc and Richard III: Sex, Saints and Government in the Middle Ages* (Oxford, 1988), pp. 12–28.

[15] *Rotuli parliamentorum*, 6 vols (London, 1782), vol. 2, pp. 52–3.

[16] F. D. Blackley, 'Isabella of France, queen of England (1308–1358) and the late medieval cult of the dead', *Canadian Journal of History*, 15 (1980), 23–47. Diana Webb notes that Isabella 'remained an enthusiastic pilgrim and collector of relics during her thirty year long widowhood', *Pilgrimage in Medieval England* (London and New York, 2000), p. 130.

[17] For the construction of Philippa's role as intercessor and model matron, see Strohm, *Hochon's Arrow*, pp. 99–105; Ormrod, 'Personal religion of Edward III', p. 850 and n. 7. For Philippa's exercise of thaumaturgical powers, see Marc Bloch, *The Royal Touch: Sacred Monarchy and Scrofula in England and France*, tr. J. E. Anderson (London, 1973), pp. 102–3.

[18] Sophie Menache, 'Isabelle of France, queen of England: a reconsideration', *Journal of Medieval History*, 10 (1984), 107–24.

[19] Ormrod, 'Personal religion', pp. 870–1.

[20] Ian Mortimer, *The Greatest Traitor: The Life of Sir Roger Mortimer* (London, 2003), pp. 191–4.

[21] See, most recently, Michael Evans, *The Death of Kings: Royal Deaths in Medieval England* (London, 2003), pp. 126–34.

[22] Edouard Perroy, *L'Angleterre et le grand schisme d'Occident* (Paris, 1933), pp. 301, 330, 341–2.

23 Michael J. Bennett, *Richard II and the Revolution of 1399* (Stroud, 1999), pp. 14–55; W. M. Ormrod, 'Richard II's sense of English history', in Gwilym Dodd (ed.), *The Reign of Richard II* (Stroud, 2000), pp. 97–110.
24 J. R. S. Phillips, 'Edward II and the prophets', in W. M. Ormrod (ed.), *England in the Fourteenth Century* (Woodbridge, 1986), pp. 189–201; Bennett, *Richard II*, pp. 140–1.
25 Note in this respect the comment of Adam of Usk on Richard's contemplation of historical examples during his period at the Tower in 1399: *The Chronicle of Adam Usk*, ed. Chris Given-Wilson (Oxford, 1997), pp. 62–5.
26 Ormrod, 'In bed with Joan of Kent', pp. 287–91.
27 Strohm, *Hochon's Arrow*, pp. 105–11.
28 Saul, *Richard II*, p. 456.
29 For Richard's emphasis on the theme of obedience, ibid., pp. 293–404.
30 For the 'father–daughter' nature of this relationship, see ibid., p. 457.
31 See the tomb of Henry IV and Joan of Navarre at Canterbury, which was probably commissioned by Joan after Henry's death, and whose tester preserves a 'punctiliously exact balance' between the heraldry of the royal couple: Christopher Wilson 'The medieval monuments', in Patrick Collinson, Nigel Ramsay and Margaret Sparks (eds), *A History of Canterbury Cathedral* (Oxford, 1995), pp. 451–510 (pp. 498–503, quote at p. 500). The case of Henry VII and Elizabeth of York, by contrast, is susceptible to a similar interpretation as applied here to that of Richard II and Anne of Bohemia, especially given the dynastic imperatives discussed later in this chapter.
32 For the development of Eleanor's posthumous reputation, see John Carmi Parsons, 'Eleanor of Castile: legend and reality through seven centuries', in David Parsons (ed.), *Eleanor of Castile, 1290–1990* (Stamford, CA, 1991), pp. 23–34.
33 For Anne's records and itinerary, see T. F. Tout, *Chapters ain the Administrative History of Medieval England*, 6 vols (Manchester, 1920–33), vol. 4, p. 201; vol. 5, p. 260–1; Chris Given-Wilson, *The Royal Household and the King's Affinity: Service, Politics and Finance in England, 1360–1413* (London, 1986), p. 93. For Westminster as the focus of the king's piety, see Nigel Saul, 'Richard II and Westminster Abbey', in W. J. Blair and Brian Golding (eds), *The Cloister and the World: Essays in Medieval History in Honour of Barbara Harvey* (Oxford, 1996), pp. 196–218.
34 Katherine J. Lewis, 'Becoming a virgin king: Richard II and Edward the Confessor', in Sarah Salih and Samantha J. E. Riches (eds), *Gender and Holiness: Men, Women and Saints in Late Medieval Europe* (London, 2002), pp. 86–100.
35 *The Miracles of King Henry VI*, ed. and tr. Ronald Knox and Shane Leslie (Cambridge, 1923); *Henrici VI Angliae Regis miracula postuma*, ed. Paul Grosjean (Brussels, 1935); Alison Hanham, 'Henry VI and his miracles', *Ricardian*, 12 (2000), 638–52.

36 McKenna, 'Piety and propaganda'.
37 Roger Lovatt, 'John Blacman: biographer of Henry VI', in R. H. C. Davis and J. M. Wallace-Hadrill (eds), *The Writing of History in the Middle Ages: Essays Presented to R. W. Southern* (Oxford, 1981), pp. 415–44; Roger Lovatt, 'A collector of apocryphal anecdotes: John Blacman revisited', in A. J. Pollard (ed.), *Property and Politics: Essays in Later Medieval English History* (Gloucester, 1984), pp. 172–97.
38 Katherine J. Lewis, 'Re-evaluating the masculinity and kingship of "St" Henry VI' (forthcoming).
39 Cf. the posthumous cult of Henry VI's son, Prince Edward: Nicholas Rogers, 'The cult of Prince Edward at Tewkesbury', *Transactions of the Bristol and Gloucestershire Archaeological Society*, 101 (1983), 187–9. It might be added that Edward IV's reign, like that of Edward III, witnessed a reconsideration of the role of the queen in political culture: see Joanna L. Chamberlayne, 'Crowns and virgins: queenmaking during the Wars of the Roses', in Katherine J. Lewis, Noël James Menuge and Kim M. Phillips (eds), *Young Medieval Women* (Stroud, 1999), pp. 47–68.
40 Paul Strohm, *England's Empty Throne: Usurpation and the Language of Legitimation, 1399–1422* (London, 1998), pp. 101–27; Joel Burden, 'How do you bury a deposed king? The funeral of Richard II and the establishment of Lancastrian royal authority in 1400', in Gwilym Dodd and Douglas Biggs (eds), *Henry IV: The Establishment of the Regime, 1399–1406* (Woodbridge, 2003), pp. 35–53.
41 Wolffe, *Henry VI*, p. 355.
42 For various treatments of these themes, see Patricia-Ann Lee, 'Reflections of power: Margaret of Anjou and the dark side of queenship', *Renaissance Quarterly*, 39 (1986), 183–217; Diana Dunn, 'Margaret of Anjou: monster-queen or dutiful wife?', *Medieval History*, 4 (1994), 199–217; Diana Dunn, 'Margaret of Anjou, queen consort of Henry VI: a reassessment of her role, 1445–53', in Rowena E. Archer (ed.), *Crown, Government and People in the Fifteenth Century* (Stroud, 1995), pp. 107–43; Thomas A. Prendergast, 'The invisible spouse: Henry VI, Arthur, and the fifteenth-century subject', *Journal of Medieval and Early Modern Studies*, 26 (2002), 305–26; Helen E. Maurer, *Margaret of Anjou: Queenship and Power in Late Medieval England* (Woodbridge, 2003).
43 Sydney Anglo, *Images of Tudor Kingship* (London, 1992), pp. 74–97.
44 There is a large literature on the gender attributes of Tudor female sovereignty. See, *inter alia*, Susan Bassnett, *Elizabeth I: A Feminist Perspective* (Oxford, 1988); Helen Hackett, *Virgin Mother, Maiden Queen: Elizabeth I and the Cult of the Virgin Queen* (Basingstoke, 1995); Susan Doran, *Monarchy and Matrimony: The Courtships of Elizabeth I* (London, 1996); Mary Hill Cole, *The Portable Queen: Elizabeth I and the Politics of Ceremony* (Amherst, 1999).

13

Making Youth Holy: Holiness and Masculinity in *The Interlude of Youth*

FIONA S. DUNLOP

> Youth, I trow that he would
> Make you holy or ye be old,
> And I swear by the rood
> It is time enough to be good
> When that ye be old.[1]

The Interlude of Youth is an early Tudor interlude, dated on internal evidence by its most recent editor to *c*.1514.[2] Like many interludes, the play was probably first performed in a noble household as part of the entertainments for the festive season of Christmas or Shrovetide.[3] Ian Lancashire has suggested the household of Henry Algernon Percy, fifth earl of Northumberland, as a likely location of the first performance.[4] *The Interlude of Youth* employs conventions familiar from other moral plays: the central character, Youth, is a figure who seems intended to have a universal significance, like Everyman; and the action of the play traces his process of fall and repentance which is meant to be taken as typical of all humankind.[5] The other characters of the play are personified vices (Riot, Pride and Lady Lechery) and virtues (Charity and Humility) who battle for man's soul, each group attempting to persuade Youth to commit himself to its guidance for the course of his life. The action of the play might be described as 'making Youth holy', a phrase derived from Pride's speech quoted above. For most of the play Youth follows a sinful lifestyle, represented by his association with his companion Riot and his servant Pride. Charity constantly seeks to make him repent, and Youth's hostility towards Charity culminates in Riot fettering Charity. Youth's repentance and dismissal of Riot and Pride forms the denouement of the play, when, finally, the arguments advanced by Charity and Humility prevail over those of Riot and Pride.

This summary stresses the universal significance of Youth, but this should not obscure the fact that the presentation of Youth is both gender- and status-specific. Youth is thoroughly gendered as male, first in the sense that he inhabits a sexed body. Indeed, Youth ostentatiously draws attention to this body in his first speech of the play.[6] Youth is also presented as masculine, in that the play draws on social norms associated with men in later medieval England to locate Youth in terms of status. As many critics have noted, Youth is presented specifically as a nobleman, a status which is marked at Youth's first entrance when Youth tells the audience that he has just inherited his father's lands.[7] In this context the battle for Youth's soul – the question of whether Youth should become holy or not – becomes a debate about masculinity, and specifically about the kind of masculinity which is appropriate to a nobleman.

This debate is not only focused on the social aspects of noble masculinity, in terms of what a nobleman's lifestyle should be like, or the ways in which a nobleman should behave. It also grapples with the question of the extent to which the male body determines the characteristics of men, whether it is *possible* for Youth to be holy when his young male body dictates behaviours which are inimical to holiness. In this respect, it is no coincidence that the play should choose to focus on the period of male youth, to the exclusion of the rest of the male lifecycle. Youth is clearly important in symbolic terms, since it is so often constructed as the liminal period between childhood and adulthood, where individuals negotiate gendered adult identities. In medieval discourses of youth, to which moral plays contribute and on which they draw, youth is a stage in the development of male bodies, which in turn determine the personality traits and behaviours of young men.[8] In this context, the idea of 'making young men holy' is highly unusual and innovative. In adopting a plot-line which makes Youth holy, *The Interlude of Youth* is arguing against two related tenets: that young men must be sinful; and that noblemen in the secular life must be sinful.

In their arguments against repentance, the representatives of evil, Riot and Pride, rely on both these tenets. Their model of masculinity constructs powerful age- and gender-related norms, which assume a biologically essentialist view of men. These norms are articulated in the climactic scene of the play, where Riot and Pride fear that Charity and Humility's arguments in favour of repentance are beginning to sway Youth. Riot and Pride counterattack by arguing that the holiness of young men is actually a violation of natural laws. Riot asserts that holiness is natural to the old, and sinfulness to the young:

> Hark, Youth, for God avow,
> He would have thee a saint now!
> But Youth, I shall you tell,
> A young saint, an old devil. (ll. 612–15)

Riot even suggests that being so unnaturally holy in youth will carry dire consequences in old age in the form of unnatural sinfulness. Youthful holiness and sinfulness in the old are both presented as inversions on the natural order. In fact as J. A. Burrow has shown, a number of late medieval texts make similarly casual references to the proverb 'young saint, old devil', which suggests that the age-related norms it implies were known to a reasonably wide audience.[9] In the passage quoted at the beginning of this paper, Pride also sets up youth in opposition to old age. His strategy is to imply that, since a long life stretches before Youth, he can afford to postpone thoughts of holiness to a later and more appropriate date. The age-related norms exploited by the vices are clearly a challenge to a religious orthodoxy which seeks to promote repentance and holy living as pressing to all people no matter what their age. Indeed the aim of much moral drama before *The Interlude of Youth* is to encourage individuals to consider their spiritual state long before old age makes them more acutely aware of the prospect of death and judgement.[10]

To an extent, *The Interlude of Youth* accepts the fact that there is a connection between male bodies and a tendency towards a particular spiritual state. This is apparent from Youth's opening speech, where he introduces himself to the audience:

> I am goodly of person;
> I am peerless wherever I come.
> My name is Youth, I tell thee.
> I flourish as the vine tree.
> Who may be likened unto me
> In my youth and jollity?

> My hair is royal and bushed thick,
> My body pliant as a hazel stick;
> Mine arms be both big and strong;
> My fingers be both fair and long,
> My chest big as a tun;
> My legs be full light for to run,
> To hop and dance and make merry. (ll. 42–54)

When Youth describes himself, he puts the stress on his physical nature, rather than on the social markers of his age, though he does also refer to the inheritance of his estates which means he must be at least 21. Youth gives an impression of vigour, and of someone feeling at the height of their physical powers. This depiction of the young male body is reminiscent of those to be found in the Ages of Man tradition.[11] For example, Bartholomaeus Anglicus describes the Age of *adolescentia* (14 to 28 and more) in the encyclopedia *De proprietatibus rerum*: 'it is ful age to gete children, so seiþ Isidire, and able to barnische and encrece and fonge myʒt and strengþe'.[12] As Philippa Tristram has shown, an attitude of arrogant self-sufficiency, based on confidence in the body, or the 'pride of life' is an aspect of the sin of pride which had long been associated with young men.[13] Indeed, this is the subject of the earliest extant, though fragmentary, moral play, which has come to be known as *The Pride of Life* (c.1350). The central character of this play, the King of Life, is pointedly described as 'ying', and his burgeoning physical powers are represented by the two knights who attend him, Streinth and Hele.[14] His arrogant assumption that he does not need to repent or fear Death is based upon his reliance on these 'doghti men of dede'.[15] In a similar way, Youth's sinfulness at the beginning of *The Interlude of Youth* is directly related to his male body.

Youth's behaviour at the beginning of the play is dictated by his bodily development. Youth is already associated with the vice, Riot, whom Youth describes as his 'brother'. Riot in turn refers to Youth as his 'compeer'.[16] Riot represents a psychological state of unstable thoughts. Indeed he announces to the audience that 'all of riot is my mind' (l. 213).[17] But he also represents the riotous behaviour which results from such a state of mind. At his first entrance, Riot has just escaped being hanged at Tyburn, and encourages Youth in his violent treatment of Charity, which culminates in the vices' putting Charity in the stocks.[18] He introduces Youth to Pride, and then deflects Youth from thoughts of marriage to an illicit relationship with Lechery.[19]

The sinfulness of Youth is also a status-related sinfulness, and *The Interlude of Youth* attacks Youth's attempts to construct an identity as a nobleman through the strategies suggested by the vice Pride. Youth's relationship with Pride originates with Youth's impulse to display the new landed wealth he has acquired by finding 'one man more / To wait upon me' (ll. 311–12). He goes on to engage Pride as his servant with 'gold and fee' (l. 330), and these terms locate Youth as a nobleman establishing a relationship with a gentleman servant.[20] In a culture which routinely used display in order to signify social status, a nobleman's household was crucial as a place for pursuing the kind of lifestyle expected of him.[21] The size of a noble household (in terms of the numbers of servants who waited on the noble) was expected to reflect the wealth and importance of the nobleman around whom it was formed. Pride's first act as Youth's servant is to suggest other ways of constructing performatively an identity which will reflect his aspirations to 'high degree' (l. 338). Pride advises Youth to display his social superiority by oppressing the poor, associating with other gentlemen, and making himself visible, through the wearing of fashionable clothing.[22] He paints a picture of the way in which such behaviours will elicit the spontaneous recognition of his noble nature by the 'pretty wenches' and 'every poor fellow' who sees him.[23]

The Interlude of Youth marks this kind of display and disdain as an inappropriate kind of noble masculinity for Youth. Youth's noble lifestyle is clearly sinful, since the impulses for it originate in the sin of pride. Youth's actions transgress other social norms for noblemen. Youth's relationship with Lady Lechery is a further example of Youth attempting to construct a noble identity through his lifestyle. Lechery presents herself as a noblewoman through her courtly manners, so that Youth describes her as 'courteous, gentle and free' (l. 425). While the relationship has a surface aristocratic glamour to it, it is nonetheless an illicit one, and a substitute for a legitimate noble marriage. Not only is such an irregular sexual relationship morally wrong, but it prevents Youth from securing his estate for the future by the birth of legitimate heirs.[24] Marriage played an important part in the dynastic strategies of noble families; but Youth is oblivious to its importance to his noble status.[25]

The Interlude of Youth also shows Youth failing an important test of his ability to exercise the lordship necessary to an adult nobleman, as Youth has to decide between the conflicting advice of the good and evil characters.[26] 'Counsel' was crucial to later medieval lordship in two ways. First, a nobleman's council was important as part of the day-to-day management of his estate, family and political business. It was usual for the late medieval lord to retain suitable counsellors – experienced, learned or influential men – whose advice would expedite his business.[27] The concept of 'counsel' was also crucial to noble identities on an ideological level. The ideology of counsel was developed in detail in later medieval mirrors for princes literature, those educational texts usually addressed at least in the first instance to named princes or noblemen, and widely read by educated men in England.[28] Such texts regularly devoted sections to the ways in which the prince should select his counsellors and evaluate their advice.[29] In *The Interlude of Youth*, Youth places himself in the hands of the kinds of evil counsellors which mirrors for princes describe as holding sway over incompetent rulers. For much of the play, Youth rejects the good counsel offered by the disinterested and truth-telling counsellors Charity and Humility. In doing so, Youth reveals a lack of that acumen in lordship which it was necessary (on a practical and on a symbolic level) for the adult nobleman to possess. The model of noble masculinity to which Youth is first attracted stands in stark opposition to the alternative noble masculinity implied by the text. This model of masculinity makes the management of estates and households into the key activity of the nobleman, and is predicated on the values of prudence, thought for the future, and the submission of personal pleasure for the good of the family.

Youth's desire to establish a gendered noble identity is evident not only in his eager acceptance of the model of masculinity offered by Pride and Riot, but in his rejection of competing kinds of masculinity which both Youth and the vices label as holiness. Indeed this rejection of holiness is enacted at the very beginning of the play, before Pride and Riot appear. After Youth's opening speech, Charity attempts to persuade Youth to repent of his sinful pride in his body. Youth rejects both Charity and his message with threats of violence. His forceful reaction against the holiness which Charity offers is at least in part connected with a rejection of what we might term 'clerkishness'.[30] When Charity refers to the writings of 'noble clerks' and quotes from the Bible in Latin, Youth instantly responds:

> What! methink ye be clerkish,
> For ye speak good gibb'rish. (ll. 113–14)

He proceeds to ask Charity nonsense questions, couched in pseudo-academic terms as a way of holding Charity to scorn. Youth's hostility to holiness is compounded by his hostility to clerks, and his suspicion that Charity, in trying to make him holy, is also trying to make him into a clerk. By implication, Youth perceives the adoption of a clerkly identity as an act which would compromise his masculinity. It seems likely that it is because Youth feels his masculinity is threatened by Charity and his clerkishness that he reacts so aggressively to them both.

The Interlude of Youth firmly associates the period of male youth not only with a state of sinfulness, but with a particular kind of noble masculinity. It renders the characteristics of young noblemen like Youth natural in the sense that it grounds them in the biological characteristics of men at this stage of their physical development. The Interlude of Youth appears to diverge sharply from other moral plays in its attitude to the possibility of over-ruling natural processes. The biological essentialism of Youth is apparent in other moral plays, which depict the life cycles of men in the guise of universal narratives of fall and repentance: that is, The Castle of Perseverance (c.1400-25), Henry Medwall's Nature (1490s) and The Worlde and the Chylde (c.1508). These texts all show the progression of their male protagonist from birth to death, and use markers recognizable from the Ages of Man tradition to denote the central character's passing from one stage of life to another. The Worlde and the Chylde makes this process particularly clear by changing the name of the central character at key moments to designate his entry into a new stage of life. These plays conflate the structure of the Ages of Man with a spiritual plot of fall and repentance, so that youth is always a period of sinfulness. As in The Interlude of Youth, these structural associations are far from arbitrary. Schemes of the Ages of Man often incorporated scientific theories, such as Aristotle and Galen's theory of the humours which makes it possible to link physical development and moral development.[31] In this kind of physiological theory, young male bodies are characterized by a preponderance of heat which drives the passionate nature of the young man.

Other moral plays are characterized by an ambiguous attitude towards youthful sinfulness. To begin with, the young protagonists of these plays may repent, but that repentance is an incomplete one, as the protagonists experience a second fall later in life, under the influence of the pressures of the worldly life or their physical desires. At the age of

60, Humanum Genus in *The Castle of Perseverance* is enticed out of the castle by the sin of avarice, who plays on his fears of a poverty-stricken old age.[32] Man in *Nature*, and Manhode in *The Worlde and the Chylde* are tempted back into riotous living despite their earlier repentance under the tutelage of Reason and Conscyence respectively. In each case, the second and lasting repentance is associated with extreme old age (in *The Castle*, Humanum Genus is in fact at the point of death). The physiological reasons behind this second repentance are spelled out most clearly in *Nature*. Man's moment of turning away from his sinful lifestyle is not shown in the performance, but is described – in rather disgusted tones, it has to be said – by the vice Sensualyte for the benefit of his fellow vice Envy.[33] Sensualyte explains that the vices can no longer hope for any influence over Man, because of the advent of a new character, Age. Age's power is derived from the nature of the ageing male body. Sensualyte describes the physical changes which mark Man's body, which include a crooked back and grey hair.[34] Sensualyte also mentions that 'Hys nose droppeth among' (2. 945), a symptom of the fact that Man's complexion is becoming increasingly cool and moist. This physiological change makes the sensual desires provoked by young male physiology die away naturally. As Sensualyte puts it, Man's 'lust ys gone and all hys lykyng' (2. 946). No longer assailed by the passions, Man is finally able to be good, through the operations of natural laws.

These texts therefore imply a rather ambivalent attitude towards youthful sin. By making sinfulness natural to youth, and holiness natural to old age, these texts appear to be taking a line similar to that of Riot and Pride. Like *The Interlude of Youth, The Castle of Perseverance* does put the argument that young men can afford to postpone holiness into the mouths of the representatives of evil, in order to discredit it. As the Bad Angel puts it to Humanum Genus:

> Wyth þe Werld þou mayst be bold
> Tyl þou be sexty wyntyr hold.
> Wanne þi nose waxit cold,
> Þanne mayst þou drawe to goode. (ll. 416–19)

This is diametrically opposed to the arguments of the Good Angel who urges Humanum Genus to consider the shortness of life and to contemplate his 'endynge day' as a spur to repentance.[35] *The Castle of Perseverance* attempts to mark the attitude of the Bad Angel as the kind of thinking which encourages sinners to deceive themselves, to their own ruin. The text appears to be aware of the dangerous implications of its own structure, which places Humanum Genus's true repentance at the end of his life, and attempts to correct anyone who might read that structure as justifying the postponement of repentance until that time. *Nature* reminds the audience of the danger of premature death, and glosses the play as an example of God's patience and mercy towards a sinner.[36] This play does, however, make the rather startling declaration that (as long as man perseveres in his repentance) 'greter reward thou shalt therfore wyn / Than he that never in hys lyfe dyd syn' (2. 1405). It is better to have sinned and repented than never to have sinned at all, according to *Nature*; a view which perhaps paradoxically presents youthful sin as essential to a superior kind of holiness in old age.

In many ways the portrayal of Youth in *The Interlude of Youth* is consistent with that in other moral plays; indeed, it depends for its full force on a familiarity with such portrayals. However, *The Interlude of Youth* breaks with earlier plays in a radical way by short-circuiting the structure they establish. Not only does the play make Youth holy, it presents his repentance as the denouement of the play. This implies that in the case of Youth there will not be another fall into sinfulness, which is characteristic of the protagonists in *The Castle of Perseverance*, *Nature* and *The Worlde and the Chylde*. Youth's repentance is the lasting repentance elsewhere associated with old age. Indeed the closing speeches of the play envisage Youth leading a life of devotion to holiness, as he applies himself to his prayers and uses the rosary beads with which Humility presents him; and as he leads other people to repent.[37] *The Interlude of Youth* is saying that it is possible for the young to be holy, overturning the association between youth and sinfulness.

The end of the play addresses the issue of Youth's specifically youthful masculinity – a masculinity dictated by the physical nature of his young male body. It also addresses, at least in part, the issue of Youth's noble masculinity – his desire to construct a masculinity as a nobleman which up until this point has been entirely at odds with achieving a right spiritual state. Youth's commitment to his conception of noble masculinity leads him into ever more outrageous excesses of pride, until he declares:

> Aback, gallants, and look unto me,
> And take me for your special!

> For I am promoted to high degree.
> By right I am king eternal –
> Neither duke ne lord, baron ne knight,
> That may be likened unto me;
> They be subdued to me by right,
> As servants to their masters should be. (ll. 589–96)

Youth not only places himself as superior to all earthly ranks of noblemen, but by implication places himself on a par with God, the 'king eternal'.

In fact, at the climax of the play, Charity makes Youth holy precisely by playing on Youth's acute understanding of status. In the cut and thrust of the debate for Youth's soul, Charity finally engages Youth's attention by describing God's salvation using the language of status:

> When thou wast bond he made thee free
> And bought thee with his blood. (ll. 710–11)

Youth is taken aback by the use of the terms 'bond' and 'free' in connection with him, who has prided himself on his noble status. Charity in describing Youth as 'bond' is calling him a churl. Youth responds:

> Sir, I pray you, tell me
> How may this be.
> That I know, I was never bond
> Unto none in England. (ll. 712–15)

Charity is then able to explain the Gospel in terms of God's redemption of man from 'the devil's bondage'; and so effects Youth's repentance. Status is in the end the only language that Youth understands. His repentance is in effect a radical recalculation of his own status, though on a cosmic scale. Youth becomes sensible of God's mercy in making him 'free' from sin, because to him being 'bond' is the most horrifying state of affairs imaginable.

The Interlude of Youth addresses a problematic masculinity which it associates with young noblemen. The text accepts that such young men are prone to sinfulness on the basis of biological essentialist principles, which explain young men's tendency to sin by reference to their physiology. However, it asserts that noblemen both can and should transcend their youthful sinfulness. The text seeks to counteract the spiritual complacency of young men who assume that old age is the time for holiness, and that they can safely indulge their sinful pleasures in youth. At the same time, the play sees dangers in a noble lifestyle radically opposed to spiritual matters in general and clerks as a social group in particular. *The Interlude of Youth* seems to be arguing back against assumptions that young noblemen are hostages to their biology and to their class: that they *must* be sinful, for reasons beyond anyone's control. Instead the text models a repentance by a young nobleman and represents it as true and lasting. We see Youth assume the signs of holiness at the end of the play: he dismisses Riot and Pride, adopts new garments, takes up his rosary and promises to convert 'misdoing men' (l. 778). Youth also confirms his masculinity by demonstrating that he has the resolve to turn away from sinful conduct while he is still young, rather than waiting for old age to take the ability and inclination to misbehave away from him.

In many ways, however, the conclusion of the play raises more questions than it answers. What remains less clear is exactly how Youth's new secular, but holy masculinity is meant to express itself. The play does make its approved form of noble masculinity contingent on the responsible management of estates. Noblemen should also marry, not devote themselves to extra-marital relationships; and they should develop the ability to weigh the counsel of their advisers correctly, rather than be duped by those who play on their weaknesses. The text offers no explicit advice on how to regulate one's dress, or on what size of a household one should keep, in order to reflect one's noble status, and yet keep oneself from the sin of pride.

The conclusion of the play does, however, see Youth transformed in terms of his appearance. Not only does Humility present Youth with 'beads for your devotion', but he renames Youth 'Good Contrition', and Charity gives Youth 'a new array' for the journey of faith before him.[38] It is a convention of later medieval and early Tudor plays that costumes reflect the moral and spiritual state of the characters who wear them, and that changes of costume indicate changes of spiritual state.[39] Youth's dress may well be a symbolic garment, rather than a model of how noblemen ought to dress. However, the play's suggestion that Youth should devote himself to a life of prayer may be an entirely serious recommendation, intended to be acted upon by the noblemen. In noble households – such as that of the earl of Northumberland, the likely patron of *The Interlude of Youth* – religious observances were built into the daily routines of nobles and other household members, and many great nobles maintained chapels and a full complement of chapel staff, including a choir, for this purpose.[40] Fifteenth-century ordinances designed to regulate the upbringing of Edward IV's son and heir to the throne indicate that ideally such devotions should punctuate the nobleman's day.[41] *The Interlude of Youth* is entirely in keeping with established conventions of a noble lifestyle in encouraging noblemen to balance the sacred with the secular in their daily lives.

Notes

[1] Pride, in *The Interlude of Youth*, ll. 642–6. All line references to this work are to *Two Tudor Interludes: Youth and Hick Scorner*, ed. Ian Lancashire (Manchester, 1980).

[2] Ibid., pp. 17–22.

[3] Ibid., pp. 24–5. On interlude drama within later medieval and Tudor noble households, see Suzanne Westfall, *Patrons and Performance* (Oxford, 1990). See also Peter H. Greenfield, 'Festive drama at Christmas in aristocratic households', in M. Twycross (ed.), *Festive Drama* (Cambridge, 1996), pp. 34–40; and Suzanne Westfall, '"A commonty, a christmas gambold or a tumbling trick": household theater', in J. D. Cox and D. S. Kastan (eds), *A New History of Early English Drama* (New York, 1997), pp. 39–58.

[4] *Two Tudor Interludes*, ed. Lancashire, pp. 27–30.

[5] On the conventions of later medieval moral drama, see Robert Potter, *The English Morality Play* (London, 1975). See also Pamela M. King, 'Morality plays', in R. Beadle (ed.), *The Cambridge Companion to Medieval Theatre* (Cambridge, 1994), pp. 240–64.

[6] *Interlude of Youth*, ll. 42–56.

[7] Ibid., ll. 57–9, 308–10. On the nobility of Youth, see *Two Tudor Interludes*, ed. Lancashire, pp. 53–4; and Westfall, *Patrons and Performance*, pp. 162–3.

[8] Nancy G. Siraisi, *Medieval and Early Renaissance Medicine: An Introduction to Knowledge and Practice* (Chicago, 1990), pp. 97–101.

[9] J. A. Burrow, '"Young saint, old devil": Reflections on a medieval proverb', *Review of English Studies*, 30 (1979), 185–96. See also idem, *The Ages of Man: A Study In Medieval Writing and Thought* (Oxford, 1986), pp. 149–50.

[10] See below, where I discuss exhortations to think forward to the day of one's death in *The Castle of Perseverance* and *Nature*.

[11] Texts in this classical and medieval tradition of writing divide the life course into stages and describe the qualities (both physical and psychological) associated with each. See Burrow, *Ages of Man*. See also Elizabeth Sears, *The Ages of Man: Medieval Interpretations of the Life Cycle* (Princeton, 1986); and Mary Dove, *The Perfect Age of Man's Life* (Cambridge, 1986).

[12] M. C. Seymour (ed.), *On the Properties of Things: John Trevisa's Translation of Bartholomaeus Anglicus De proprietatibus rerum*, 2 vols (Oxford, 1975), p. 292, ll. 3–5. *De proprietatibus* is dated to the early thirteenth century; Trevisa's tr. to 1389.
[13] Philippa Tristram, *Figures of Life and Death in Medieval English Literature* (London, 1976), pp. 34–48.
[14] *The Pride of Life*, ll. 240, 431. Line references to *The Pride of Life* are to *Non-Cycle Plays and Fragments*, ed. N. Davis, EETS SS 1 (London, 1970).
[15] Ibid., l. 260.
[16] *Interlude of Youth*, ll. 207, 216.
[17] See also Youth's ironic comment at ll. 245–8.
[18] *Interlude of Youth*, ll. 227ff., 282–8, 297–305.
[19] Ibid., ll. 314–20, 360–76.
[20] On fees paid to household staff, see Christopher M. Woolgar, *The Great Household in Late Medieval England* (New Haven, 1999).
[21] On later medieval noble households, see Mark Girouard, *Life in the English Country House* (New Haven, 1978); David Starkey, 'The age of the household: politics, society and the arts', in S. Medalf (ed.), *The Later Middle Ages* (London, 1981), pp. 225–90; Kate Mertes, *The English Noble Household, 1250–1600: Good Governance and Politic Rule* (Oxford, 1988); Woolgar, *Great Household*.
[22] *Interlude of Youth*, ll. 342–53. The wearing of fashionable clothing frequently indicates youthful pride in early moral plays. See T. W. Craik, *The Tudor Interlude: Stage, Costume, and Acting* (Leicester, 1958), pp. 57–8. On Youth and other young male protagonists of moral plays as 'gallants', see Tony Davenport, ' "Lusty fresche galaunts" ', in P. Neuss (ed.), *Aspects of Early English Drama* (Cambridge, 1983), pp. 111–28.
[23] *Interlude of Youth*, ll. 349–52.
[24] *Two Tudor Interludes*, ed. Lancashire, p. 54.
[25] Kate Mertes, 'Aristocracy', in R. Horrox (ed.), *Fifteenth-Century Attitudes: Perceptions of Society in Late Medieval England* (Cambridge, 1994), pp. 42–60. See pp. 45–7.
[26] *Two Tudor Interludes*, ed. Lancashire, p. 53. On the influence of princely mirrors on *Youth*, see Daryll Grantley, *Wit's Pilgrimage: Drama and the Social Impact of Education in Early Modern England* (Aldershot, 2000), p. 150.
[27] Carole Rawcliffe, 'Baronial councils in the later Middle Ages', in C. Ross (ed.), *Patronage, Pedigree and Power in Later Medieval England* (Gloucester and Totowa, NJ, 1979), pp. 87–108.
[28] On 'Mirrors for Princes' in later medieval England, see Richard Firth Green, *Poets and Princepleasers: Literature and the English Court in the Late Middle Ages* (Toronto, 1980), pp. 135–67; Nicholas Orme, *From Childhood to Chivalry: The Education of the English Kings and Aristocracy, 1066–1530* (London and New York, 1984), pp. 86–106; John Guy, 'The rhetoric of counsel in early modern England', in D. Hoak (ed.), *Tudor Political Culture*

(Cambridge, 1995), pp. 292–310; Charles F. Briggs, *Giles of Rome's De Regimine Principum: Reading and Writing Politics at Court and University, c.1275–c.1525* (Cambridge, 1999). See also Katherine J. Lewis's essay in the present volume.

29 This is particularly true of versions of the pseudo-Aristotelian *Secretum secretorum*: see Mahmoud A. Manzaloui, *Secretum Secretorum: Nine English Versions*, EETS OS 276 (Oxford, 1977).

30 Grantley reads this passage as Youth's rejection of a noble masculinity which puts a high value on humanistic values of the pursuit of learning. See Grantley, *Wit's Pilgrimage*, p. 141.

31 On Aristotelian and Galenic complexion and humoral theory in the later Middle Ages, see Siraisi, *Medieval and Early Renaissance Medicine*, pp. 97–101.

32 *Castle of Perseverance*, ll. 1491–2504. All line references to *The Castle* are to *The Macro Plays*, ed. Mark Eccles, EETS OS 262 (Oxford, 1969).

33 *Nature*, 2. 932ff. All line references to *Nature* are to *The Plays of Henry Medwall*, ed. Alan H. Nelson (Cambridge, 1980).

34 *Nature*, 2. 944.

35 *Castle of Perseverance*, ll. 402–10.

36 *Nature*, 2. 1378–91.

37 *Interlude of Youth*, ll. 770–5.

38 Ibid., ll. 762–71.

39 Craik, *Tudor Interlude*, pp. 73–92.

40 On the chapels maintained by early Tudor noblemen, including that of the fifth earl of Northumberland, see Westfall, *Patrons and Performance*, pp. 13–62. On the household as a religious community, see Woolgar, *Great Household*, pp. 176–9; and R. G. K. A. Mertes, 'The household as a religious community', in J. Rosenthal and C. Richmond (eds), *People, Politics and Community in the Later Middle Ages* (Gloucester, 1987), pp. 123–39. The importance of private chapels to noble and gentry religious practice in this period is also discussed by Sarah Bastow in the present volume.

41 Nicholas Orme, 'The education of Edward V', *Bulletin of the Institute of Historical Research*, 57 (1984), 119–30. Ordinances for noble households also set out a daily round of religious observance for the inmates: see Woolgar, *Great Household*, pp. 84–9.

14

The Catholic Gentlemen of the North: Unreformed in the Age of Reformation?

SARAH L. BASTOW

The early modern period has often been portrayed as a time of gender crisis, when traditional masculine superiority was challenged.[1] For Anthony Fletcher, the period was one where there was a general crisis in gender relations, leading to what Mark Breitenberg has categorized as 'anxious masculinity'.[2] Taking these assertions as a starting point this paper will explore the changing way in which Catholic belief was expressed in the north of England, with particular reference to the Catholic gentlemen of Yorkshire, in contrast to Catholic women's demonstrations of religious commitment. The ways in which religious expression changed is illustrative not just of the need to mask Catholic activities from the Protestant authorities, or of changing modes of religiosity, but also of the wider debates concerning the performance of early modern masculinity and authority.

The north of England is still often portrayed as a traditional place, and, more negatively, as backward and repressed. In the sixteenth century an additional negative term was generally applied to the north: Catholic.[3] Even for the modern historian the Catholic north frequently carries with it this detrimental baggage, compounded by an emphasis on the Catholic mission and its failure to reconvert England. In addition to this, the progress that has been made in the fields of women's and gender history in the study of medieval and early modern England has no parallel in examinations of Catholic communities of the period.[4] The presupposition has been that the discussion of gender could not be applied to the Catholic community, for Catholicism was about priests, and priests were male, therefore a discussion of gender relations was irrelevant (gender being understood here as something pertaining only to women).[5] The recent strides made in scholarship on historical formulations of masculinity provide us with a means of exploring the ways in which gender was an issue for both men and women in their practice of Catholicism. This paper will centre on examination of three points: first, how secular Catholic gentlemen expressed their religious commitment after the Reformation; secondly, whether the religious laws of the period created 'anxiety' about the relative status of men and women in the period; and, thirdly, whether a specifically 'masculine anxiety' was expressed amongst those with religious vocations.

Expressions of piety in public and private

During the 1530s Henry VIII and his government passed a series of Acts which removed papal authority from England and established an English church with the monarch at its head.[6] This was the first stage of religious reformation in England which was to continue throughout the Edwardian, Elizabethan and Jacobean eras, with only the unsuccessful and short-lived era of Marian restoration to interrupt the reforming proceedings.[7] From the 1530s onwards those adhering to the Catholic faith found themselves in a difficult situation, but it was from 1558 and the accession of Elizabeth I to the throne that the position of many Catholics became increasingly demanding and dangerous as they faced prosecution and persecution for maintaining their faith. Convicted Catholics faced fines and imprisonment for non-attendance at church, but risked even more by harbouring priests, holding Catholic masses or engaging in communication with foreign Catholics, including travel to the continent. Catholics could be prosecuted for failing to attend Protestant services at their parish church under the Act of Uniformity.[8] Those who failed to attend were guilty of the specific legal offence of recusancy, which entailed not just the failure of Roman Catholics to attend Church of England services, but the failure of an individual to accept the state's authority as well. The state was very keen to ensure conformity via church attendance, not least because a clear association was drawn between religious non-conformity and political dissent. For example, the Elizabethan government became increasingly anxious about rooting out nonconformity following the 1569 Northern Rebellion.[9] In the north recusancy commissioners searched houses and prosecutions increased as the Courts of High Commission became more permanent under the new president of the Council of the North, the earl of Huntingdon.[10] By the Jacobean era the restrictions had progressed even further, with recusants being forced to apply for licences to travel.

So, what affect did these dramatic developments have on the religious conduct of those who wished to remain Catholic? Pre-Reformation Catholicism had seen men's piety expressed in both public and private. The religious devotion of a gentry family and in particular the head of the family, was often demonstrated via physical constructions. There was an expectation that men should express their piety much more publicly than women in this respect, because the building of chapels and monuments within the parish church provided a lasting reminder of the benefactor's religious fervour as well as attesting to his standing in the community and acting as an expression of his authority. For example, Goldsborough parish church in North Yorkshire contains the fourteenth-century monument of Sir Richard Goldsborough who died in 1333.

But the institution of the Church of England and the outlawing of Catholicism had changed the situation. Catholicism became a hidden religion. For those who still adhered to it, these more public displays of religious commitment were now no longer an option. After the Reformation the local parish church was, in theory at least, the enemy of the Catholic. General interaction with local parish churches could therefore become difficult and even the semi-private expressions of religious dedication Catholics used to make in their wills were looked on unfavourably as, within a Protestant ethos, people were not permitted to appeal to the Virgin Mary and the saints. So the secular Catholic male was left with the problem of how to express his beliefs and demonstrate his religious piety.

In practice, however, many Catholic gentlemen maintained a tolerable relationship with their local parish church and the Anglican authorities there. For example Richard Cholmley used the local Anglican church as a place to conduct business with his conformist neighbours despite being a convicted recusant.[11] The full role that they had played prior to the Reformation was out of bounds to recusant gentlemen and beyond most Catholics who engaged in surface conformity to Protestantism. However, some early modern gentlemen whose religion was doubtful, yet who presented themselves as conformists, were still able to practise these public acts of piety, as Marmaduke Wyvill showed with the erection of his own memorial in his local parish church of Masham. Marmaduke was a conformist gentleman despite coming from a predominantly Catholic family, having a Catholic son and heir and a convicted recusant as a daughter-in-law. Similar depictions can be found of Sir Thomas Vavasour at Haselwood and Sir William Bellasis who were both in similar circumstances. William Bellasis had been suspected of being a Catholic in his youth, was from an inherently Catholic family and had recusants amongst his younger sons.[12]

Aside from this there is evidence that Catholic gentlemen continued to express their private piety in the same ways that they had in the medieval period. Felicity Heal and Clive Holmes state that 'the expectations of male private piety were not significantly different' from female piety in this period, which meant that 'patterns were gendered by outcome rather than intent'.[13] Although the differentiation between outcome and intent is left vague, it is clear that a woman's private devotions were not supposed to be expressed outside her closet and contact with her confessor and priest; whereas male private devotion was expected to be a prelude to more public worship, even within the household. Thus prayers said in private by the male head of the family should be followed by mass or devotion in the more public sphere to include servants and the rest of the household. Surviving evidence of Catholic gentlemen's private writing shows that the prayers and devotions of the late Middle Ages remained popular. Thomas Meynell's book written at the turn of the sixteenth century contains prayers expressing devotion to the Virgin Mary, which was shared by much of his family, to All Saints, to the Virgin Martyrs and to the Holy Name of Jesus.[14] On the death of his daughter Ann, who had been married to Thomas Grange and had produced four children, Thomas Meynell writes a prayer asking for mercy from both God and the Virgin Mary.[15]

The gentry had long favoured private chapels. This was a trend begun in the late Middle Ages which suited the practice of Catholicism, with its increasing need for secrecy, after the 1530s.[16] By the Elizabethan era Catholic worship largely occurred within the privacy of family chapels. These could be little more than a room set aside in a gentleman's farmhouse, although private chapels on a grander and more semi-public scale did exist and were used despite the dangers. At

Haselwood, in the West Riding, the Vavasour family had a private chapel which was well-known as a Catholic chapel throughout the post-Reformation period. Similarly, in the North Riding, the ruined Lady Chapel at Mount Grace remained a place of Catholic pilgrimage and was within reach of several Catholic families including the Granges.[17] Yet these semi-public places were increasingly a rarity as Catholicism became a hidden and primarily a household religion. This had ramifications for the role of laymen within it, as we shall now see.

Secular piety: the gentleman as 'second fiddle'?

Scholarly discussions of early modern masculinity and patriarchy have paid particular attention to the household sphere. Elizabeth Foyster argues that 'above all else, men from whatever social status were only held worthy of honour if they could demonstrate control over their wives, children and servants'.[18] But as the post-Reformation practice of Catholicism was a household activity, women rather than men were frequently the main players. It is here that the issue of gender roles is brought into question. Ideologically men were at the head of the household, but in practice women controlled the practical elements of the day-to-day running of the house, allocating space, giving orders to the servants and in many cases having responsibility for hiring them.[19] Thus, for recusant Catholics, religious activities that had previously occurred in a church or chapel under the auspices of a priest, were brought into the female-run sphere of household management.

There is often a perception that female independence of thought and action in relation to religious expression was a key part of radical Protestantism.[20] This was not accepted without challenge and caused conflict and condemnation from both secular and religious Protestant authorities.[21] However, whereas those women involved in radical Puritanism, particularly in the north, could be dismissed as an aberration, within the Catholic community of Yorkshire women were in the majority: in fact Catholicism needed women to survive.[22] Women were active in housing priests, arranging masses within the household and retaining Catholic servants. For example, in the West Riding in 1604 Anne Holmes was recorded as retaining a Catholic maidservant.[23] In the North Riding Dorothy Scrope was recorded as retaining three Catholic servants, Marie Beseley, Isabel Sparling and Richard Skelton.[24] Priests were housed and masses conducted in the houses of several women including Margaret Clitherow in York and Dorothy Lawson in Durham. Furthermore Dorothy was recorded as inviting the local populace to hear the priests who were regularly found to be staying with her.[25]

It was frequently women who made a public expression of their religious commitment by absenting themselves from church and even by being charged under the Recusancy Acts, whilst their husbands often gave evidence that they were unable to control their wives or enforce the religious conformity required by law. A role reversal seems to have occurred, with women playing the dominant role in making public expressions of religious devotion and retaining their influence in household piety. But how far did this reflect the reality of relations between men and women, or their relative status? And what were the implications for the masculinity of a man whose wife was more piously active than he, and who had publicly admitted that he could not control her? I shall explore this in relation to the famous case of Margaret Clitherow.

Anxious men, obstinate women and the law

The concept of patriarchal male authority was reinforced by the early modern legal system. In law once married women were protected by their husbands but also lost any individual identity; man and wife became one person with the male subsuming the female.[26] This established the superiority and authority of men over women, but also made men accountable for the actions of their wives, daughters and sisters. However, as noted above, men often appeared in the recusancy courts testifying that they were unable to compel their wives to conform. In the post-Reformation north this displayed itself most prominently through the series of prosecutions which took place in the York High Commission. John Clitherow appeared at York several times in the 1570s and 1580s to testify that he could not make his wife, Margaret, conform. Margaret Clitherow was an active Catholic, despite her conformist husband and Protestant background. Her house became a centre for Catholics in the city. Mass was regularly held there, priests sheltered and Margaret actively tried to convert people.

Margaret appeared regularly before the High Commission between 1578 and 1586 and during this time John was forced to enter into bonds to secure her release, pay her fines and appear before the commission himself to explain his wife's behaviour. In 1586 John was imprisoned in the castle for nine days and when released was ordered to leave the city whilst his wife prepared herself for her final trial. She was condemned to death by pressing, having been found guilty of possessing Catholic altar goods and on suspicion of harbouring the known Catholic priest Francis Ingelby.[27] Her actions won her recognition as a martyr for the Catholic faith and she was canonized in 1970.[28]

In some ways early modern thinking could explain away this aberrant female behaviour, for women's emotions were more volatile and it had long been accepted that this explained why their religious expression and commitment was likely to be fervent.[29] Yet it still posed a problem for male authority, both within family structures and in regulating and stabilizing volatile female emotions. As far as the Protestant authorities were concerned, such men, in failing to govern their wives properly, were seriously compromising their masculinity. This had dangerous ramifications for the premises upon which patriarchal authority was based. One Dorothy Scrope was forcibly removed from her house and imprisoned in Thirsk as a result of her continuing adherence to Catholicism. It was recorded that Thomas Marr and Richard Braithwaite came to her house, violently broke down the door and arrested her. However, as she was 66 years old, 'impotent and very sicklye', they carried her on a barrel to Thirsk, calling her 'vile and most Reproachfull words Callinge her hoore bitche & ould Rotten papiste Queane and such lyke termes wth muche othes, unseamly and barbarouse behavior to her not fytting for this deponent to set downe'.[30] The case continues with the deponent recording that Dorothy was imprisoned in a chamber in Thirsk, threatened with a knife and concludes that she was released only after the two men acquired 45 shillings from her. One Anthony Pybus brought this to the attention of the authorities, stating that Marr and Braithwaite did not confine themselves to attacking Catholic women, but also targeted Catholic men. But Pybus's testimony stated that it was only in Dorothy's case that physical violence was used, as the threats on the Catholic men were aimed far more directly at their livestock and possessions. This suggests that a man would be attacked largely for what could be taken from him, but a woman was more likely to be attacked simply for being a woman who refused to uphold the religious status quo.

While Catholic women faced the particular opprobrium of the Protestant authorities, Catholic men faced possible hostility from the

Catholic hierarchy itself, stemming from a different cause. Whilst the Catholic authorities were willing to excuse women who engaged in conformist activities, because they were weaker beings, they did not extend the same excuses to men. By contemporary standards of masculinity, no allowance could be made for men who did not stick staunchly to their religious convictions. This is clear from the texts circulated among the recusant community in the later sixteenth century, composed by exiled Catholics on the continent such as Allen, Campion and Persons who provided guidance on various theological questions which faced both English lay Catholics and the missionary priests who served them.[31] For example: 'Is it lawful for wives, children or servants to serve their husbands, fathers or masters in their heretical activities?' These activities covered many aspects of daily life including eating or serving meat on what, to a Catholic, should be a meatless day. This answer was given:

> it is lawful for inferiors to obey their superiors in this way . . . they are allowed to do this because of their subjection to their superiors and it does not seem that they co-operate in the sins of their superiors . . . but, on the other hand, superiors sin if they help their inferiors in these things.[32]

Inferiors could refer to anyone in the household under the authority of a male head, but these instructions have particular ramifications for perceptions of the religious conduct of men in relation to women. Clearly while Catholic men were expected to remain strong and unwavering in their religious commitment, Catholic women were permitted the occasional transgression because their inferior position made them naturally subject to the orders of men. Therefore we can see that ideologies of gender, with respect both to ideals of masculinity and of femininity, underpinned expectations of desirable Catholic behaviour in both men and women. But did this really mean that men who conformed to Protestantism (even if only outwardly) were actually seen to be unmanly by their fellow Catholics?

Masculinity in the home

In the light of the preceding argument let us consider in more detail apparently conformist gentlemen with Catholic wives, for it could be argued that they faced a crisis of masculinity and authority. From 1536 onwards many northern gentlemen's wives and daughters continued to practise Catholicism, whilst they conformed. As we have already seen, this could be taken to be a challenge to male superiority, as it appeared that women who were in a subordinate position were flagrantly disobeying both their husband's and the state's authority. But is this what was actually happening within individual households? For instance, in managing to hide and finance missionary priests, many women were drawing upon monies which were, at least in law, the property of their husbands. The Catholic Church, although still maintaining that husbands and fathers were the superiors of their wives and daughters, was willing to allow that women were within their rights to finance Catholic activities, even without their husbands' permission. The instructions given to priests providing set guidance and answers for difficult questions stated:

> out of the property of their husbands, wives may pay debts which the husbands do not want to pay, even against the express will of the husbands. It follows that Catholic wives may maintain priests who administer the sacraments to them; for their husbands should provide them with priests. They can also dispose freely of whatever property they possess over and above the dowry for similar purposes.[33]

Evidence suggests that many husbands in fact tacitly approved of their wives' behaviour and in this way male authority was preserved intact, as it was disobedience sanctioned by men and understood as such within the community in which it occurred. For example Maior/Mauger Vavasour of Newton near Ripley had entered into a bond 'for wife and family all to receive communion except him', yet at a further session of the High Commission he stated that his family had conformed, but not received communion.[34] He had clearly not enforced conformity upon his wife and family, despite the bond, suggesting that he did not feel that their display of religious disobedience and spiritual independence affected his standing or authority. The memoirs of another gentleman, Sir Hugh Cholmley, provide further explanation as to why this should be. He praised the women of his family as extremely virtuous in continuing to adhere to Catholicism, but continues that, regardless of this dedication, their actions 'could not bee soe exactly done with out mentioning their husbands, who in respect of their sex may nit clyme to have the greatest honour and reverence ascribed to them, but commonly are the princypall Actors in the seane'.[35]

Appearances could therefore be deceptive – the gentlemen who apparently conformed while allowing his wife to remain a Catholic could use her as a shield to disguise the crucial role that he played in maintaining Catholicism. Thus perhaps the secular men of Yorkshire were not at all anxious, because despite outward appearances, or the perceptions of Protestants, they securely held the principal position in all things within the domestic sphere.

Masculine authority within the Catholic Church

Within Catholicism the role of priestly authority was well established by this period. Medievalists have questioned whether this authority was strictly masculine, for the priest lacked the means to prove his masculinity in the more conventional secular ways.[36] Procreation and taking up arms were not options legitimately open to the post-Reformation Catholic clergy either, but in some ways the ambiguities of medieval masculinity had been clarified by the early modern era and the challenge of being a Catholic priest in Protestant England carried with it an automatic heroism which was entirely masculine. When women attempted to display the same kind of traits they were roundly condemned by contemporaries and even to some extent by later historians, underlining perceptions (then and now) of the intrinsically masculine nature of this sort of conduct.

The role of missionary priest was a dangerous one, with English laws specifically focused on preventing Catholic priests operating in England. Thus priestly masculinity was defined as heroic; for these men defence of the faith was a practice, not just a theory.[37] Yet even here priests faced challenges in new ways. Once in England priests were heavily reliant on gentry households for shelter and protection. This often meant that Catholic women were influential and the role priests were forced to assume as tutors or visitors to the house was much less authoritative than the roles priests had been used to performing in the past. This further illustrates the ways in which some manifestations of traditional masculine authority were being eroded by the enforced circumstances of the Reformation. The missionary and Jesuit priests still played a vital role in maintaining Catholicism, for it could not exist without them, but women began to play a crucial role in protecting and extending the Catholic community. They would even assist priests in their duties – thus, in 1575, one Elizabeth Tetlowe, a midwife, is recorded as 'going up and down the country with chyldren to be baptysed of popyshe prestes'.[38] Dorothy Lawson's chaplain complained of her that 'When any was to be reconcil'd there-abouts shee played the catechist, so as I had no other share in the work but to take their confession.'[39] He continued to say that he was with her seven years and that during that time all received help and baptism, and that she ensured no child went to the grave unbaptized.[40] Dorothy thus filled the role of a priest in many respects, serving the community in the ways in which a local Catholic parish priest would have done in the past. So here we do have some conflict of interests and whilst these complaints often take the form of fairly minor disagreements over boundaries (where a midwife's duties ended and a priest's began) issues of gender and authority were clearly at work as well, for the actions of these women trespassed into an area where masculine priestly authority should have ruled.

Monastic piety: masculinity reasserted

The removal of the monastic communities in England meant that those Englishmen who wished to take up a Catholic vocation were forced to travel to the continent. Whereas the women who travelled to the continent were left with only the option of an enclosed order, their brothers had a greater range of options. Their religious expression could take the traditional form of joining the priesthood, enclosed orders or the new Jesuit orders. The Society of Jesus (Jesuits) had been founded in 1540 by St Ignatius Loyola and placed a great emphasis on education and an active life. Jesuits were seen as undertaking the dangerous task of reconverting England and men such as Edmund Campion led eventful lives. In 1581 Campion undertook the Jesuit mission in Yorkshire; he was housed by several families in Yorkshire including the Harringtons in the Thirsk area. Yorkshire families had already sent sons to Douai to train as priests and the dangerous times were illustrated by the number of priests arrested and even killed. Five seminary priests were executed in York in 1582–3.[41] Men such as Campion were seen as inspirational in terms of their activities and subsequent martyrdom. He was a fugitive from the English authorities, tracked down by spies and eventually captured, whereupon he was paraded through London, imprisoned and then had an audience with Queen Elizabeth. He was subsequently tortured, tried and condemned to a traitor's death. During the Elizabethan period five Jesuits were condemned to death and became martyrs to the cause. These activities were seen as forerunners to the Jesuit-directed Yorkshire mission of the 1590s led by Richard Holtby and John Mush. Their mission was heroic, dangerous and involved endeavours which it was deemed unthinkable for a woman to undertake.

The continental orders placed a great emphasis on education, which was very much in line with contemporary priorities regarding the early formation of masculinity.[42] The importance of education increased in the sixteenth century for large sections of the population and it had become part of a gentleman's training. Thus gentlemen such as Thomas Meynell of North Kilvington deemed a formal education necessary for his sons and sent them abroad to ensure that their young minds and concepts of self were formed under Catholic tutelage.[43] Once trained, both secular and Jesuit priests were also expected to take part in the 'mission', which for Englishmen involved the reconversion of Protestant England to Catholicism. The mission was not envisaged as something in which Catholic women on the continent would play a part. In fact women were actively discouraged, as witness the experience of the Order of the Blessed Virgin Mary begun by Mary Ward in 1609. This was intended to have a similar brief to the Jesuits, performing a missionary role in England, but Ward and her followers were condemned for this by the Catholic hierarchy, which even sent spies to monitor the order's activities in Rome.[44] The Jesuits also attacked the order, considering its activities unsuitable for a woman's temperament and condemning its emphasis on education and an active life in the world when an enclosed life was still considered preferable for religious women, as it had been in the Middle Ages. The mission and the risks involved were regarded as masculine religious activities, illustrating that male and female expressions of Catholic piety within religious orders in the early modern period were intended to be entirely different. The male role involved being active and proselytizing in the world, while the female role was to be passive, contemplative and enclosed.[45]

Conclusion

This essay has argued that there were, on the surface, signs of tensions between male and female Catholics in their modes of religious expression. The increasing importance of the household meant that male authority in religion was in some ways redefined as Catholicism moved from a public to a private environment. But limited access to Catholic priests and a close-knit familial community resulted in Catholic families' increased reliance on each other. So these tensions were not always as real in practice as the evidence suggests: co-operation was essential. Private worship had always had a role, but now it was the dominant one which, in some instances, appears to have given women a more active and authoritative role in the maintenance of religious practice. But men still remained vital as priests and heads of families, the latter, at least, apparently not seeing their wives' increasing profile in religion as a threat to their social standing or masculine authority. This was, presumably, in part because their wives' activities were ultimately predicated on traditional ideas about the roles of women and female piety within the household. Their activities were unusual in degree, not in form. It was only really amongst the hierarchy of the Catholic authorities on the continent that we can discern serious and sustained anxieties about the threat which might be posed by women who did seek to go beyond approved areas of female religiosity and participate in activities such as missionary work which were theoretically the preserve of men. Thus it was not only practices of religion which remained unreformed among the Yorkshire Catholic gentry, but perceptions of the relationships between religiosity and gender as well.

Notes

[1] A. Fletcher, *Gender, Sex and Subordination in England 1500–1800* (London, 1995), p. 28.
[2] M. Breitenberg, *Anxious Masculinity in Early Modern England* (Cambridge, 1996); Breitenberg, 'Anxious masculinity: sexual jealousy in Early Modern England', *Feminist Studies*, 19 (1993), 377–98; Fletcher, *Gender, Sex and Subordination*, pp. 28–9 .
[3] C. Haigh, *Reformation and Resistance in Tudor Lancashire* (Cambridge, 1975), p. 63.
[4] This is an argument made by Christopher Haigh in several books and articles, but most forcibly in 'The Church of England, the Catholics and the people', in C. Haigh (ed.), The *Reign of Elizabeth I* (London, 1984), p. 202, and in 'From monopoly to minority: Catholicism in early modern England', *Transactions of the Royal Historical Society*, 5th series (1981), 129–47.

5 Thelma Fenster, 'Preface: why men?', in C. E. Lees (ed.), *Medieval Masculinities: Regarding Men in the Middle Ages* (Minneapolis and London, 1994), pp. ix–xiii, discusses the wider prevalence of this correlation between women and gender.
6 G. R. Elton, *The Tudor Constitution* (Cambridge, 1975), 329–68.
7 Mary reigned for only five years (1553–8) and the restoration of the Catholic religion came to an abrupt end with the re-establishment of the Protestant religion and royal supremacy over the church in 1559.
8 Elton, *Tudor Constitution*, pp. 401–4.
9 A. Fletcher and D. MacCulloch, *Tudor Rebellions* (London, 1997).
10 C. Cross, 'The third earl of Huntingdon and trials of Catholics in the north 1581–1595', *Recusant History*, 8 (1965–6), 136–46; A. Dures, *English Catholicism 1558–1642* (London, 1984).
11 North Yorkshire County Record Office (NYCRO), Northallerton, ZQG/MIC 1456, fo. 2; *The Memoranda Book of Richard Cholmley of Brandesby 1602–1623* (NYCRO, 44, Northallerton, 1988), p. 29.
12 J. T. Cliffe, *The Yorkshire Gentry from the Reformation to the Civil War* (London, 1969), p. 128.
13 F. Heal and C. Holmes, *The Gentry in England and Wales 1500–1700* (London, 1994), p. 365.
14 J. C. H. Aveling (ed.), 'Recusancy papers of the Meynell family', in *Miscellanae*, CRS, 56 (1964), pp. 42–3.
15 Ibid., p. 41.
16 See Heal and Holmes, *Gentry*, p. 352, for the trend towards private chapels.
17 Aveling, 'Recusancy papers', p. xv.
18 E. Foyster, 'Male honour, social control and wife beating in late Stuart England', *Transactions of the Royal Historical Society*, 6th Series (1996), 215–24.
19 Fletcher, *Gender, Sex and Subordination*, p. 205.
20 P. Lake, 'Feminine piety and personal potency: the emancipation of Mrs Jane Radcliffe', *Seventeenth Century*, 2 (1987), 147–9.
21 D. R. Woolf, 'A feminine past? Gender, genre, and historical knowledge in England, 1500–1800', *The American Historical Review*, 102 (1997), 645–79 (657).
22 S. L. Bastow, '"Wilful and worth nothinge": the Catholic recusant women of Yorkshire', *Recusant History*, 25 (2001), 591–603.
23 E. Peacock (ed.), *A List of the Roman Catholics in the County of York in 1604: Transcribed from the Original MS in the Bodeleian Library* (London, 1872), p. 17.
24 Ibid., p. 64.
25 W. Palmes, 'The life of Dorothy Lawson of St. Antony's, near Newcastle-upon-Tyne in Northumberland', in J. Fenwick (ed.), *Local Tracts: Tracts Relating to the Counties of Northumberland and Durham and the Borough and County of Newcastle-upon-Tyne*, vol. 3 (Newcastle-upon-Tyne, 1856), pp. 17, 32.

[26] Discussion of the *feme covert* can be found in J. Eales, *Women in Early Modern England, 1500–1700* (London, 1998), p. 79.
[27] P. Caraman, *Margaret Clitherow* (York, 1986); R. Connelly, *Women of the Catholic Resistance in England 1540–1680* (Durham, 1997), pp. 48–52.
[28] David Hugh Farmer, *The Oxford Dictionary of Saints* (Oxford and New York, 1978; this edn 1987), p. 92.
[29] Fletcher, *Gender, Sex and Subordination*, pp. 68–74; S. Mendleson and P. Crawford, *Women in Early Modern England 1550–1720* (Oxford, 1998), pp. 18–30.
[30] C. Talbot (ed.), *Miscellanea: Recusant Records*, CRS, 53 (1960), p. 279.
[31] P. J. Holmes (ed.), *Elizabethan Casuistry*, CRS, 67 (1981), pp. 6–7.
[32] Ibid., p. 119.
[33] Ibid., p. 29.
[34] J. S. Purvis, *The Elizabethan High Commission of York: The Act Book 1561/2–1580* (York, 1979), pp. 68, 79 (68^v, 96^v and 97).
[35] J. Binns (ed.), *The Memorials of Sir Hugh Cholmley of Whitby 1600–1657*, YAS RS, 153 (2000), p. 61.
[36] R. N. Swanson, 'Angels incarnate: clergy and masculinity from Gregorian Reform to Reformation', and P. H. Cullum, 'Clergy, masculinity and transgression in late medieval England', both in D. M. Hadley (ed.), *Masculinity in Medieval Europe* (London, 1999), pp. 160–77, 178–96.
[37] The focus on Catholic priest martyrs has been a constant theme of Catholic historiography. The most notable Yorkshire priest martyr was Nicholas Postgate who died in York in 1679.
[38] J. S. Purvis (ed.), *Tudor Parish Documents of the Diocese of York* (Cambridge, 1948), p. 80.
[39] Palmes, 'Life of Dorothy Lawson', p. 45.
[40] Ibid., p. 46. Palmes also stated that Dorothy was involved in the more conventional lay Catholic activities, placing special emphasis on the seven works of charity.
[41] J. C. H. Aveling, *Northern Catholics: The Catholic Recusants of the North Riding of Yorkshire 1558–1790* (London, 1966), pp. 58–60, 136–7.
[42] Heal and Holmes, *Gentry*, pp. 250–61, provides a discussion of the formative nature of early education in determining the future of the gentleman's son. This section relates to practical matters, but does indicate that informal education was designed to train young men in gentlemanly activities which were often designed to illustrate the differences between themselves and their female siblings.
[43] Aveling, 'Recusancy papers', p. 73.
[44] M. C. E. Chambers, *Life of Mary Ward*, vols 1 and 2 (London, 1882) provides an account of both Mary Ward and the Institute of the Blessed Virgin Mary.
[45] For a similar attitude to the roles of men and women within more recent scholarship see, for example, J. C. H. Aveling, *Post Reformation Catholicism in East Yorkshire, 1558–1790* (York, 1960), pp. 21–46; *The*

Catholic Recusants of the West Riding of Yorkshire 1558–1790 (Proceedings of the Leeds Philosophical and Literary Society, 10, 6 (1963)), pp. 211–29; *Northern Catholics*, pp. 112–98; *Catholic Recusancy in the City of York, 1558–1791*, CRS, monograph series, 2, 1970), pp. 14–76; *The Handle and the Axe: The Catholic Recusants in England from the Reformation to Emancipation (*London, 1976). Aveling places great emphasis on the role of Catholic men in all three of his studies of Yorkshire. The idea that women should be enclosed and passive, rather than in the world and active, was a theme inherited from medieval Catholicism, as Meri Heinonen's essay in this volume demonstrates.

Index

Abbo of Fleury 145, 159, 171
Abelard, Peter 27–8, 122
Absolom 114
Absolon 119
Adam of Eynsham 36
Ælfric of Eynsham 144–6, 149, 153, 155, 171
   Natale Sancti Oswaldi Regis et Martyris (Life of St Oswald, King and Martyr) 144–6, 149–50
   Passio Sancti Eadmundi Regis et Martyris (Passion of St Edmund, King and Martyr) 144–6, 150–2
   Lives of Saints 144
Aelred of Rievaulx 31–2, 35
   Mirror of Charity 31–2
Aeneid 37
age 2, 35, 84, 109, 116, 162, 194–5, 198–9
Aidan, bishop 145
Aldhelm, abbot of Malmesbury, bishop of Sherborne 4, 8–23, 157
   Opus Geminatum De virginitate 8–23
Alkmund, king 162
Ambrose
   De virginibus ad Marcellinam 10
Anglicus, Bartholomaeus
   De proprietatibus rerum 195
Anglo-Saxon Chronicle 145, 159
Angoures, Baanes 102, 108
Anna 62
Anna the Younger 96
Anne of Bohemia, queen 180–2, 190
Anthony, St 48

Antony the Younger, St 95
   Life of St Antony the Younger 95
Antioch 44–6, 53, 109
Antonello de Messina 143
Aphrahat the Persian 46
Aristotle 198
Assyria 93
Athanasius, St 98
Augsburg 65

Babylas 96
Bardas 98, 100, 102, 106
Basil I, emperor 98
Basil, St 98
Beatrix of Nazareth 79
Beauchamp, Richard, earl of Warwick 160, 169
Becket, Thomas, St 33
   holy oil of 180
Bede 8, 144–5
   Historia Ecclesiastica 8
Bellasis, Sir William 209
Benedictines 31
Beowulf 144, 147–50, 154
Bernard of Clairvaux 28, 32–3, 36
Beseley, Marie 210
Blacman, John 183, 185
body 2, 11, 16, 17, 33, 35, 47, 52–3, 82–4, 87, 94–5, 101, 115, 119, 137, 143–6, 151–2, 153–4, 168–9, 175, 193–5, 198–202
Bonaventure 112–13
Boniface VIII 161
Bonvisnus, Razo 69

INDEX 223

Bosphorus 44
Botticelli, Alessandro 143
Braithwaite, Richard 212
Bromyard, John 119
Bury St Edmunds, abbey of 159
Byzantium 2, 44, 93, 95, 96, 100, 102–3

Cadwalla, king 145, 149–50
Caesarius of Heisterbach 28–9, 30, 31, 32, 33, 34, 40
Campion, Edmund 213, 216
Canterbury 1
Capet, Hugh 129
Capgrave, John
   The Book of Illustrious Henries 168
Cappadocia 97
Carthusians 36
Castille, arms of 136
Castle of Perseverance 198–200
castration 94, 97, 98, 101–3, 115, 122, 151, 153, 155
Catherine of Alexandria, St 58
Catherine of Siena, St 58, 124
celibacy 4, 10, 25–7, 30, 36–8, 45, 117, 123, 125
Chalcedon 44
Chararic, king 115
Charlemagne 26
Charles IV, king 135
Charles the Bald 129, 142
chastity 4, 10, 12, 24, 25, 27, 29–30, 33–7, 39–40, 82–3, 94, 96, 101–2, 111, 135, 166–7, 182
Chaucer, Geoffrey
   Shipman's Tale 116–17
   Miller's Tale 119
Chertsey, abbey of 183–4
China 93
Cholmley, Sir Hugh 214
Cholmley, Richard 208
Chrysostom, John, St 44, 98, 117
Cistercians 29, 30, 34, 40, 69, 152
Clare of Assisi, St 86, 113
Clement of Alexandria 114
clergy 4, 5, 10, 19, 25–30, 33–4, 37–9, 93, 109, 111–12, 114, 117–20, 122–3, 125, 197–8, 200, 215
Clitherow, John 211–12
Clitherow, Margaret 211–12
Clotild, queen 115
Clovis, king 115
Cologne 59, 62, 69, 71
Constance 59

Constantine 132
Constantinople 44, 45, 95
   Hagia Sophia 98
   Petra monastery 97
   St Agathos monastery 100
Councils 112
   of Chalcedon 55
   of Ephesus 44
   Second Lateran 38
   Fourth Lateran 111
   of London 112
   of Toulouse 111
   of Vienne 86
Crusade 6, 138
   Second 129
   Third 134
Curtesys, William, abbot 159, 170
Cyra 45, 52
Cyrrhus 44, 45

Damietta 134
Danes 145, 159, 164, 168
Daniel 15
Daniel 154
Daniel, Walter 31–2, 35
David, king 114, 130
Delilah 114
Denis, St 134–5, 138, 142
Diocletian, emperor 146
Diodore 44
Dogmael, St 36
Dominicans 59, 79, 80, 81, 82, 85–6
Domnina 45, 52
Douai 216
Dream of the Rood 150
Durham 211

East Anglia 145, 154, 159, 172
Ecclesiasticus, book of 61
Eckhart, Meister 59, 74, 86
Edmund of Abingdon, St 69
Edmund of East Anglia, St 5, 144–6, 148–54, 158–73
education 5, 120, 158–69, 192–205, 215, 217, 220
Edward, prince 185
Edward II, king 4–5, 175–80, 182–6
Edward III, king 4, 178–80, 182, 184–5
Edward IV, king 169, 183–4, 191, 203
Edward the Confessor, St, king 4, 169, 182
effeminacy 31–2, 34, 37, 42, 95, 166–7

Eleanor of Castille, queen 181
　Eleanor crosses 181
Elizabeth I, queen 186, 207, 216
Elizabeth of York, queen 185–6, 190
England 3, 159–60, 168–9, 174–6, 187, 193, 201, 206, 215, 217
　Anglo-Saxon 4, 8, 10, 11, 18, 144–55, 159
Ephraim the Syrian 46
Eudes, king 133
Eugenia, St 17, 96
eunuchs 2, 3, 93–108, 116
Euphrosine, St 113
Euthymios, patriarch 100
Eve 94–5
Exeter Riddles 152–3

family 5, 25, 37, 111, 128, 196–7, 207–8, 218
femininity 3, 5, 11–12, 14–16, 43, 45, 49–50, 53, 62, 69, 73, 79–84, 88, 94, 104, 148, 151–2, 175–6, 178, 180, 182, 187, 213
Flanders 134
France 4, 127, 129–30, 134–8, 161, 178
Fredegar, chronicler 148
Fremund, St 168
friars *see* mendicants

Galen 198
Gautier de Coincy 69
Geoffrey le Baker 178–9
Gerald of Aurillac 24–5
Gerald of Wales 32–6, 41
Germany 59, 83
Giles of Paris 135
Gloucester Abbey 177, 179
Goderic, St 36
Godfrey of Viterbo 168
Goldsborough, Sir Richard 208
Grange, Thomas 209
　family 210
Gregory of Nazianus, St 98
Gregory of Tours
　History of the Franks 115
Grosseteste, Robert 35
Guy de Chauliac 116

Hadewijch of Brabant 58, 86
Harrington family 216
Haselwood 209–10
Heidelberg law book 111, 113
Henry I, king 129

Henry V, king 164–5, 184
Henry VI, emperor 168
Henry VI, king 5, 158–73, 175–7, 183–6
Henry VII, king 177, 184–6, 190
Henry VIII, king 207
Hermann-Joseph, St 3, 59, 69–73, 77
Herrenfrage 25, 38
Hilarion, St 15
Hildelith, Abbess of Barking 10
Hingwar 145–6, 150–4, 164–6, 168
Holmes, Anne 210
Holofernes 151
Holtby, Richard 217
Hoven 69
Hugh of Avalon, bishop of Lincoln 30, 33, 36–7
Hugh of St Victor 113

Ignatios the Younger, St 95, 98–103, 106–8
　Life of Ignatios the Younger 98, 100–3
Ingelby, Francis 212
Interlude of Youth 192–203
Isabella of France, queen 176, 178–80, 182, 185–6, 189
Isabelle of France, queen 181, 183
Isidore of Seville 195

Jacobus de Voragine 33, 109, 111
　Golden Legend 33
　Legenda aurea 109–10, 120, 123
James of Mesopotamia 45
Jerome, St 42, 114
Jesuits 215–17
Jews 85, 111
Joan of Kent, princess of Wales 180
John, St 95, 102
John, bishop of Heraclea, St 97, 103
John the Faster, St 97
Joseph, St 70–2, 77
Judith 151
Julian Saba 49–51

Kings Langley 184
kingship 4, 5, 8, 113, 115, 127–30, 132–8, 142, 143–57, 158–73, 174–91, 201, 207
knighthood 4, 29–30, 31, 32, 36, 39–40, 79, 81–5, 88, 134, 160–2, 164–5, 168

Langland, William
　Piers Plowman 116, 120

INDEX

Lawson, Dorothy, 211, 216, 220
Leo V, emperor 98
Leo VI 100
Leo the Armenian 101
Lincoln 181
London 181, 216
   Council of 112
   Newgate prison 112
   Tower of 183
Lothbrok, king 165
Louis VI, king 129, 133–5
Louis VII, king 129, 135, 137
Louis VIII, king 135, 137
Louis IX, St, king 4, 129, 133–8, 142, 161, 169, 177
Loyola, Ignatius, St 216
Luttrell Psalter, The 117–19
Lydgate, John, 159–69, 171
   Life of St Edmund 159, 162–9, 171

Mantegna, Andreas
   St Sebastian 143
Marana 45, 52
Marcellina 10
Marcianus 50–1
Margaret of Anjou, queen 176, 185–6
Marguerite de Porete 79
Maris of Cyrrhus 45
Mark, king 116
Maron 52
Marr, Thomas 212
marriage 24, 25, 34, 38, 42, 69, 101, 113, 178, 183, 195–6, 202
Martin, St 14
martyrdom 4, 5, 13, 16, 96, 102, 123, 143–7, 160, 166, 174–91, 212, 217, 220
Mary, Blessed Virgin 29, 32, 58, 69-72, 76–8, 94, 135, 187, 208–9
   Order of the BVM 217
   as *Theotokos* 44
Mary I, queen 186
Mary of Egypt, St 117
masculinity
   and authority 4, 5, 18, 94, 122, 123, 150–1, 158, 182, 210–16, 218
   and autonomy 3, 4
   and body 3, 4, 30, 31, 32, 40, 109–23, 143–55, 193–4, 197, 200–2
   and power 14, 17, 142, 144, 149–51
   and strength 12, 16, 48, 83, 95, 149–50, 167

   and violence 108, 143–9, 151–4, 165, 168, 193–5, 197
   and will 3, 4, 5, 6, 30, 35–6, 40, 47, 82–3, 122, 147, 149–50, 152, 154–5, 162, 167
   contested 175
   symbols of
      regalia, oriflamme 134
masculinities 24, 122–3, 129, 170, 172
Maserfield 145
Masham 209
masochism 143–4, 151
Matrona 96
Matthew of Vendôme, regent of France 129
Mechtild of Magdeburg 58, 86
Medwall, Henry
   Nature 198–200
mendicants 81–2, 85–8
Mercia 8, 145
Methodius 98
Metrical Life of St Hugh of Lincoln 37
Meynell, Ann 209
Meynell, Thomas 209, 217
Michael I, emperor 97, 98, 101
Michael II, emperor 101
Michael III, emperor 98
monasticism 4, 8, 12, 24–6, 28–30, 32–3, 35, 39, 45, 48, 83, 96, 98, 127–9, 134, 152, 216
   double monasteries 10, 18
monks 4, 5, 8, 9, 10, 13, 25, 28–38, 44–5, 50, 65, 93–5, 97, 103, 111, 116–18, 127–9, 135, 137–8, 142, 159, 161, 177, 179
Mortimer, Roger 178
Mountgrace 210
Mush, John 217
mystical marriage 3, 49–54, 57, 58–78, 82, 128–9
mysticism 3, 46–57, 58–78, 79–92

Nebuchadnezzar 154
Nestorius 44, 48, 53, 55
Nicerte 44
Nikephoros, bishop of Miletus, St 97
Nikephoros I, emperor 98
Nikephoros II Phokas 97
Nikephoros Gregoras 97, 103
Nikephoros Kallistos 97
Niketas David the Paphlagonian 98, 100–3, 107

Niketas Stethatos 97
Niketas the patrician, St 97, 103, 108
Nikolaos, patriarch 100
nobility 3, 4, 8, 17, 19, 24, 26, 31, 38–9, 41, 81, 147–8, 159, 164–5, 192–3, 196–8, 200–3, 206–21
North Kilvington 217
Northumbria 144–5

Odes of Solomon 51
Odo of Cluny 24
Orange 132
ordination 25, 33, 71, 113, 122
Oswald, St 144–6, 148–9, 151, 153

Pachomius 48
Paris 138
Paul, St 102, 113
  Corinthians 61, 113
Pelagia, St 96
Penda, king 145, 149
Percy, Henry Algernon, fifth earl of Northumberland 192, 202
Peter, St 107, 109
Peter Lombard
  Sentences 112
Peter of Mt Silpius 46, 51
Philip I, king 133–4, 137
Philip III, king 135
Philip IV (the Fair), king 134, 178
Philip Augustus, king 137
  'Dieudonné' 135
Philippa of Hainault, queen 178–80
Photios, patriarch 98, 100, 102, 108
Piero de la Francesca 143
Plato 49
Pontefract 180
Pride of Life 195
priests 9, 25, 26, 28, 33–6, 38, 65, 69, 96, 100, 115, 118, 120, 132, 148–9, 207, 209–18
  priesthood 33, 113, 216, 220
Prokopia 98
Proverbs, book of 61
Pybus, Anthony 212

Reformation 2, 5, 186, 206–21
Reims 133
Richard II, king 172, 174–7, 179–85, 188
Richard III, king 184
Robert de Neuby 112
Robert of Molesmes, St 69
Roland 26

Rolle, Richard 120
Rome 93, 146, 217
Roncesvalles 26–7
Rueland Frueauf the Elder's circle
  Carrying of the Cross 121
Saint-Denis
  abbey of 4, 127–42
  Grandes Chroniques, Chroniques de Saint-Denis 129
  Porte de Suger 130
Samson 114
sanctity 4–5, 10–11, 13–16, 21–2, 24, 32, 35–6, 39–40, 43, 52–3, 59, 80, 93–8, 100–4, 109, 117–18, 127, 130, 134–8, 142–6, 152–4, 159–61, 164, 166, 169–70, 175–80, 182–7, 194, 208, 212
Scrope, Dorothy 210, 212
Scrope, Richard, St, archbishop 177
Sebastian, St 143–6
Secreta secretorum 158–62, 164, 166–8
semen 27, 35, 116
sexuality 9, 24, 25–7, 29–30, 32–4, 36–7, 39, 41, 45, 51, 76, 82, 84, 85, 94, 96, 104, 108, 116–18, 134, 154, 166–8, 176, 179, 182, 195–6, 198–9, 202, 212, 215
Sheen, palace of 182
Sicily 97, 101
Sigebert of East Anglia 8
Silvester, St 15
Simon de Montfort, St 177
Skelton, Richard 210
soldiers 93–5, 101–2
Solomon 130
  Song of Songs/Song of Solomon 51, 58–9, 71
  Wisdom of Solomon, book of 61
Sorg, Anton 65
Sparling, Isabel 210
Steinfeld, abbey of 69
Stephen of Hungary, St 161, 169
Suger, abbot 128–32, 134
  Libellus Alter de Consecratione Ecclesiae Sancti Dionysii (On Consecration) 128
  Liber de Rebus in Administratione Sua Gestis (On Administration) 128, 130
  Ordinatio A.D. MCLX uel MCLXI (Ordinance of 1140 or 1141) 130
Sulpicius Severus 14

INDEX

Sunder, Friedrich 80
Gnadenleben 80
Suso, Henry 2, 3, 4, 59–69, 72–3, 75, 77, 79–92
Büchlein der ewigen Weisheit 88
Büchlein der Wahrheit (Little Book of Eternal Wisdom) 60, 61, 72
Exemplar 60–2, 65, 67, 68, 75, 89
Horologium sapientiae (Clock of Wisdom) 60, 61, 65, 66, 72, 75
Leben 60, 61, 80–9
Symeon the New Theologian, St 97, 103
Synaxarion A 97
Syria 2, 43–6, 48, 51

Tarasios, patriarch 100
Tetlowe, Elizabeth 215
Thekla 96
Theodora, Empress 98
Theodore of Mopsuestia 47
Theodoret of Cyrrhus 43–57
Historia Religiosa 43–57
Theodosius II, emperor 44
Thirsk 212, 216
Thomas of Lancaster, St 177
Toledo 29
Tonsure 3, 98, 109–26
Tractatus de regimine principum ad regem Henricum Sextum (A Tract on the Regiment of Princes to Henry VI) 160
Trajan, emperor 120
Tristan legend 116
Turpin, archbishop 26–7, 37
Tyburn 195

Ulm 59–60, 62, 67, 80
Ursula, St 71

Vavasour, Major 214
Vavasour, Sir Thomas 209
family 210
Vbba 165–6, 168
Vegetius
De re militari (On Military Matters) 164, 167
Venus Pudica 62, 75

Victoria, St 14–16, 22
Vikings 145–6
Villon, François
Testament 120
virginity 10–11, 12, 13, 15, 35, 37, 40, 52, 71, 96, 113, 166–9, 172–3, 182
Ward, Mary 217
warfare 8, 12, 25-27, 30, 37, 101, 130, 134, 144, 151, 164–5, 168
spiritual warfare 4, 11, 12, 16, 17, 29, 30, 36–7
warriors 4, 8–9, 12, 16, 18, 27, 37, 147–8, 152, 154, 165
Wessex 10, 159, 172
Westminster Abbey 181–2, 184
Wild man 117–18
Wilfrid, St 36
William of St Thierry 28
William the Breton 135
Windsor 184
women 3, 13, 26, 29, 32, 33, 35, 42, 58–9, 80–1, 94, 96, 113, 114, 142, 167, 188, 207–9, 212–15, 217
and authority 3, 17, 178, 185, 217
as ascetics 43, 48, 52, 55, 83–4, 86–7, 91, 96
as beguines 86
as concubines 34–5
as mothers 35, 69, 101–2, 128, 148, 178
as nuns 9, 10, 11, 18, 25, 32, 37, 59, 67, 69, 76, 80–3, 86–8, 113, 216–17
as queens 170, 175–6, 178–83, 185–7, 191
as transvestites 17, 96, 113
as wives and daughters 5, 26, 33, 37, 128, 175–6, 178, 186, 210–14, 218
Worlde and the Chylde 198–200
Wyvill, Marmaduke 209

York 1, 2, 211, 216
Yorkshire 206, 210, 215–18
North 208
West 210
youth 31–2, 97, 128, 162, 192–205
Yseut, queen 116

Zoe Karbonopsina 100